Themes in modern European history 1780–1830

D0222911

Themes in Modern European History 1780–1830 is an authoritative and lively exploration of a period of revolution and war whose events have shaped modern Europe. It ranges from Revolutionary France to the Russian Empire tracing emerging conflicts over liberalism and nationalism. In a series of articles, six leading academics ask some controversial questions:

- How far can it be said that the nineteenth century was shaped by the impact of the Napoleonic Wars rather than by the reforming projects of the Revolutionaries?

- Was the conservative Europe of 1814 more an invention of the Romantic imagination than the restoration of the old regime?

Spanning political, social, economic and demographic facets of revolutions, this is an indispensable textbook for all students of the nineteenth century, and for all those interested in understanding the nature of Europe today.

Pamela M. Pilbeam is Reader in Modern European History at the University of London. She is the author of *The Middle Classes in Europe 1789–1914* (1990), *The 1830 Revolution in France* (1991), and *Republicanism in Nineteenth-Century France 1814–71* (1994).

THEMES IN MODERN EUROPEAN HISTORY
General editor: Michael Biddiss, University of Reading

Already published

Themes in Modern European History 1830–90
Edited by Bruce Waller

Themes in Modern European History 1890–1945
Edited by Paul Hayes

Themes in Modern European History 1780–1830

Edited by Pamela M. Pilbeam

London and New York

First published 1995
by Routledge
11 New Fetter Lane, London EC4P 4EE

Simultaneously published in the USA and Canada
by Routledge
29 West 35th Street, New York, NY 10001

Typeset in Palatino by
Ponting–Green Publishing Services, Chesham, Bucks
Printed and bound in Great Britain by
Redwood Books, Trowbridge

British Library Cataloguing in Publication Data
Themes in Modern European History,
1780–1830. – (Themes in Modern European History Series)
   I. Pilbeam, Pamela M. II. Series
   940.2

Library of Congress Cataloging in Publication Data
Themes in modern European history, 1780–1830 / edited by
   Pamela M. Pilbeam.
      p.   cm. – (Themes in modern European history)
   Includes bibliographical references and index.
   1. Europe–History–1789–1815.
   2. Europe–History–1815–1848.
   I. Series.
   D803.T44   1994
   940.2'7–dc20   94–28278
                        CIP

ISBN 0–415–10172–7 (hbk)
ISBN 0–415–10173–5 (pbk)

Contents

Maps

Figures

Tables

Notes on contributors

Robert Alexander is Associate Professor at the University of Victoria, British Columbia, Canada. He has written *Bonapartism and the Revolutionary Tradition in France* (1991) and is currently writing a monograph on grass-roots opposition to the Restoration Bourbon Monarchy.

Michael Biddiss is Professor and Head of the Department of History at the University of Reading. His interest is in the history of ideas and publications include *Father of Racist Ideology* (1970), *The Age of the Masses* (1977), *Thatcherism: Personality and Politics* (co-editor, 1987) and *The Nuremberg Trial and the Third Reich* (1992). He is General Editor of the series.

Colin Heywood is Senior Lecturer in Economic and Social History at the University of Nottingham. His publications include *Childhood in Nineteenth-Century France* (1988) and *The Development of the French Economy, 1750–1914* (1992). He is currently preparing a history of the town of Troyes in the nineteenth century.

Pamela M. Pilbeam is Reader in History, Royal Holloway, University of London. Her publications include *The Middle Classes in Europe 1789–1914; France, Germany, Italy and Russia* (1990), *The 1830 Revolution in France* (1991) and *Republicanism in Nineteenth-Century France* (1994). She is currently writing a comparative study of early French socialists and the 'social question'.

Brendan Simms is Official Fellow and Director of Studies in History, Peterhouse, Cambridge. His publications include '"The worker correspondents" movement in Wurttemberg during the Weimar Republic: 1928–1933', *European History Review*, 21 (4)

(1991), pp.481–514 and *The Impact of Napoleon: Prussian Policy, Politics and Executive Reform, 1797–1806* (1995).

Julian Swann is Lecturer at Birkbeck College, University of London. He has written several articles on eighteenth-century French politics and *Politics and the Parlement of Paris under Louis XV, 1754–1774* (1995).

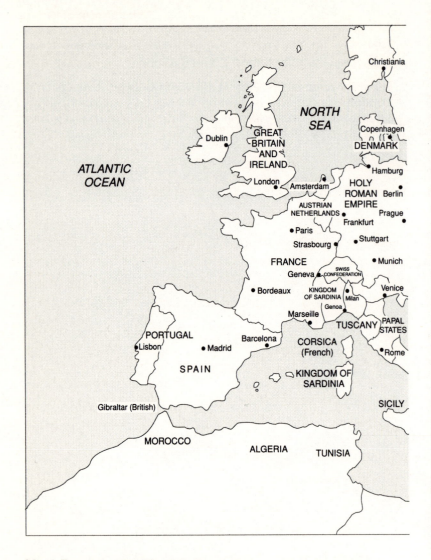

Map 1 Europe in 1780 (The Holy Roman Empire consisted of nearly 400 states under the leadership of Austria.)

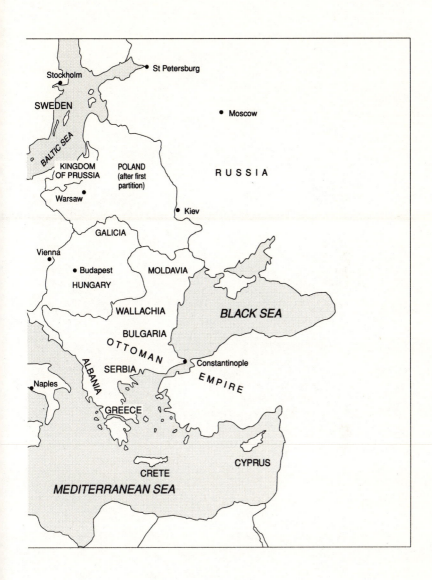

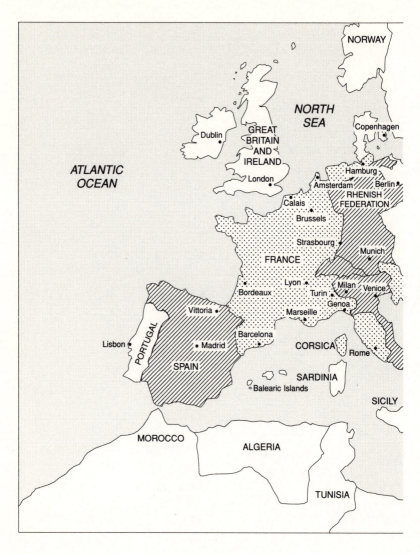

Map 2 Europe in 1812, after the Congress of Vienna

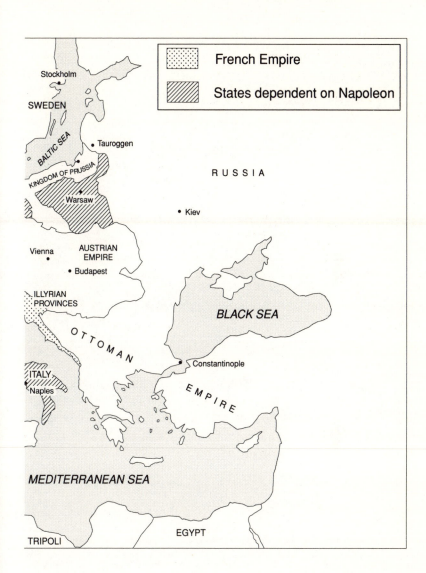

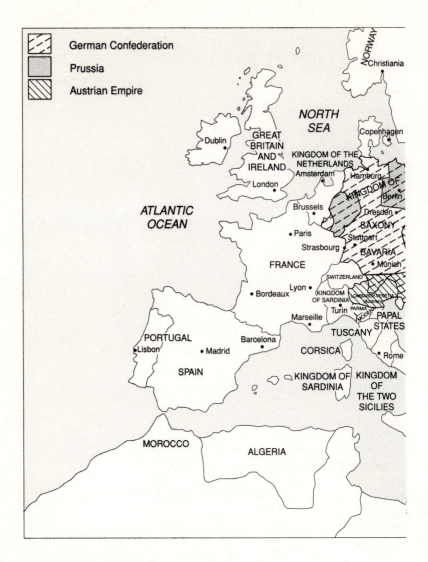

Map 3 Europe in 1815, after the Congress of Vienna

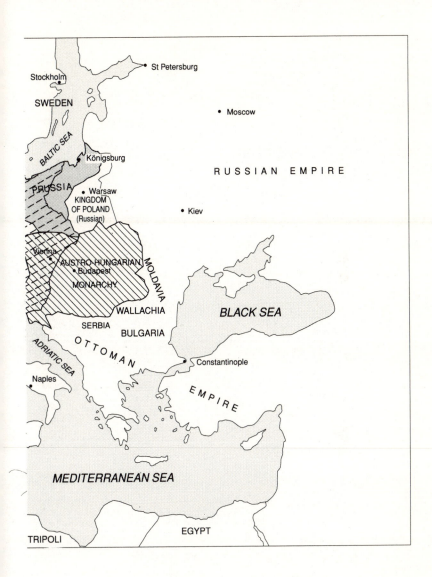

Chapter 1

Introducing Europe in revolution and war

Pamela M. Pilbeam

'Men are born free and remain free and equal in their rights. Social distinctions can only be founded on public utility.'[1] In the socially privileged Europe of the 1780s this confidently optimistic claim of the French Declaration of the Rights of Man and of the Citizen of 1789 was indeed revolutionary. Much of this volume will concern itself with the ways in which the Declaration was interpreted – and neglected. The themes we shall consider include why the attempt to reform the French state led to cataclysmic revolution and military dictatorship, the impact of the 1789 Revolution and Bonapartist Empire, the expanding role of the state, the emergence of liberal, national and conservative ideas, and the significance of economic change and population growth.

The purpose of this volume, like the series to which it belongs, is to allow a number of specialists, who enjoy discussing broad themes, to offer a guide through the compelling issues of the period to those who want an outline of the main problems and points of contention among historians. Our contributors hope to have captured the style of a good lecture course and have a debt to undergraduate audiences (on two continents) whose tutorial comments have helped to clarify these themes – certainly for the editor! We hope that the overviews which follow will be an encouragement to try the original sources or delve into the historical controversies in more depth. France is dramatically, inescapably centre-stage in this period and we make no apologies for our emphasis on her role.

Historians cannot escape time. The significance of the dates they emphasize is often a mystery to their readers. The contributors to this volume make no claims that the precise dates 1780 and 1830 indicate any more of a specific and tidy beginning and ending than time itself. But they do believe that they signify a broad period of revolutionary upheaval in ideas, politics, society and economic life, and that they serve to cover an era that constituted a major turning point in European history.

Until roughly the middle of the twentieth century historians approached the French Revolution believing that it was an enormously significant epoch, either in the progress of mankind, or in its doom, depending on their political sympathies. Those who believed in the perfectibility of man were again divided into liberals who thought that individual freedom and parliamentary democracy held the key to progress, and socialists who argued that progress was determined by economic development. For both of the latter groups 1789 was a key event. For liberals it was a stage in the struggle for political freedom which was continued by subsequent revolutionary upheaval in France and elsewhere in the nineteenth century. For socialists 1789 marked the first stage in the decline of a feudal, landed, aristocratic elite and the transfer of economic and political power to a commercial and industrial middle class. The revolutions which followed, climaxing within Russia in 1917 and China in 1949, were part of the inevitable narrowing of the capitalist class and its overthrow by proletarian revolution.

Until a generation ago any account of the French Revolution and the years which followed would have had either a liberal or a socialist agenda. A cursory glance at the essays which follow will reveal the absence of such rather optimistic explanations of history. Julian Swann, Robert Alexander and Pam Pilbeam all resist any whiff of determinism in their explanations of the incidence of revolution. While noting the existence of serious socio-economic problems due to demographic and economic change, revolution is seen more as the product of the coincidence of a number of issues, in which the ideals and decisions of individuals or groups, and the problems of containing mass violence in large and crowded cities are significant.

Much ink has been spilled, to the torment of undergraduates anxious to grasp 'significant' dates, to try to determine when the French Revolution began and ended; 1780 is a conveniently unspecific date to launch the debate on causation. Julian Swann, in common with other present-day historians, naturally focuses on the immediate and political factors in the downfall of the Bourbon Monarchy. The final act is more problematic. Some writers might even claim that the Revolution is still in progress. When Professor Alfred Cobban taught a Special Subject on the French Revolution at the University of London, he, like Julian Swann, ended with the fall of Robespierre and the demise of the radical Revolution in 1794. The Directory (1795–9) is nearly always the Cinderella of Revolutionary studies, depicted as the rule of a self-interested middle class keen to curb both popular unrest and popular power. These years are shrouded in failure as well as selfishness, the last oligarchical act of a tragedy which ended with the military dictatorship of Napoleon.[2] The byzantine Directorial structure of indirect elections barely concealed a desire to emasculate the electoral principle itself. A very narrow, virtually self-selected oligarchy of anti-Jacobins ruled a France where counter-revolutionary movements posed a threat to the survival of the Revolution.[3] But it must be remembered that it suited Bonapartist propaganda to compare the glories of the Napoleonic edifice with an anarchic and chaotic predecessor. There have been attempts to resuscitate the image of the Directory. Its unexciting but not inefficient administrators did much to construct the institutions and codes for which the Revolution and Empire are famed[4] and its military record in exporting the Revolution was not inconsiderable.[5] The Directory is often scored as a prelude to the Napoleonic era and it is appropriate that Robert Alexander, in tracing the links between Bonaparte and the Revolution, has far more to say about its history than does Julian Swann.

The raw material of history is the surviving record, written or artifact. Yet much remains hidden. Apart from government documents and the accounts of educated contemporaries, we have very little direct evidence of the motivation of artisans and peasants who formed the shock-troops of revolutionary unrest. We know very little about the ideas of half the adult population, women, apart from the writing of exceptional individuals such as Mary Wollstonecraft[6] and Madame de Staël.[7] The work of historians such as Maurice Agulhon,[8] Olwen Hufton,[9] Alan Forrest[10] and Peter Jones[11] has begun to offer some insights into the concerns of the vast majority of the population of all countries who were virtually invisible to most historians until relatively recently.

This half-century was dominated by French ideas and institutions and by French military expansion on a scale unmatched by any state since the days of Charlemagne. The victories of the French armies led to the further decline of the Ottoman Empire and the break-up of the already barely sustainable Holy Roman Empire. Nearly four hundred separate components in the territories we would call Germany were turned into the Confederation of the Rhine. The Italian peninsula was reorganized, a large part being absorbed into France, while the rest was ruled by puppets appointed by Napoleon. The Austrian Emperor, former head of the Holy Roman Empire, was confined to a much smaller domain, as was the king of Prussia. The Polish provinces, which Russia, Austria and Prussia had divided among themselves in the later eighteenth century, were welded by Napoleon into the Grand Duchy of Warsaw. Driven back to Moscow by invading French troops in 1812, the Tsar was able to hold out mainly because of the winter. In 1814 the new French Empire was destroyed by a coalition of Great Britain, Russia, Prussia and Austria. She was stripped of all her conquests, leading to a second major reorganization of frontiers. Thus twenty-five years of this half-century were dominated by war and its effects. During them France rose to her peak of influence, although by 1830 the permanence of the eventual downturn was not perceived by her nervous neighbours.

The impact of France extended well beyond the shunting of frontier-posts and the redrawing of maps. Enlightened writers such as Rousseau demanded a new approach to politics and society, while the decisions of politicians and the popular violence of the 1789 Revolution made institutional changes an urgent necessity. Contemporaries believed that institutions and education could remake society and the individual for the better. The educated prosperous elite elected to successive revolutionary assemblies in France tried to legislate for a measure of liberty and equality which would favour the better-off, while not ignoring the needs of the poor. Their limited altruism was snuffed out by escalating popular expectations and violence, the pressures of virtual famine plus civil and foreign war. Naive optimism tended to be replaced by fear of the revolutionary process. For the wealthy elites in France and the rest of Europe the experience of the 1790s left a profound fear of popular unrest, which underlay the attempts to restore monarchies and conservative attitudes in post-1814 Europe.

Despite the alarm and disillusion, the institutional legacy of the Revolutionary and Imperial years ultimately rendered French institutions uniform, rational and (in principle at least) egalitarian.

Notwithstanding the initial decentralizing euphoria of 1789, they were also highly centralized. This blueprint was transferred to the Italian peninsula, the Low Countries and the Confederation of the Rhine, often to be retained, particularly in the Rhineland and the Italian states, after Napoleonic troops had been repelled. Out of revolution came new state structures, making government more effective and more interventionist. However, it did not always take revolution to commence such rationalization. The pressures of war and defeat obliged other states, especially Prussia, but to some degree Russia also, to continue a process of remodelling and centralization begun in the second half of the eighteenth century. Thus by 1830 not only were frontiers much altered, but the scope of government itself was often very different from the beginning of the period.

The urge for change came not only from French philosophers, armies and bureaucrats. These were years of an unprecedented population explosion which, as Colin Heywood explains, was by no means limited to areas which were also experiencing accelerated economic change. Although, as Heywood emphasizes, only very isolated pockets of territory were directly affected by fundamental structural economic change such as the introduction of large-scale factory production in the cotton industry, contemporaries were as much alarmed by the potential social consequences of industrialization and urbanism as by the effects of the French Revolution. The economies and peoples of Europe seemed to be, willy-nilly, victims of cyclical depressions which governments were helpless to control. At roughly ten-year intervals (on the eve of the meeting of the Estates General of 1789 until the mid-1790s, 1810–11, 1816–18, 1827–32) communities were thrown into disarray when harvest failure coincided with financial, commercial and industrial recession. High food prices and actual shortages were exacerbated by the traditional reluctance of rural communities to permit the free passage of food stuffs. Nervousness on the money markets of Europe led to reduced rates of pay for manufactured goods and to short-time working. The situation was made worse by war and the deliberate attempts of the British and the French to 'adjust' international commerce to their own taste. Cyclical depression, in association with the beginnings of long-term structural change, made violent protest endemic in both rural and urban areas as the poor not only blamed government policies for causing their misery but also expected official intervention to alleviate their problems.

Educated contemporaries were divided in their view of the social misery which many were beginning to explain as the consequence of capitalist competition. Some observers were convinced that the disequilibrium was temporary, and were prepared to change the law and to use soldiers to bully the less well-off to accept structural changes in the economy such as the abandonment of communal and artisan traditions.[12] Some, like Saint-Simon and Fourier, argued that industrialization must invoke new forms of government to alleviate the effects of the growing disparities of wealth and the social cleavages endemic in capitalism. Others retreated into an idealized, often artificially constructed past. The culture of the Romantic Movement offered historical novels (Walter Scott was the darling of Europe in the 1820s) and re-created a safe and orderly past in verse, on canvas, in music, historical writing and even by building new 'ruins'.

How terrifyingly different was post-Napoleonic Europe? What had changed by 1830? A comparison of the essays in this volume dealing with western and eastern Europe reveals a dramatic contrast. In the west the French Revolution was inescapable and its structural institutional changes were not questioned when old monarchies were 'restored' in 1814. In the east, even in lands conquered by French armies, its impact appeared to be limited to the need for top level diplomatic and military deals to expel invading armies. Most major states, particularly the east European empires of Russia, Prussia and Austria, were still absolute monarchies, unchecked by formal, written constitutional arrangements and still justified principally by the military successes of their ruling dynasties. Brendan Simms stresses the primacy of foreign policy in their approach to government. During the French Wars disaster rather than triumph became the norm for the Romanovs, Hohenzollerns and Habsburg families. In this half-century rulers and their governing servants were keen to centralize, eliminating the power of intermediate bodies such as municipal and guild corporations and the remnants of estates and corporate judicial bodies. The centralizing impetus was grounded in the need for money to fight wars to reverse French conquests; for attempts at setting up viable tax structures; for efforts to rationalize government so that similar institutions operated in different provinces, a tricky problem because some states, such as

Prussia, were an amalgam of provinces gathered through war and marriage and physically widely scattered. Rulers were dependent on doing deals with local elites, as in Hungary, to secure the compliance of the wealthy both to pay for war and to lead the armies, even though such arrangements might detract from centralization.

In 1830 the enlargement of the authority of the state was far from complete, but rulers had made further progress in the refinement of two vital props for centralized authority, the army and the bureaucracy. Armies were no longer merely dynastic. Conscription meant that they were beginning to represent the interests of the whole community. The concept of the army of the 'nation' was beginning to emerge. Moreover the growth in the size and in the centralization of bureaucracies gave absolute rulers far more authority. The professionalization of government took away both the independence of local notables and that of a corps of state servants, as in Prussia, which had previously considered itself a fairly autonomous arbiter of royal authority.

Although rulers reinforced the foundations of their command structures, in some respects these years seemed to mark the end of an era of states based solely on dynastic justification. France survived the execution of the king; Napoleon constructed even greater power for himself, justified by a combination of military success abroad and 'popular' acclaim manufactured through plebiscites. After 1814 the Bourbons might claim to be God's anointed, but politicians were conscious that the new written constitution was a negotiated deal. No one pretended that Louis-Philippe, made king 'of the French people' by the Chamber of Deputies in August 1830, or that the German Leopold of Saxe-Coburg, who was elected king of the new rebellious Belgian state,[13] owed their crowns to anything more than political manoeuvring. By 1830 it had become transparent that authority in the state was based on consent, but it was still far from clear whose agreement was required.

In this half-century there were serious challenges to the two vital props of old-style monarchy, the church and the nobility, but, as we shall see, the extent to which their authority had been undermined by 1830 varied. The idea that royal initiative should be circumscribed by written constitutions was intimately associated with the 1789 Revolution and the development of liberal notions. What did liberalism mean? In exploring the ideas of

Benjamin Constant and others, Michael Biddiss reveals the ambiguity of liberal thought, which was to prove disastrous for liberals throughout the new century. Liberals called for written constitutions establishing power-sharing in government plus freedom of speech, religion, etc. for the individual. How were such liberties to be defined and guaranteed? This half-century exposed many of the problems and found no solutions.

The attempt to create constitutional governments, in which elected assemblies shared some measure of legislative power with an hereditary executive, was fudged by the failure to define who should 'bell the cat' and who should be excluded. Liberals were essentially part of an educated wealthy elite, who wanted a share in the political action and were keen to protect their own property. Many were anxious to moderate the impact of economic change and try to ensure that the poor were healthy, non-destitute and even rudimentarily educated, but by 1830 almost none wanted democratic political structures. The problem for those of liberal sympathies, whose sentiments were vague, amorphous and usually defined in negatives, was that the circumstances in which the opportunity to set up constitutional government occurred were usually ones created by popular unrest.

The experiences of the Revolutionary and Imperial years in France exposed the problem and cast a long shadow. In the 1790s the attempt to set up constitutional government had ended in repeated popular upheaval and dictatorship. The human legacy of this experience in France, and in the areas taken over by her armies, was an educated elite which had served either the Revolution, or the Empire, or both. Their loyalties lay with the ideals of 1789, but these were likely to be tempered in some, if not all cases, by a fervent detestation of popular violence, often based on personal experience.

In France and some of the smaller south German states, the constitutional monarchies created after Napoleon's defeat seemed to have solved the impasse. A constitutional assembly was discussed for Prussia. Alexander I initially proposed a constitutional framework for the Polish provinces and Spanish liberals did not forget their constitutional scheme of 1812. The French Charter of 1814 was a marker for the rest of Europe. It was forged by compromise and consent, the White Terror notwithstanding, and at first seemed viable. Demands for written constitutions and the involvement of the wealthy in the process of law-making became the fundamental plank of liberal programmes of reform elsewhere in the 1820s. The events of 1830 again exposed the contradictions between liberalism and revolution, even when the upheaval of that year in Paris was later advertised as 'Three Glorious Days'.

In 1830 liberal and national sentiments were still closely linked. A form of patriotism might be invoked, tracing love of country to an historic, even mythical, past and to a common language and culture. Yet nationalism was still regarded as a subversive, radical phenomenon, associated with the French Revolution, with liberal constitutional demands to restrict absolute power, and even with popular upheaval.[14] Nationalism was seen, by those in control, as a threat to European peace, visible whether in the dramatic if temporary expansion of France or in the destruction of traditional order associated with the fight for Greek independence. Patriotic feelings had been invoked in the closing stages of the struggle against Napoleon, and the Russian Emperor expressed sympathy for the Polish nation when Russia absorbed the former Grand Duchy of Warsaw in 1814. During the same year a German Confederation was invented to link together the new thirty-nine German-speaking states of central Europe, under the leadership of the Austrian Emperor. However, its organizers had no intention of using this loose association, consisting of no more than periodic meetings of the ambassadors of each of the states in Frankfurt, as the basis for a national Germany. In 1830 the Belgians successfully divided themselves from the Dutch in a nationalist revolt. Mazzini was to found a Young Italy society committed to inspiring the inhabitants of the peninsula with a common purpose.[15]

In 1830 nationalism was an even more diffuse notion than liberalism. Its future as a doctrine of state power was as yet uncharted, although the beginnings were there in the writings of some German thinkers, as Michael Biddiss argues. Later in the century nationalist sentiment was employed to justify burgeoning centralization and state power.

In one respect our terminal date marks a substantive break: 1830 was a year of revolutions, with hints of nationalist and claims of liberal sentiments, although it should be noted that the largest state, Russia, was as untouched by upheaval then as she was in 1848, and that the German states were little affected. The political discord of 1830 was kick-started into revolt by the impact on the major cities and rural areas of an economic crisis. This was the last 'year of revolution' in which socialist ideas played no significant part, although their development was already under way. The period began with a revolution which aimed at 'Liberty, Equality and Fraternity'. It ended with another revolution in France whose watchwords were 'Liberty and Order'. 'Equality and Fraternity' were soon to be recalled by those who found 1830 a very bad date at which to end the story.

NOTES

1 *Archives Parlementaries*, IX, pp.236–7, quoted in J. Hardman, *The French Revolution* (London, 1988), p.116.
2 D.M.G. Sutherland, *France 1789–1815. Revolution and Counter-Revolution* (London, 1985), pp.279–307.
3 C. Lucas, 'The first Directory and the rule of law', *French Historical Studies*, x (1977), pp.231–60.
4 C.H. Church, 'In search of the Directory', in J.F. Bosher (ed.) *French Government and Society, 1500–1850. Essays in Memory of Alfred Cobban* (London, 1973).
5 D. Woronoff, *The Thermidorean Regime and the Directory 1794–1799* (Cambridge, 1984).
6 M. Wollstonecraft, *A Vindication of the Rights of Women* was first published in 1792 (London, 1992, ed. Miriam Brody).
7 See R.S. Alexander, ch.3, p.42.
8 M. Agulhon, *The Republic in the Village: The People of the Var from the French Revolution to the Second Republic* (Cambridge, 1970, trs. Janet Lloyd).
9 O. Hufton, *Women and the Limits of Citizenship during the French Revolution* (Toronto, 1992).
10 A. Forrest, *The French Revolution and the Poor* (Oxford, 1981).
11 P.M. Jones, *Politics and Rural Society. The Southern Massif Central c.1750–1880* (Cambridge, 1985).
12 Such as the *Loi le Chapelier* of June 1791 which banned artisan organizations; for the text see J. Hardman, *The French Revolution* (London, 1981), pp.112–14.
13 C. H. Church, *Europe in 1830* (London, 1983), p.92.
14 M. Hughes, *Nationalism and Society. Germany 1800–1945* (London, 1988).
15 D. Mack Smith, *Mazzini* (London, 1994).

FURTHER READING

The background to the period is succinctly explained in W. Doyle, *The Old European Order, 1660–1800* (Oxford, 1978) and O. Hufton, *Europe: Privilege and Protest 1730–1789* (London, 1980). The whole period was examined in a brisk and stimulating way in G. Rudé, *Revolutionary Europe 1783–1815* (London, 1964) and E. Hobsbawm, *The Age of Revolution 1789–1848* (London, 1962) and both are still well worth reading. Useful specific references can be found in C. Cook and J. Stevenson, *Modern European History 1763–1985* (London, 1992).

Recent surveys of individual countries include B. Jelavich, *Modern Austria: Empire and Republic, 1815–1986* (Cambridge, 1987) and A. Sked, *The Decline and Fall of the Habsburg Empire, 1815–1918* (London, 1989). An introduction to France can be gained from the very brief R. Price, *A Concise History of France* (Cambridge, 1993), F. Furet, *Revolutionary France 1770 – 1870* (Oxford 1992, trs. Antonia Nevill), an anti-Marxist account by a leading revisionist, which could usefully be read in conjunction with R. Magraw, *France 1814–1914. The Bourgeois Century* (London, 1983). The latter offers a detailed survey of the literature delivered in a somewhat Marxist tone. A. Cobban, *History of Modern France*, vols 2 and 3 (London, 1969) still provides the most readable and comprehensive summary despite the enormous amount of research completed since its publication. Recent research on the period is brought together in F. Furet and M. Ozouf, *The Transformation of Political Culture 1789–1848*, vol. 3 of *The French Revolution and the Creation of Modern Political Culture* (Oxford, 1989).

J. Sheehan, *German History 1770–1866* (Oxford, 1989) is lucid and knowledgeable and M. Fulbrook offers a crisp survey in *A Concise History of Germany* (Cambridge, 1992). W. Carr, *History of Germany 1815–1990* (London, 1991) gives an efficient summary of political events. S. Woolf, *A History of Italy 1700–1860. The Social Constraints of Political Change* (London, 1979) is well informed and thoughtful on social change and its repercussions. Russia is concisely summarized by E. Acton, *Russia* (London, 1986) and examined in more detail by D. Saunders, *Russia in the Age of Reaction and Reform 1801–1881* (London and New York, 1992). S.G. Payne, *A History of Spain and Portugal. Volume 2: 1700–Present* (Madison, 1973) offers an introduction to the Iberian peninsula, R. Carr, *Spain 1808–1939* (Cambridge, 1966) is valuable. H.V. Livermore, *New History of Portugal* (Oxford, 1966) gives more detail on her history, while A. Shubert, *A Social History of Modern Spain* (London, 1990) should not be missed.

Chapter 2

The French Revolution

Julian Swann

The French Revolution was one of the greatest social and political upheavals in European history, and its tremors can still occasionally be felt.[1] In the popular imagination, the magical figure 1789 conjures up conflicting images of Liberty, Equality and Fraternity alongside the *tricoteuse* and the guillotine, of a revolution that offered individual choice and freedom, but that was transformed first into terror and subsequently the Caesarism of Napoleon. These events have never ceased to fascinate historians, nor to divide them, and the causes and consequences of 1789 remain a rich source of debate. In order to steer a path through this minefield, it is necessary to understand why the monarchy lost control in 1789. It is also important to examine the reforms of the revolutionaries, their successes and failures, and to consider why, despite so much goodwill and optimism, political stability proved elusive. Finally, we need to confront the horrors of the Terror and to assess its origins and relationship to the revolution as a whole.

The doors of revolution were prised open by the political repercussions of a financial crisis which began in the summer of 1786.[2] Louis XVI was informed by his controller general of finances, Calonne, that the budget deficit had reached astronomical proportions and that only drastic remedies could save the state. His proposed solution was a thorough overhaul of the taxation system with the introduction of a new land tax, or *subvention territoriale,* plus a host of measures designed to encourage trade and industry by the abolition of internal tolls and duties. There was nothing very remarkable about these suggestions. Calonne was the latest in a long line of ministers with grand projects of reform, and his plans to free the grain trade or to replace the *corvée* with a cash payment had been part of fashionable physiocratic doctrine since at least 1763. It was not, therefore, his proposals, but the means of implementing them that were revolutionary. Rather than pass the relevant edicts to the Parlement of Paris, Calonne urged Louis to summon an Assembly of Notables in order to provide a semblance of public consent for his measures. When the king agreed, he ended a tradition of royal absolutism dating back to the time of cardinal de Richelieu. Such an Assembly had last met in 1624 and ever since successive French kings had ruled without the cooperation of any national representative body. Not that Calonne intended to abrogate royal authority. He was detested by the parlements and saw the Assembly of Notables as a convenient means of side-stepping their opposition. Others were more prescient, and the vicomte de Ségur, a notorious wag, was soon informing the salons of Paris that 'the king has just resigned'.[3]

His quip was a little premature, but the monarchy had taken a potentially dangerous step by asking nearly one hundred and fifty notables, including princes of the blood, clergy and magistrates to interest themselves in its financial affairs. They gathered in February 1787 and problems quickly became apparent. Despite Calonne's efforts to pack the Assembly with his own creatures, the notables were highly critical of his plans. Not only did they refuse to rubber-stamp his policies, but they even began to question his integrity, comparing the massive deficit of 1787 with the surplus reported by Necker in his *compte rendu* of 1781. Calonne replied with a direct appeal to the people in the form of the *avertissement* read from the pulpits in April, accusing the notables of defending their own selfish interests. It was a last desperate gamble and it failed; on 8 April 1787 he was dismissed. His replacement was one of his chief critics, Lomenie de Brienne, a worldly archbishop strongly suspected of atheism. Brienne was as skilled in intrigue as he was ill-versed in finance, and Louis was obliged to correct his minister's sums before a new fiscal package could be presented to the notables. With extra taxation the only realistic option available, Brienne could only add a new gloss to Calonne's original programme. Not that it mattered. The Assembly proved no more amenable than before, and on 25 May it was dismissed.

The crown was now forced to employ its traditional strategy of registration in the Parlement of Paris. Since 1756, it had been common practice to impose unpopular taxation at a *lit de justice*, where the king presided in person. After the ceremony, the *parlementaires* would protest about the insult to the fundamental laws of the kingdom and arbitrary government, while the crown collected its taxes. By summoning an Assembly of Notables, the king had refused to play by these old rules, and in July and August 1787 the Parlement did the same. Not only did it declare the forced registration of Brienne's edicts to be illegal, but it also echoed the notables by calling for the convocation of the Estates General. The ancient representative body of the nation had last met in 1614, but according to the government's critics it was the only body qualified to grant new taxation. Louis XV had once declared that he would 'rather abdicate than call the Estates General', and courtiers speculated upon the punishment Louis XIV would have inflicted upon a minister foolish enough to make such a suggestion. Not surprisingly, therefore, Brienne did his best to put off the fateful day. After a brief exile to Troyes, the magistrates were recalled in September 1787, and presented with a revised financial policy, the centre-piece of which was a massive loan.

In exchange for a promise to call the Estates General in 1792, it was expected that the Parlement would register Brienne's proposals, thus buying time for serious reform. Hopes of reconciliation were dashed because of a misunderstanding about the nature of the ceremony held on 19 November. The princes and magistrates believed they were participating in an open royal *séance*, whereas Louis behaved as if he was holding a *lit de justice*. Protests and recriminations followed, and the king was obliged to exile the rebellious duc d'Orléans. In a last desperate effort to restore the king's authority, Brienne and the guardian of the seals, Lamoignon, attempted a full-scale reform of the Parlement. These draconian measures implemented in May 1788 destroyed what was left of royal credit, and in August 1788 Brienne found himself staring into an empty treasury. He could not even raise money against future taxation, the classic expedient in moments of crisis, and in a panic-stricken effort to restore confidence he persuaded Louis to advance the meeting of the Estates General to May 1789. It was not enough to save him, and on 25 August he was disgraced. His replacement, the recalled Necker, was content to stabilize the fiscal situation and await the Estates General.

It was, therefore, financial weakness that forced Louis XVI to take a decision that neither of his two predecessors would have contemplated. Yet both Louis XIV and Louis XV had faced crises which matched that of 1787–8, so what was different? It has usually been assumed that Louis XVI's problems were the result of an enormous debt accumulated in the wars of the eighteenth century and, above all, that of American Independence (1776–83).[4] There is no doubt that the figures were terrifying. At least 997 million *livres* were borrowed to pay for French involvement in the conflict, and to repay the debt and accumulated interest would cause immense strain. The key was the ordinary peacetime budget: if that could be kept roughly in balance and the debt amortized the monarchy would remain solvent. Instead, after the fall of Necker in 1781, and especially during the ministry of Calonne, a number of fatal errors were committed. A programme of gradual reduction of expenses, notably by the suppression of offices in the fiscal administration, was reversed, while borrowing continued on a grand scale in order to finance Calonne's ambitious plan of economic expansion and public works, inflating interest payments in the process. Finally, the return of peace and the desire to honour engagements contracted during the war prevented increases in taxation. This unhappy combination caused a ballooning deficit, which gradually undermined confidence in the crown's ability to repay, eventually forcing Calonne to make his ill-fated gamble with the Assembly of Notables. The only realistic alternative was a partial bankruptcy, as had occurred in 1770. A truly determined government could probably have repeated the exercise, but Louis XVI was personally opposed to the idea. His caution was understandable because in the intervening two decades the desire for public accountability had grown appreciably.

There was, of course, more to the crisis of 1787–8 than simply balancing the budget. Calonne for all his faults was a dedicated servant of Louis XVI, and his ideas reveal much about contemporary views on reform. Before 1789, the social and administrative map of France resembled a patchwork quilt, and at every level privileges and anomalies were to be found. One did not have to be a cleric or noble in order to possess special rights, but those two groups were extremely pampered. Although the fiscal exemptions of the nobility have frequently been exaggerated, its dominance over positions of power has not. Rapid social mobility was possible, but, in 1789, nobles effectively monopolized high office whether at court or in the church, army, judiciary or royal bureaucracy. Yet, there was much more to the idea of privilege than just the three orders of the state. Provinces such as Brittany, Languedoc and Burgundy had retained powerful local Estates, and were relatively lightly taxed when compared with Normandy or the Ile de France. Recently conquered territories such as French Flanders or Franche-Comté had also retained local privileges, and over the years many towns had bought, or acquired, their own rights and exemptions. These fiscal inequalities were compounded by the myriad internal tolls and duties which littered the country-side, hindering trade and causing resentment. Paris was ringed by nearly fifty toll gates, enforcing the taxes levied on goods entering the capital, and it was not a coincidence that they were one of the first targets of the popular revolution. Corporations and institu-tions including, among others, the Catholic Church, parlements and other law courts, municipal councils and trade guilds, all possessed their own rights and status.

The crown was in a very ambiguous position relative to this society because it was both the guarantor and principal threat to the world of privilege. French monarchs had contracted obliga-tions on a one-to-one basis with these institutions, and their successors felt duty bound to honour them. As the eighteenth century progressed, these corporate rights began to look in-creasingly anachronistic, harmful to the economy and even unjust, to enlightened eyes. Ministers such as Machault, Bertin and Turgot made a conscious effort to reduce fiscal anomalies and promote the idea of a more rational and egalitarian state. The results were mixed. Machault failed in his campaign to tax the French church between 1749 and 1751. Nor was Bertin able to impose a national property survey for fiscal purposes in 1763. The free trade experiment in grain conducted between 1763 and 1770 also ended in disappointment, as did Turgot's efforts to abolish the guilds and *corvée*. Not that the picture was uniquely sombre. The crown did have its successes, building an impressive road network, and encouraging arts and industry. The financial col-lapse of 1787–8 has, however, inevitably focused the attention of historians upon the failure of fiscal reform and the supposedly damaging role of class and vested interests. There is some truth in these allegations. The Catholic Church proved especially adept at protecting its fiscal privileges, paying no direct taxes and instead negotiating a 'free gift' to the crown. The parlements were another hindrance, frequently denouncing government policy and obstructing its implementation. Yet neither the clergy, nor the *parlementaires*, would have been able to thwart a truly determined government, and the parlements had been effectively broken between 1771 and 1774. The real problem was the monarchy itself.

All important decisions were made in the king's councils, where the sovereign consulted with his ministers and personally chosen advisers. In order to work effectively, the king needed to listen to the arguments presented and then decide. If his decisions were consistent and other than in exceptional circumstances irreversible the system could function effectively. Louis XVI was conscientious and full of good intentions.[5] His ultimately fatal weakness was a lack of confidence in his own judgement, and an inability to surmount the ministerial and aristocratic cabals that surrounded him. Aware that the king could be manipulated, the members of his council intrigued against each other, undoing their own reforming initiatives in the process. Turgot was felled by the plotting of Miromesnil and Maurepas, while Calonne was, in part, a victim of the circle of courtiers around the queen, Marie-Antoinette. Louis needed a first minister, but after the death of Maurepas in 1781 he preferred to maintain the fiction that he was ruling alone in the manner of Louis XIV. It was not a coincidence that the government lost its reforming impetus thereafter. Indeed, the problems of factionalism at Versailles were accentuated by the growing political independence of the king's brothers, Artois and Provence, not to mention his frondish cousin, Orléans, the future Philippe Égalité. Finally, the period saw the gradual emergence of the queen as political power-broker, with disastrous consequences after 1787.

If factionalism at Versailles dissipated the energies of the government, then there is no doubt that public opinion reduced its scope for drastic action. In the course of the eighteenth century, educated French opinion became increasingly seduced by the idea that legitimate authority needed a check, especially after the publication of Montesquieu's classic *L'Esprit des lois* in 1748, and the highly influential *Lettres historiques* of Le Paige, published in 1753. Within the context of mid-eighteenth-century France, the only feasible intermediary body between the king and his subjects was the Parlement of Paris.[6] Its members gradually warmed to their role, publishing their remonstrances to the king and styling themselves as 'the defenders of the people and the *patrie*'. Their illusions were shattered in 1771 when Louis XV and his chancellor, Maupeou, exiled the magistrates, replacing them with loyal judges in a reformed Parlement. For the majority of enlightened opinion, the monarchy had crossed the threshold into despotism, and the first calls for the summoning of the Estates General were heard. Although recalled after Louis XVI's accession, the Parlement was a shadow of its former self, but the belief that power exercised without restraint equalled despotism was solidly entrenched. Despite their weakness after 1774, the *parlementaires* were unlikely to give their consent to radical change, and in order to win confidence and consent for its measures, the crown needed to cooperate with some form of representative body. Such aspirations were given an additional fashionable gloss by the American War of Independence which inspired a generation of liberal opinion, especially amongst the aristocracy. The provincial assemblies favoured by both Calonne and Brienne were perhaps the most manageable method of conducting a representative experiment, but before they had time to prove their worth they were swept away by the political avalanche of 1787–8.

The financial crisis has, therefore, to be seen against the wider political and intellectual background of a society increasingly convinced of the need for government accountability. As the elections for the Estates General took place in the spring of 1789, the three estates of the kingdom drew up their *cahiers de doléances* listing both their grievances and hopes for change. Generalizing about such a vast collection of documents is always hazardous, but certain key themes recur. The desire for a constitutional check via regular meetings of the Estates General, or some other representative institution, was prominent, as were calls for freedom of speech, equality before the law and open competition for public office. Moreover, even the nobility, which theoretically had most to lose, echoed these sentiments, revealing a willingness to sacrifice its fiscal privileges for the common good.

Louis XVI was personally popular, and had he, or his ministry, seized the initiative by designing a programme that reflected these hopes then the crown and Estates General could conceivably have worked in harmony. Instead, the behaviour of Louis and his ministers before July 1789 offered the final and most compelling evidence of the total inability of the monarchy to reform itself. Despite his good intentions, the king offered no lead, nor did he invest any of his ministers with the necessary backing or confidence. The result was a government that resembled a rabbit trapped in the headlights of the oncoming juggernaut known to history as the Estates General. When the deputies assembled on 1 May, there was no royal programme to discuss, nor was any lead given about how to tackle the thorny question of whether voting should be by order or head. The political initiative was not so much lost as given away, and ambitious or radical deputies such as Mirabeau, Lafayette, Sieyès and Le Chapelier allowed to come to the fore.

Under their influence the third estate, admittedly representing at least 98 per cent of the population, declared itself the National Assembly on 17 June. In doing so, the deputies broke the umbilical chord connecting them to the society of orders. It marked the birth of the sovereign nation and, to push a clumsy metaphor that bit further, the death of the old regime. The revolution had begun. The audacity of the third estate stung the government into action with the royal *séance* of 23 June, when Louis finally presented his own proposals for reform. Only a few weeks before they would have been greeted as bold and imaginative, but by mid-June they were obsolete. When the third estate, headed, it is true, by the aristocratic Mirabeau, protested, the king characteristically backed down. A few days later his surrender was confirmed when the two other orders were instructed to join the triumphant National Assembly. By the end of June effective power was draining away from the monarchy, and the political eclipse of Louis XVI was complete after the violence in the capital culminating in the storming of the Bastille on 14 July.

It was traditionally argued that the dismissal of Necker on 11 July, and the appointment of a more robust ministry under baron de Breteuil was part of a failed royal counter *coup* against the National Assembly.[7] Troops were certainly moved up to Paris and the *clique* around the comte d'Artois was demanding firm measures. Moreover, the fear that force would be used to restore the royal authority triggered a popular rebellion in the capital. For the vast majority of Parisians, the summer of 1789 was a period of acute hardship as the effects of two poor harvests drove bread prices to their highest level since 1770–1, causing bankruptcies, unemployment and hunger. Even in normal circumstances the population would have been agitated, but the peculiar political climate, combined with the atrophy of the royal administration, provoked an explosion. While understandable, this revolution was attacking an enemy which was more imagined than real. There was nothing in the conduct of Louis XVI before or after 1789 to suggest that he was prepared to risk civil war in order to restore his position. Nor can his ministers be represented as hard-headed counter-revolutionaries. They were worried about public order in Paris and insubordination in the army, and definitive proof of an attempted *coup d'état* remains elusive. The Estates General had been assembled because of the crown's financial crisis, and a military *coup* was very unlikely to boost either public confidence or royal credit.

The fall of the Bastille was nevertheless highly significant both as a political symbol and as a result of the municipal revolutions that followed. In Paris, order was restored by the newly created National Guard, headed by another ambitious aristocrat, Lafayette, and effective power passed into the hands of the elected municipality, leaving appointed royal officials with little more than their titles. Throughout France, the traditional authority of governors, parlements and intendants melted away. The task of replacing them fell to the National Assembly, and between the fall of the Bastille and the formal promulgation of a new constitution in September 1791 France witnessed an unprecedented wave of reform. Amongst those responsible were liberal nobles including Lafayette, Mirabeau, Lameth, Montmorency-Laval and Lally-Tollendal, assisted by their fellow-patriots from the third estate, notably Barnave, Sieyès, Bailly, Le Chapelier and Target. Acting in the name of the sovereign nation, they assumed powers and authority beyond the wildest dreams of absolute monarchs such as Louis XIV. As for Louis XVI, he paid the price of his earlier inertia by being largely excluded from the process of national regeneration. In a sense, his discomfiture symbolized one of the revolution's most striking achievements, namely the transfer of sovereignty from the king to the National Assembly, but both would pay a high price for that separation.

No sooner had calm been restored in Paris than frightening reports of a rural revolution began to flood into the capital. The history of the revolution is nearly always written from a Parisian perspective. Yet, in 1789, approximately 80 per cent of the population lived in towns or villages with less than 2,000 inhabitants, and their lives were shaped by the rhythms of an agricultural economy. Debate continues to rage about the attitudes of the peasantry in 1789, but despite its overwhelming numerical superiority it had few spokesmen in a National Assembly dominated by middle-class lawyers and liberal nobles. Although not directly involved in the political upheavals of Versailles and Paris, the peasantry was nevertheless sensitive to their repercussions. Excited reports from the capital provided an additional source of rumour and anxiety for a population already nervous about the harvest after two years of dearth. With large numbers of poor and destitute already roaming the countryside, this anxiety produced outbreaks of popular panic and wild fears about invading foreign armies, or bands of brigands. Perhaps two-thirds of the country was touched by what has been termed 'the great fear', and by arming themselves and taking to the road in order to warn neighbouring communities, the peasantry helped to give substance to its own nightmare.[8] Not that the great fear was purely imaginary because this movement was accompanied by a highly effective and largely peaceful attack upon the seigneurial system.

Historians continue to disagree about the extent of social tension in the countryside, but there is no doubt that the seigneurial system was resented. As the peasants invaded the *châteaux* of the nobility, the principal targets, other than the wine cellars, were the legal deeds confirming their obligations to the lord. These documents were thrown onto celebratory bonfires, while dovecots, weathervanes, ovens, presses and other symbols of seigneurial authority were destroyed. Such large-scale unrest had not been seen since the early seventeenth century, although the flour wars of the 1770s had demonstrated that the capacity for rural violence was undiminished. On previous occasions, peasant revolts had been brutally suppressed, but in the summer of 1789 normal chains of authority were broken. The National Assembly feared the army, and rather than use force to calm the countryside chose to sanction the peasant revolution instead. In a night of patriotic euphoria, the deputies renounced personal, institutional, provincial and other privileges as the corporate edifice of the old regime came tumbling down. Many would subsequently regret their decision, and the legislation giving final form to these promises was less generous. The peasantry, however, proved itself to be far more tenacious than the revolutionary politicians, and by July 1793 had won a complete victory as seigneurialism and tithes disappeared from the French countryside forever.

The night of 4 August was vital for the future path of reform because it swept away the particularist obstacles and corporate mentality that had so often impeded the monarchy. However, it was the Declaration of the Rights of Man, adopted by the National Assembly on 26 August, which most clearly indicated the new philosophy of government. Written by Lafayette, probably in conjunction with his colleague from the War of American Independence, Thomas Jefferson, the Declaration was a manifesto for the liberal revolution. Men were declared equal in rights, and such basic principles as freedom of speech and of the press, religious toleration, equality before the law, freedom from arbitrary arrest and open competition for public office, decreed in a series of imposing articles. No less important was the claim that sovereignty belongs to the nation, which justified everything accomplished thereafter. However, for the leading revolutionaries, most of whom believed in a constitutional monarchy, that basic doctrine would cause a dangerous clash with the reality of a king who remained in his own mind Louis by the grace of God, king of France and Navarre. Producing a constitution that could solve this riddle was one of the most urgent tasks of the National Assembly, and it was not until September 1791 that a solution was finally reached.

Taken together the night of 4 August and the Declaration of the Rights of Man symbolized a revolution that literally tore up the old social and institutional map of France, and sought to apply rational and enlightened principles to the construction of its successor. Many of the measures implemented recalled the unfulfilled ambitions of earlier ministers of the crown. Internal tolls and duties were abolished, free trade in grain restored and guilds and professional monopolies destroyed. More novel was the replacement of the old provinces by eighty-three departments of comparable size and identical administrative structure. With geometric precision, each department was divided into districts, which in turn were sub-divided into communes. In harmony with the principles of the revolution, office in the new administration was elective, although candidates were expected to meet certain property qualifications. The reform of the judiciary was no less dramatic. In August 1790, the parlements were abolished, and the legal hierarchy reconstructed on fresh foundations. Henceforth, there was a new legal pyramid with courts at communal level, dealing with minor cases, climbing upwards in degree of seriousness to district and ultimately departmental level. Finally, only in exceptional circumstances were cases subject to appeal to Paris. Under the old regime, offices in the parlements and many of its inferior courts had been bought on the open market. That abuse was reformed, and once again the democratic principle brought

into play – in future judges were to be elected. When Louis XV
and Louis XVI had tried to reform the parlements they had been
denounced as despots, but no such objections were levelled at the
representatives of the nation, who introduced change on a hitherto
unimagined scale. One final example of their power was the
decision to abolish nobility, which disappeared with scarcely a
murmur in June 1790. There could now be no doubt that the
society of orders had passed away. Only equal citizens remained.

Yet for all these worthy reforms, it was the financial crisis that
had been the immediate cause of the monarchy's collapse, and the
revolutionaries were expected to provide a solution. That task was
rendered more complicated by the almost total collapse of the
existing administrative and fiscal system and the disturbances in
the countryside where taxes were not being paid. Despite these
difficulties, the National Assembly rejected the idea of outright
bankruptcy and like Louis XVI before them guaranteed the state's
debts. This would have provided the perfect recipe for complete
financial collapse were it not for the addition of a vital ingredient,
paper money. In order to meet its obligations, the state began to
print money which, initially, benefited from the public confidence
in the National Assembly. More tangible grounds for confidence
were provided in November 1789, when the Assembly, under the
prompting of Mirabeau, voted to confiscate the lands of the
church. The effective nationalization of between 5 and 10 per cent
of the land in the kingdom provided collateral for state credit and
a source of income when the decision was taken to sell these *biens
nationaux*. By continuing to print paper money – or *assignats* –
against the value of the land seized from the church, the revolutionaries solved, in the short term, their financial worries. Moreover the problem of inflation was sidestepped by accepting the
assignats as payment for the *biens nationaux*. The revolution had
thus bought a breathing space in which to accomplish more
substantial fiscal reform; war and continuing revolution would
see the opportunity go to waste.

The revolution gained another vital asset when despoiling the
church because by selling the *biens nationaux* it acquired an
influential and grateful constituency. Those who had invested in
church land had a vested interest in the consolidation and defence
of the new regime. Not that the effects of the measure were wholly
positive. The nationalization of church property had deprived the
clergy of their revenues, and the National Assembly had promised

that the state would provide for their financial needs. Following the old adage that he who pays the piper calls the tune, the revolutionaries embarked upon a complete reform of the church.[9] Aided by dissident Jansenist priests, such as the *abbés* Camus and Gregoire, they drafted the Civil Constitution of the Clergy, which was unveiled in July 1790. In this document, rational and enlightened thinking was brought to bear upon the workings of the Catholic Church. For orderly minds the existence of 136 bishops in dioceses of varying physical size and population made little sense. In order to restore a sense of symmetry, each of the eighty-three departments was to have a bishopric, while those considered surplus to requirements were abolished.

Now that stipends were to be paid by the state, the clergy was expected to conform to prevailing bureaucratic norms. Like judges and officials in the administrative and political hierarchy, parish priests were subject to elections by district electoral assemblies. Nor did this exercise in democracy stop there, for bishops were also to be elected and not appointed by the king with the blessing of the pope. Some reform of the French church was perhaps desirable. The episcopate was exclusively noble and two centuries after the Council of Trent still contained scions of the aristocracy lacking both faith and vocation. Anger amongst the ranks of the priesthood had been demonstrated during the elections to the Estates General, when many lordly prelates had been shocked not to be chosen as delegates. Yet there was a world of difference between reform of the church and the Civil Constitution. Not only did it create the theoretical possibility that a priest or bishop could be elected by Protestants, Jews, or, even worse, atheists, but it also stood centuries of church tradition on its head by investing authority in the laity and priesthood (as electors) and not the bishops. To call the Civil Constitution an unmitigated disaster would be an understatement, and it was a prime cause of many of the revolution's later difficulties.

As this brief survey has indicated, the National Assembly was responsible for a programme of reform which transformed the social and institutional life of France. The patchwork quilt of particularist rights and privileges was replaced by a greater emphasis upon the rights of the individual and the concept of equality before the authority of the state. In areas such as local government, or in the basic principles of the Declaration of the Rights of Man, its work can still be seen in contemporary France.

The driving force behind these changes was the coalition of a minority of liberal aristocrats and the leaders of the wealthy, legally trained, bourgeoisie. The contribution of the nobility is particularly striking. Lafayette led the National Guard and was the author of the Declaration of the Rights of Man. The duc d'Aiguillon made the opening speech of the famous night of 4 August 1789, Mirabeau proposed the nationalization of the church lands and Mathieu de Montmorency, a member of one of the most distinguished aristocratic houses in Europe, led the campaign to abolish the nobility. Yet, if the revolution of 1789 was in large measure the work of a section of the nobility, its chief beneficiaries were the bourgeoisie. After the reforms of the National Assembly, it was inconceivable that the effective stranglehold of political power and public office enjoyed by the pre-revolutionary nobility would return. Moreover, as the revolution developed after September 1791, the active participation of former nobles noticeably diminished both at national and local level.

If the National Assembly had reinvigorated France, the constitution that it bequeathed to the country was a disaster. Providing a constitutional settlement that could provide stable government was, together with solving the financial crisis, a crucial test for the National Assembly. In September 1789, an attempt to transplant an English-style bicameral legislature had been defeated. Thereafter the deputies had spent nearly two years wrangling about the franchise and, above all, the prerogatives reserved for the crown. When it was finally published, the constitution provided for biennial elections to a legislative assembly, with a restricted franchise when compared to that of 1789. Government ministers were chosen by the king, although legislation was to be initiated by the assembly. The king could veto legislation, but if two successive legislatures adopted the measure his verdict could be overridden.

Such an unwieldy constitution was a recipe for disaster. Within twelve months the monarchy had been overthrown by the second revolutionary wave of August 1792, and after a show trial Louis XVI was executed in January 1793. There is no simple explanation for this dramatic turn of events, but the constitution of 1791 was severely handicapped from the moment of its conception. Had Louis XVI's sanction been freely given, then there is no doubt that he could have done much to consolidate the new regime. Instead, from the outset, the constitution was built upon the lie that the king had willingly participated in its creation. The truth was very different. Dragged to Paris against his will after the women's march to Versailles of October 1789, the king had become increasingly hostile to the revolution. In June 1791, Louis and his family had escaped from Paris and made a desperate dash for the frontier. Before departing, the king penned a detailed memorandum denouncing much of what had been achieved since July 1789. After having been trapped at Varennes, the royal party was obliged to return under guard to Paris, where a sullen populace was convinced that it had been betrayed. In punishment the king was suspended, and it was only after signing the constitution that he was symbolically put back on his throne. It was in these inauspicious circumstances that elections were held for the first, and only, Legislative Assembly. Although the king subsequently fulfilled his constitutional duties with precision, he displayed neither enthusiasm, nor commitment. Not unreasonably, he expected the constitution to be unworkable, but typically did nothing to shape events and simply observed developments with an air of resigned fatalism.

Trying to establish a totally novel constitutional government with a head of state who gave the impression that he was being held prisoner was a testing proposition. Nor was there any shortage of other obstacles. Perhaps the most damaging was the absence of any form of cohesion amongst the revolutionary leadership. Throughout the period after 1789, politics moved at a tremendous pace and the radical of one day was the conservative of the next. In September 1791, it was the liberal alliance that had led the revolution of 1789, including Lafayette, Lameth, Bailly and Barnave, who were determined to uphold the constitutional monarchy. Weakened by the disaffection of the king, they were confronted by an increasingly powerful radical movement to their political left. In the Legislative Assembly an ambitious faction of deputies including Brissot, Guadet, Isnard, Louvet, Roland and Vergniaud, known variously as the Brissotins, or more commonly the Girondins because of their strong links with the department of the Gironde, were at best ambiguous in their relationship to the monarchy. Even more outspoken were the Parisian radicals who numbered Danton, Marat and Robespierre amongst their most famous spokesmen. In the immediate aftermath of the flight to Varennes many had shifted to a republican stance, and their distrust of the constitutional monarchists had been given a bitter edge by the political clamp-down that had accompanied the massacre of the Champs de Mars of 17 July 1791, when National Guards under the command of Lafayette had fired on a crowd of peaceful protesters.

It is not surprising that the revolution had spawned conflicting factions or ideologies, but it had also politicized French society, and especially life in the capital.[10] The old regime had permitted few channels for meaningful political expression, and Versailles, the parlements and provincial estates had been dominated by a small, largely noble, elite. After August 1788, controls and censorship had vanished, allowing the proliferation of newspapers, pamphlets and manifestos of every description, as would-be politicians and journalists competed in a hitherto unimaginably free political debate. Every taste was catered for, from the staid pages of *Le Moniteur*, to the incendiary *L'ami du peuple* published by the noxious Marat.

The political clubs which flourished first in the capital and subsequently throughout the kingdom were another significant innovation. By July 1791, the Jacobin club of Paris, named after its meeting place in a former monastery, had no fewer than 920 affiliated institutions. Amongst its competitors were the Cordeliers, also occupying a former monastery although catering for a more popular clientele, and break-away movements from the mother society such as the Feuillants, which after 1791 grouped together moderate constitutional monarchists. Although originally a meeting place for the deputies to the National Assembly and a largely affluent membership, the Jacobins gradually broadened their social base. At its height, it became a sort of parallel legislative assembly, and few major decisions were taken without having been thrashed out in the club first. Other mediums for the politicization of daily life included membership of the National Guard, and participation in the numerous elections at communal, district or national level. The public meetings and debates which accompanied these first steps in democracy were undoubtedly a novel and exciting experience for the participants, and historians have recently begun to place great emphasis upon the role played by such factors in creating a new form of political culture. The democratization of politics was one of the revolution's most striking legacies. However, for those struggling to re-establish order after 1791 it was certainly a mixed blessing. The existence of an attentive popular audience which, as the events of July and

October 1789 had shown, could be mobilized for political purposes added a volatile extra dimension to the situation.

An already grim political horizon was darkened further by a string of errors and miscalculations committed after September 1791. One of the most intractable problems facing the Legislative Assembly was the opposition of much of the Catholic hierarchy, including the pope, to the Civil Constitution of the Clergy. Matters had been made worse by the National Assembly's foolish decision of November 1790 to force the clergy to swear a constitutional oath.[11] Attempting to use legislation and coercion in matters of conscience only irritated existing wounds and the result was to confirm the schism with a slight majority of the clergy bowing to the authority of the state. Those who refused the oath found themselves dismissed from their livings. Talk of dechristianization in the French countryside has probably been exaggerated and deeply conservative communities were incensed by external meddling in their affairs. Not surprisingly, they could not understand why perfectly good priests, many of whom were local men, were being forced out in favour of outsiders. Not content with treating the church as if it was an extension of the civil service, the revolutionaries proceeded to persecute the dissenters. Stripped of their livings, forbidden to use religious buildings and from May 1792 threatened with deportation, non-juring priests were forced to flee or go into hiding. Even those who sided with the government enjoyed only a brief period of peace and quiet. As the revolution slid into Terror after 1792, the clergy, constitutional or otherwise, was increasingly seen as the agent of counter-revolution. During the dechristianization campaign of 1793–4, churches were ransacked and closed, while priests were obliged to abjure or face imprisonment and frequently death. These tragic events launched a bitter war between the Catholic Church and the French state that would continue periodically until the twentieth century.

In the short term, the religious policies of successive governments after 1790 created unnecessary enemies for the revolution. To draw a direct line between interference in the church and counter-revolution is too simplistic, although from Louis XVI to the humblest of his subjects the schism posed a problem of conscience, and in areas like the Vendée and parts of Normandy, Languedoc and Brittany it could be an important ingredient in the popular counter-revolution.

However, the principal cause of the monarchy's fall was the decision taken in April 1792 to declare war on Austria and Prussia.[12] In doing so, the revolutionaries began a conflict that would continue with few interruptions until the defeat of Napoleon in 1815. The official justification for beginning hostilities was Austrian toleration of émigré armies in the Rhineland towns of Mainz and Trier. The king's brothers, Artois and Provence, and sundry other aristocratic plotters had long fled the country and had sought help from the crowned heads of Europe in order to mount a military campaign against the revolution. Initially their pleas had fallen on deaf ears as the other powers were content to profit from the misfortunes of the Bourbons. After Varennes, however, the plight of Louis XVI was evident and the fear of contagion by the revolutionary virus caused a hardening of opinion in Germany. Vienna and Berlin buried their differences, which dated back to Frederick II's invasion of Silesia in 1740, and signed a joint declaration in August 1791. Yet, with Catherine II of Russia glancing covetously at what remained of Poland, the two German powers were unlikely to have favoured an early war. It was France that precipitated matters, although for some very curious reasons.

Louis XVI and especially Marie-Antoinette were in favour of the war because they believed that the French armies, depleted by the emigration of large sections of the noble officer *corps*, would be no match for their enemies. Defeat would, according to their logic, bring a return to power on the backs of the victorious émigré and German forces. Such bizarre reasoning might be considered a joke, or the result of revolutionary propaganda, were it not for the fact that the dim-witted Marie-Antoinette sent French military plans to Austria in March 1792. Not that the king and queen were the only ones who hoped to profit from the conflict. Generals such as Lafayette and Narbonne also saw war, in their case a victorious one, as a means of furthering their own careers while reinforcing the position of the monarchy. They argued, not unreasonably, that a dash of military glory would strengthen the crown against republican sentiment. Amongst the deputies of the Legislative Assembly martial spirit was also in evidence. Brissot and his supporters engaged in what appeared to be a competition to present the most vainglorious speech in favour of war. Isnard probably deserves the prize for a ludicrous outburst in which he claimed that the 'moment the enemy armies begin to fight ours, when the light of philosophy opens their eyes, the peoples will embrace each other in the face of dethroned tyrants'. Underneath their posturing was a more insidious desire to use war as a means of forcing the king, and any other waverers, to declare themselves whole-heartedly for the revolution.

It was, therefore, with mixed motives that the French began their crusade to export the revolution to Europe. Initially the campaign was disastrous. French troops in Flanders fled at the first sight of Austrian uniforms, and discipline and organization were poor. Further embarrassment was avoided because of the second partition of Poland, which distracted the Austrian and Prussian forces at a crucial moment. These setbacks did nothing to calm the fears and anxieties of the capital, and although Marie-Antoinette may have been surprised, much of the blame was heaped upon the king and his 'Austrian bitch'. On 20 June 1792 a crowd of Parisian artisans, shopkeepers and tradesmen, known collectively as the *sans-culottes*, invaded the royal palace of the Tuileries, insulting the king and forcing him to spend several hours indulging the whims of his least affectionate subjects. As news of the king's ill-treatment spread there was something of a reaction in his favour, although it proved short lived. Once the German and émigré armies crossed the frontier into France their commandant, the duke of Brunswick, issued a blood-curdling manifesto threatening Paris with the sack in the event of any harm befalling the royal family. These threats produced the result they were intended to prevent. Urged on by radical leaders such as Danton and Marat, a popular insurrection of National Guards and *sans-culottes* attacked the Tuileries on 10 August. The royal family fled in desperation to the Legislative Assembly, putting themselves under its protection while over 600 royalists and Swiss guards defending the palace were massacred. It was a second revolution. In a last gesture, the Legislative Assembly dissolved itself and called for fresh elections to a National Convention. It was that body which would declare France a republic in September 1792, and judge and condemn the king a few months later.

As we have seen, the dice had been loaded against a constitutional monarchy from the very beginning and a series of miscalculations had destroyed what little hope was left. Nor was the monarchy the only victim of the events of 1792. Many of those who had taken a leading role in the revolution of 1789 and who had invested their reputations in the constitution of September

1791 fell with the king. Lafayette, after a failed attempt to march his army on Paris, fled across the border into an Austrian prison. Moderates, including Barnave, Bailly and the Lameth brothers, were now accused of being monarchists and counter-revolutionaries, and either emulated Lafayette or risked imprisonment in France. The election of the Convention marked another step to the revolutionary left, and the formerly radical Girondins found themselves transformed into conservatives in the sense of wishing to uphold a constitutional republican government. To their left within the Convention were the Montagnards or Mountain, so called because they occupied the highest benches within the chamber, including Robespierre, Danton, Desmoulins, Marat and even Louis XVI's treacherous cousin, Philippe Égalité, the former duc d'Orléans. The Montagnards dominated the Parisian Jacobins and possessed the confidence of the *sans-culottes*. Yet even their position was capable of being redefined and they were under increasing competition for the affections of the *sans-culottes* from the extreme left in the form of the *enragés* led by Jacques Roux, or the followers of René Hébert, the journalist responsible for the infamous *Père Duchesne*. Although distinct both the *enragés* and the *Hébertistes* advocated radical social and economic policies and the latter were to the fore in the dechristianization campaign. It is clearly very difficult to do justice to the shifting sands of revolutionary politics, but it is important to remember that issues such as the fate of the king, or popular insurrection in Paris, were constantly redefining the contours of the political map.

If anything the overthrow of the monarchy heightened the tension in Paris. The fall of the key fortress of Verdun on 1 September reinforced the impression that the advance of the enemy was unstoppable. As Paris mobilized its men for the front, demagogues such as Marat played upon popular fears of a counter-revolutionary insurrection from amongst the many prisoners crammed into the city's jails. Public authority was divided between the revolutionary city government in Paris known as the Commune, the Legislative Assembly and a ministry composed largely of Girondins, but dominated by Danton. All turned a blind eye, or in some cases encouraged, a wholesale massacre of the prisoners. After mock trials, men and women were brutally hacked to death during three days of sickening violence. Perhaps 2,000 perished in what is often described as the first Terror. Its political ramifications were also profound. Just prior to the massacres, Robespierre, acting on behalf of the Commune, signed warrants for the arrest of several leading Girondins. Had his instructions been carried out they would almost certainly have died. It is not difficult to imagine the mutual loathing that subsequently existed between these two groups which formed rival camps in the National Convention.

From the election of the Convention until June 1793, the struggle between Girondins and Montagnards provided the principal political drama. The Montagnards drew their strength from the capital, and after August 1792 held the potential ace in the form of their ability to conjure a popular insurrection in Paris. Given their perceived close escape in September, the Girondins sought to neutralize that advantage by concocting schemes for a defence force from the provinces to protect the integrity of the nation's deputies. As the crisis intensified in the late spring of 1793, Isnard delivered a memorable speech threatening Paris with annihilation if it dared harm the Convention. With rhetoric hyperbolic even by the standards of the Girondins, he claimed that future generations would search the banks of the Seine in vain for signs of the city. His outburst was to no avail. After a botched attempt on 31 May, his opponents succeeded in provoking an insurrection on 2 June. Orders for the arrest of twenty-nine members of the Convention were issued and the leading Girondins either escaped to the provinces or were imprisoned. The era of constitutional republicanism had been brief. The Terror had begun.

Before discussing the Terror we are, however, obliged to offer an overview of the general military and political situation after September 1792. Despite its fearsome reputation, Brunswick's invading army was defeated at the battle of Valmy on 20 September. His troops were driven back across the frontier, further French successes followed in Belgium and by the end of November the Austrians had been expelled. Despite the rhetoric of international fraternity that had accompanied the French declaration of war, the revolutionary government showed a distinctly old regime attitude to the 'liberated' territories. Parts of modern Belgium and the Rhineland were annexed, and its staunchly Catholic population subjected to, amongst other things, French-style reforms of the church. Inspired by their victories, the revolutionaries declared war on much of the rest of Europe and crucially the English in February 1793. Resentment in the conquered territories ensured that when the military tide turned against the French, after the battle of Neerwinden on 15 March, the return of the Austrians was greeted by popular rejoicing. Pushed out of Belgium and defeated in the Rhineland, France once again faced the prospect of invasion.

Conscription was introduced to meet the threat, but in the short term it made matters worse by acting as a catalyst on the already disaffected population of the Vendée which rose in revolt. The west of France was thinly garrisoned and the rebels of what was christened the Royal and Catholic Army achieved a series of quick victories. Thouars and Saumur were captured and by June the vital Atlantic port of Nantes was threatened. It was against this sombre background of war and civil war that the Girondins were expelled from the Convention. Their fall provoked indignation in many of the great provincial cities, where traditional suspicion of Paris combined with growing fear of its political radicalism. Among others, Lyon, Bordeaux, Marseille, Caen and Toulon rose against the authority of the capital in what was described as the Federalist revolt. At its peak no fewer than sixty of the eighty-three departments openly defied Paris, and when the civil war in the Vendée and the conflict with the other European powers are taken into consideration the danger to the revolution becomes clear.

These details are vital because the period of revolutionary government that we call the Terror was the child of that military and political crisis.[13] To save the republic from its enemies required the ruthless mobilization of manpower and economic resources. By 1794, a conscript army of at least 750,000 men was in the field, and the arms and supplies for this formidable force had to be guaranteed. Given the limitations of eighteenth-century bureaucracy and the opposition, passive or otherwise, of large sections of the population, ruthlessness was understandable, if not inevitable. Coordination of this vast effort fell to the Committee of Public Safety, created by the National Convention in April 1793, which after the expulsion of the Girondins provided France with its first strong government since 1788. In strictly military terms its achievements were remarkable. By December 1793, the Vendean army had been destroyed. Lyon fell in October 1793 after a prolonged siege, and the other cities that had sided with the Federalists capitulated. Even Toulon, which had surrendered to the English and declared for Louis XVII was defeated by a young officer with a future, Napoleon Bonaparte. Finally, the victories of Hondshoote (September) and Wattignies (October) relieved the danger of an enemy invasion. The safety of the republic was temporarily assured.

If this was the positive side of the balance sheet, the human cost was heavy. In the Vendée the repression that followed defeat was horrific. Determined to wipe out any potential for further resistance, the government ordered its troops to impose what amounted to a scorched earth policy against its own citizens. Men, women and children died by their thousands, victims of what contemporaries dubbed the Hell columns. Yet without mitigating the horrors of the Vendée, it has to be remembered that civil wars then, as now, are particularly powerful agents of human callousness and cruelty. Tragic scenes were also enacted in Lyon and Toulon, although the repression of the Federalist cities was less severe than that of the Vendée. The degree of persecution depended, in part, upon the attitude of the individuals charged with fulfilling these unpleasant duties.

There was, however, another Terror, the more familiar one of guillotine and *tricoteuse*. Louis XVI, Marie-Antoinette, Barnave, Brissot, Danton, Saint-Just and Robespierre, to name but a few, all died beneath the democratic blade. Their deaths reflected the use of show trials and judicial assassination for political purposes. Louis was executed more because of who he was than for anything he actually did, although his wife had fewer grounds for complaint given her treachery in March 1792. As for the politicians, they fell victim to their own fratricide. After the failure of the Federalist revolts, the remnants of the Girondins were put on trial, condemned, and executed in October 1793. They were victims of the Revolutionary Tribunal which, after its creation by the Convention in March 1793, was synonymous with the Terror in Paris. Before its abolition in May 1795, this extraordinary court was responsible for the deaths of over 2,000 people in the capital, while perhaps 15,000 died at the hands of similar tribunals in the country as a whole. The vast majority were neither aristocrats nor politicians; ordinary men and women were arrested and condemned. Moreover, the number of victims of the Revolutionary Tribunal was increasing in a kind of deadly symmetry with military success, not failure. It is this fact which undermines the argument that the Terror was a necessary, if nasty, means of saving the republic. Instead, it had acquired a momentum and logic of its own.

As the military threat receded there was an attempt by a faction known as the Indulgents, led by Danton and Desmoulins, initially backed by Robespierre, to end the Terror. Desmoulins started a campaign through a newspaper entitled the *Vieux Cordelier* in November 1793, in which he denounced the tyranny that had rendered every citizen, high or low, suspect. Desmoulins and Danton, formerly stalwarts of the revolutionary left, were now redefined on the right in their bid to halt the Terror. They failed in the short term, but the radical revolution was losing its momentum. In March 1794, the Parisian militants headed by Hébert were arrested and executed. However, the purge of the radical left was balanced by the sacrifice of Danton, Desmoulins and their supporters, who were given a parody of a trial before being guillotined. These events were the perfect illustration of the use of Terror as a form of political strategy because the Committee of Public Safety sought to maintain its precarious equilibrium by striking simultaneously at both left and right.

Yet in the minds of, for example, Robespierre or Saint-Just, there was more to the Terror than just defending the republic or settling political scores. In their rhetoric we can detect a theme that would echo in the totalitarian ideologies of both the extreme left and right in the twentieth century. They believed that they were creating a new society, a new man – for they rarely considered the position of women – and to do so they needed to destroy the ideas, beliefs and patterns of behaviour of the old. Terror could, therefore, pave the way to a republic of virtue, and those who stood in the way of the onward march of progress to the New Jerusalem could legitimately be disposed of. Terror was, for the true believer, an integral part of the vision and ideology of revolution.

The power of the Terror should not, however, be exaggerated, and when compared with the twentieth-century tyrannies of Stalin, Hitler and Mao its reign was mild and mercifully brief. Although they would not live to see their ideas bear fruit, the Indulgents had started a movement that would check the revolution and ultimately propel it in a more moderate direction. The Committee of Public Safety had proved dynamic and effective, but it was never more than an arm of the Convention and powers given could always be taken away. The membership of the Committee of Public Safety after the summer of 1793 was far from united. Moderates like Carnot, Lindet and Prieur de la Côte-d'Or had a professional, bureaucratic mentality, well removed from the bloodthirsty Billaud-Varennes or Collot-d'Herbois, and they in turn were distant from icy ideologues such as Saint-Just and Robespierre. Through his uncompromising personality and involvement in elaborate charades such as the Festival of the Supreme Being held on 8 June 1794 as part of the attempt to replace Christianity with an Enlightened civic religion, Robespierre was increasingly accused of dictatorial aspirations. This was perhaps unfair, but he served as the chief target for the opponents of the Committee of Public Safety, and rumours that he planned a further purge provoked the Thermidorean reaction. After two days of deadly political conflict, Robespierre and his allies were defeated. Arrested on 9 July, he survived a bungled suicide attempt and together with Couthon and Saint-Just was guillotined the next day. Robespierre has served ever since as the symbol and the scapegoat for the Terror, but others with more blood on their hands survived and, in some instances, prospered. Nor did Thermidor bring an immediate return to the rule of law, but the era of permanent revolution was over.

It is for this reason that my account of the French Revolution ends with the fall of Robespierre. While the subsequent government of the Directory was a continuation of the republican regime established in September 1792, it was already a conservative force struggling to protect itself against the would-be heirs of the Jacobin left and the various strands of royalist and counter-revolutionary right. Hopes of consolidating the republic were dashed by the military reverses suffered during the campaigns of 1797–9. With the revolution once more in danger, it was the brilliant young general, Napoleon Bonaparte, who presented himself as its saviour. Unfortunately the new Caesar had come not to save the republic but to bury it.

Between 1789 and 1794, the French Revolution had offered a spectacle which has inspired and horrified the people of France and Europe ever since. The overthrow of the monarchy, the destruction of seigneurialism, the attack on the church, and the declaration of the principles of civic equality and national sovereignty were a warning to the other crowned heads of Europe and a model to their critics. For liberals the principles of 1789 and the Declaration of the Rights of Man offered a model that continues to find a resonance today. As the bicentennial celebrations of 1989 demonstrated, they represent the official acceptable face of the French Revolution. By comparison, the anniversary of the declaration of the republic was passed over in comparative silence, and when in 1993 the Russian writer Alexander Solzhenitsyn inaugurated a monument to the victims of the revolution in the Vendée the sense of official embarrassment was tangible. With a metro station in Paris now named after him, the image of Robespierre has ceased to frighten the French public. However, throughout the nineteenth century the radical revolution was the source of inspiration for republican and left-wing movements everywhere. Conservatives, on the other hand, were constantly fearful of a further outbreak of revolutionary fervour and were obliged to rethink their justification of political authority. The French Revolution was a defining moment in the development of all shades of political opinion. It left no one indifferent.

NOTES

1 Two of the best general studies of the revolution are D.M.G. Sutherland, *France 1789–1815: Revolution and Counter-Revolution* (London, 1985), and W. Doyle, *The Oxford History of the French Revolution* (London, 1989).

2 J. Egret, *The French Pre-revolution, 1787–88* (Chicago, 1977) offers the best analysis of the crisis that followed.

3 Comte d'Allonville, *Mémoires secrets de 1770 à 1830 par m. le comte d'Allonville*, 2 vols (Paris, 1830), vol.I, pp.220–1.

4 E.N. White, 'Was there a solution to the financial dilemma of the ancien régime?', *Journal of Economic History*, XLIX (3) (1989), offers a stimulating reappraisal of these events.

5 J.D. Hardman, *Louis XVI* (London, 1993), provides by far the best study of the king and his government.

6 J. Egret, *Louis XV et l'opposition parlementaire* (Paris, 1970), has written the best guide to the conflict between the crown and the parlements.

7 M. Price, '"The ministry of the hundred hours": a reappraisal', *French History*, 4 (1990), pp.317–39, provides a new version of these events.

8 The classic account is that of G. Lefebvre, *The Great Fear of 1789: Rural Panic in Revolutionary France* (London, 1973).

9 For an introduction to the religious policies of the revolutionaries, see J. McManners, *The French Revolution and the Church* (London, 1969).

10 Political culture is currently the fashion amongst historians of the revolution and the volumes edited by K.M. Baker and C. Lucas, *The*

French Revolution and the Creation of Modern Political Culture (Oxford, 1987–8), are the essential starting point.

11   T. Tackett, *Religion, Revolution and Regional Culture in Eighteenth-Century France: The Ecclesiastical Oath of 1791* (Princeton, 1986), is the indispensable guide.

12   T.C.W. Blanning, *The Origins of the French Revolutionary Wars* (London, 1986), offers an excellent introduction.

13   The works of N. Hampson, *The Terror in the French Revolution* (London, 1981), and *The Life and Times of Maximilien Robespierre* (London, 1974), are especially helpful.

FURTHER READING

Amongst the best general surveys of the French revolution are W. Doyle, *The Oxford History of the French Revolution* (Oxford, 1989), S. Schama, *Citizens* (London, 1989), and D.M.G. Sutherland, *France 1789–1815: Revolution and Counter-Revolution* (London, 1985). There is also much to be gained from reading A. Soboul, *The French Revolution, 1787–1799. From the Storming of the Bastille to Napoleon* (London, 1989), which offers the classic Marxist interpretation. T.C.W. Blanning, *The French Revolution: Aristocrats versus Bourgeois?* (London, 1988), provides a brief and stimulating account of the historiographical debates provoked by the revolution. C. Jones, *The Longman Companion to the French Revolution* (London, 1989), is an invaluable work of reference.

G. Lefebvre, *The Coming of the French Revolution* (Princeton, 1947), is the ideal starting place for a study of the origins of the revolution. W. Doyle, *The Origins of the French Revolution* (2nd edn, Oxford, 1988), shows how the debate has developed since Lefebvre and offers an important interpretation of his own. J. Hardman, *Louis XVI* (London, 1993), is by far the best study of the king and his government, while J. Egret, *The French Pre-Revolution, 1787–1788* (Chicago, 1977), is vital for the financial and political crisis of 1787–8. In recent years, the political and intellectual origins of the revolution have provoked a lively debate, and the works of K.M. Baker, *Inventing the French Revolution. Essays on French Political Culture in the Eighteenth Century* (Cambridge, 1990); J.W. Merrick, *The Desacralization of the French Monarchy in the Eighteenth Century* (Baton Rouge, 1990), and R. Chartier, *The Cultural Origins of the French Revolution* (London, 1991), should all be consulted. The volumes edited by K.M. Baker and C. Lucas in the series *The French Revolution and the Creation of Modern Political Culture* (Oxford, 1988–9), are full of interesting essays assessing political and cultural change both before and after 1789.

T.C.W. Blanning, *The Origins of the French Revolutionary Wars* (London, 1986), explains why France went to war in 1792. The effects of war and the origins and role of the Terror are examined by, among others, R. Cobb, *The People's Armies* (London, 1987); N. Hampson, *The Terror in the French Revolution* (London, 1981), and his *The Life and Opinions of Maximilien Robespierre* (London, 1974); C. Lucas, *The Structure of the Terror: The Example of Javogues and the Loire* (Oxford, 1973), and A. Patrick, *The Men of the First French Republic: Political Alignments and the National Convention of 1792* (Baltimore, 1972). There are also some fine studies of counter-revolution, notably C. Tilly, *The Vendée* (London, 1964), and D.M.G. Sutherland, *The Chouans* (Oxford, 1982).

Chapter 3

Napoleon Bonaparte and the French Revolution

Robert Alexander

Although his preferred symbol was that of the bee, perhaps a more suitable image of Napoleon Bonaparte would be that of the chameleon. He had the ability to make his contemporaries see in him what he wanted them to see, although the images were often contradictory. Because contemporaries often used their understanding of the French Revolution of 1789 as a gauge by which to measure him, it was often in his interest to pose either as the champion of the Revolution, or the man who had ended it. Because the Revolution, then as now, stood for many different things, determining his precise relation to it was never easy. Moreover, Bonaparte was nothing if not an opportunist; he altered his policies according to circumstance and struck the pose that best suited these shifts. Thus if the Revolution was by no means uniform, neither was Bonapartism.

The subject of Napoleon's relation to the Revolution has subsequently exercised many learned minds; indeed it remains central to discussion of the Napoleonic period. Given that he more or less directed attention towards it in *Le Mémorial de Saint-Hélène*, we can conclude Bonaparte himself would have approved, but the reader well might ask whether there is much point in rehashing the subject. Beyond the usefulness of inclusion in a series of works on major themes in European history, one good answer is probably the most familiar – historical investigation continues to evolve. Not only has there been a plethora of recent work on the meaning of the Revolution, the Napoleonic era has also undergone reinterpretation. Moreover, what is considered fertile ground for enquiry changes. While the Empire has not been a focal point of women's studies, some authors have drawn broad conclusions about the period from the standpoint of women's rights and these have been linked to experience during the Revolution. But perhaps a better response is that by viewing Bonaparte from the various angles taken by academics, we can see just how difficult it must have been for contemporaries to pin him down. Each angle reveals a different Bonaparte.[1]

Interpretation of the Napoleonic epoch can vary greatly according to periodization. A recent work on the Revolution covers up to 1802, suggesting significant linkage at least for the period of the Consulate. Other authors have terminated their consideration of the Revolution at the *coup d'état* of Brumaire, in November 1799; some, including Julian Swann in the preceding chapter, have considered the Revolution to have effectively ended with the fall of Robespierre in July 1794. Concerns of periodization may seem trivial, but they alert us to a complicating problem: we must make choices as to what constituted the Revolution before we can determine Napoleon's relation to it. Moreover, a similar issue arises at the other end of the Napoleonic epoch. The Hundred Days of 1815 have often been treated as an anomaly, an episode amusing for its drama but hardly typical of the period. Yet it has been argued that the Hundred Days were crucial to the development of Bonapartism and that they reshaped understanding of the meaning of the epoch.[2]

So choices have to be made. For the purposes of this essay, we shall consider the Revolution to have ended with the *coup d'état* of Brumaire and the Napoleonic era to have commenced at that point and continued until the second abdication in June 1815. In doing so we shall want continually to bear in mind that there are other ways of viewing matters and draw attention to how this can alter interpretation. But the dates 1799–1815 seem most in keeping with the theme of this essay; when contemporaries tried to evaluate where Napoleon stood they took 1799 as their starting point and worked forwards or backwards. Dividing the Revolution into separate blocks came later.

There are many ways of approaching this topic, but for the purposes of this essay we shall look at Napoleonic rule from the standpoint of the three famous watchwords of the Revolution – Liberty, Equality and Fraternity. By way of conclusion, the evolving nature of Bonapartism will be considered in order to explain why the Napoleonic legacy was to prove so complex.

NAPOLEON AND LIBERTY

Napoleon has often been described as the heir of the Revolution, but what precisely this means is not always clear. Certainly the Revolution afforded him opportunities which would not have existed previously. His mercurial rise to the position of general would have been unthinkable during the ancien regime, and even the way for the *coup d'état* of Brumaire had been paved by previous military interventions. Moreover the Revolution, with its internecine political factionalism, apparently endless wars, economic dislocation and breakdown of civil order, heightened the appeal of a strong man who might bring peace with victory and put an end to internal strife. Yet Bonaparte's attitude towards the Revolution was ambivalent. A fervent advocate of the early Revolution, Bonaparte later developed an almost pathological fear of the revolutionary crowd. When in power he could ably portray himself as the champion of the *menu peuple*, and indeed he was well loved in the lower-class quarters of Paris, yet his Empire became increasingly hierarchical over time and his proclivity for order often amounted to severe repression. In this ambivalence he was not untypical of his age, for there was no consensus then, as now, as to what exactly constituted the Revolutionary legacy.

In her *Considérations sur la Révolution Française*, first published during the Second Restoration, Madame de Staël sought to equate the Revolution to the triumph of liberty. She divided the Revolution into phases, arguing that the constructive work of the Revolution had been the overthrow of despotism prior to the September Massacres of 1792. From this perspective all that followed was essentially negative, and she particularly warned the friends of liberty to eschew Bonapartism.[3]

There was plenty of evidence that Bonaparte was no friend of liberty. Through a combination of force, guile and bribery, at the national level he turned Sieyès's constitution of December 1799 in effect into a dictatorship. Royalist attempts to assassinate him were cynically exploited to strike ruthlessly against critics of both the Jacobin left and the royalist right. While he was always willing to take advice in private and delegate responsibility, the bottom line was that all ultimate authority rested with the First Consul or Emperor; even Louis XIV would have been impressed by the way Bonaparte vetted the decisions of his government ministers. The same stripping of independence from representative bodies took place at departmental and local levels. Powers previously held by elected councils were transferred to prefects, who in turn were appointed by the central government. The mayors of major cities were appointed by Bonaparte, and those of significant towns by prefects. A facade of democracy was retained in that members of municipal and departmental councils were elected by narrow plutocracies, but these bodies could only act in advisory capacities. Local notables could exercise indirect influence, but representative institutions yielded no direct authority. In similar fashion, the election of judges was abolished in favour of appointment by the central government.

Civil liberties also received rough treatment. Bonaparte's equation of political parties to factionalism inevitably led to repression of freedom of association. Neither the Parisian nor the provincial press fared well. The number of newspapers was systematically cut back, and those which remained increasingly became instruments of Napoleonic propaganda. Bonaparte wished a controlled public opinion, not an informed one.

On the other hand, the Napoleonic Concordat of 1801 did mark an advance for freedom of religious opinion. While the Roman Catholic faith was formally recognized as that of the majority of the French, this did not in practice mean a return to the intolerance of the ancien regime. While the Concordat did not put an end to feuding among Catholics, it did begin recovery from the trauma of the Revolution. Yet, as with other institutions, Bonaparte intended to use the church for his own purposes; his treatment of the Pope in the later years of the Empire gave strong warning against making any church a forum for discussion which might be considered hostile to the government. And although arbitrary actions against the individual may not have been as great in number as once thought, Bonaparte was not hesitant to set aside due process of law when the occasion suited him or his administrators. Under Joseph Fouché a network of agents and spies moved France in the direction of a modern police state.

There is much in common between Madame de Staël's view of what constituted the essence of the Revolution and the currently predominant school of Revolutionary interpretation associated most often with François Furet. If the central meaning of the Revolution was a halting but seminal step towards democracy and political liberty, then the Napoleonic period does indeed look like a great leap backwards.[4]

Yet if Napoleonic government appears consummately illiberal from the standpoint of the early Revolution, it must be recognized that the Revolution also included marked authoritarian tendencies, perhaps inherent in the Rousseauean concept of the 'general will'. Indeed there is another line of interpretation which sees in the Revolution not the emergence of liberal democracy, but rather the emergence of the modern totalitarian state. One can trace this back as far as Edmund Burke, but more crucial are the fears expressed by Alexis de Tocqueville concerning how the Revolution had continued a process of centralization of power begun during the ancien regime. Concepts such as divine right and monarchical sovereignty had simply been replaced by those of popular sovereignty and the absolute will of the majority; all were used to justify state intrusion into individual rights. For certain writers Napoleon and his plebiscites represent a logical next step towards fascism by giving tyranny an apparent mass justification. Viewed from this standpoint, Napoleon merely perfected tendencies already manifest in the Revolution.[5]

The clawing back of powers granted to local bodies dated at least from the advent of the Terror, and while the Committee of Public Safety may have formally recognized that its special powers were meant to be temporary, Robespierre, Saint-Just *et al.* showed few signs of reducing central government authority during their pursuit of the republic of virtue. The Law of Suspects and the arbitrary nature of revolutionary justice if anything went well beyond Napoleon's tampering with the rule of law. Prior to the purge of June 1793, even the liberal Girondins had themselves laid the ground for Terror, not least of all when they attacked the parliamentary immunity of citizen Marat.

The Terror thus gave Bonaparte many precedents for authoritarian government. Cowing of legislative assemblies through force and reducing the representative principle by altering constitutions were then further refined during Thermidor and the Directory. From 1795 onwards the national electorate was a plutocracy, and the Directors were more than willing to reshape constitutional provisions whenever their interests required it, calling in the military when necessary. The temporary powers of *représentatives en mission* became permanent with the creation of the Directory's *commissaires en mission*, blazing a path for the prefects. Placing entire departments under states of siege became a mechanism for systematically substituting more rapid and arbitrary military justice for civil justice.

Thus if Napoleon was more successful in gathering up the threads of power, he certainly had a wealth of experience to draw on. Much, though not all of this came from the Terror and the periods following. But unless we grant Madame de Staël's very restrictive definition of what constituted the Revolution, we must accept that he was not entirely out of line with his immediate predecessors.

Yet viewing dictatorship as the central characteristic of Napoleonic rule overlooks several points. Bonaparte later claimed that the centralizing measures he took were a product of necessity, and not meant to be permanent. Such claims could be easily dismissed were it not for the Hundred Days. During his brief return to power in 1815, France enjoyed extensive freedom of the press and a measure of the right to political association. Moreover, Napoleon called in the arch-liberal Benjamin Constant to revamp the Imperial constitution in what came to be known as the *Acte Additionnel aux Constitutions de l'Empire*. While the *Acte* was a disappointment to many, it did represent an improvement over the Bourbon Charter of 1814 in terms of the franchise and it did set up a parliament with at least some independent powers. Whether it was anything more than a product of desperate circumstance can be questioned. Yet the only definite answer is that we simply do not know whether Bonaparte would have respected a return to effective constitutional monarchy following military victory. More importantly, despite de Staël's warnings, the Hundred Days did affect the image of Bonaparte, and enable Bonapartists to claim a part of the liberal Revolutionary heritage. If he was not history's most notable liberal, neither was he its most perfect tyrant.

The view from beyond France's shifting borders was rather different. To other Europeans Bonaparte was unequivocally a tyrant. Yet even here the distinction between Bonaparte and the Revolution was by no means perfectly clear. The Revolutionary claim to be exporting liberty had been all too hollow for most Europeans. True, in annexing the former Austrian Netherlands and dividing it into French departments Revolutionary governments had given citizens the right to vote for representatives in the French parliament, but there had been little consultation as to whether the citizens wanted this. Nor did they have much choice over taxation, requisitions and conscription by the government in

Paris. Forced tributes, depredation of church property and imposition of French rule raised serious questions wherever Revolutionary troops imposed their version of liberty. From the perspective of Italians, Germans and Dutch, Napoleon was not so very different when it came to political liberty.[6]

Indeed in some regards Napoleonic government might be considered an improvement. In a recent work, Stuart Woolf has argued that Napoleon's essential contribution was a new administrative model which rationalized government and made it more effective. There was of course little room for political liberty in it, but this did not mean a return to the old corporatist order. The Revolutionary work of abolishing feudal privileges was continued, and the Revolutionary elements of the Napoleonic codes were applied. The French presence also brought at least a measure of religious toleration to regions which were unaccustomed to it. Improving communications and transport systems were intended to serve the twin purposes of encouraging economic production and civil order. Establishment of order was of course a means of wooing local elites and would ensure their ascendancy. But, varying in accordance to the nature of the regime being replaced, much of this actually increased the civil liberties of ordinary subjects. It was under Bonaparte that French troops knocked down signs demarcating Jewish ghettos in Italian cities. To Europeans Napoleon could appear a tyrant, but his rule could also mean freedom from feudal and clerical privilege. Bonaparte and his administrators were just as convinced as Revolutionary agents that they carried progress; they did not view the lands they came to conquer as simply fodder for France and they lasted long enough to implement their reforms in a meaningful way.[7]

NAPOLEON AND EQUALITY

De Tocqueville's opinion that the French were inclined to sacrifice liberty in the name of equality would at first appear to have some merit when viewed from the standpoint of the Napoleonic period. Under Bonaparte there would be no return to the formal, legal social hierarchy of the ancien regime. In more concrete terms, the vast land redistribution of the Revolution would remain largely permanent. Although the ancien regime nobility was not as grievously affected by this as was once thought, still the economic basis of their power had at least been eroded, especially when one takes into account who had most benefited from church wealth prior to 1789. Yet under Napoleon French society underwent extensive hierarchical militarization under the guise of meritocracy, provisions were made to ensure a self-perpetuating elite, and the patriarchal features of law and convention were strengthened. If this did not amount to a return to the ancien regime, neither did it amount to social levelling, and if Bonaparte may have given lessons in the leadership principle, he certainly was not building a modern, mass totalitarian society.

Bonaparte wished to base his regime on the support of the notables – in essence, the wealthy, landed bedrock of society. To this end he favoured a fusion of former ancien regime nobles with wealthy non-noble elements, many of whom had risen to prominence during the Revolution. It was to the notables that Bonaparte turned when staffing the administration; the same group was encouraged to enter into the departmental and local councils. Although such a fusion had, perhaps, already been taking place prior to the Revolution, producing an homogeneous 'mass of granite' (as Napoleon described his corps of administrators) in fact proved difficult. Bonaparte persistently wooed ancien regime nobles to enter his service; while usually willing to return from emigration or accept the return of unsold nationalized lands, aristocrats generally preferred to maintain a certain distance from the regime. Even so, those who did take up local positions were sufficient in number to antagonize local Jacobin elites.[8]

It is instructive to keep in mind that many Jacobins had supported Bonaparte in 1799; thereafter their allegiance had been slowly eroded. The assault upon liberty undoubtedly played a part in this, but probably more disruptive was the return to hierarchy. The process occurred in stages, beginning with the creation of the Legion of Honour and a host of titles which were not hereditary. By 1804, and the replacement of the Republic with the Empire, Napoleon had begun the creation of a court with hereditary princely titles; this subsequently became part of a full hereditary Imperial nobility, replete with entail. While the new Imperial nobility did not enjoy the fiscal and legal privileges of the ancien regime nobility, land endowments helped assure economic ascendancy and there could be no doubt the titles granted enhanced influence and opportunity in governmental matters. While ability remained an important qualification within the administrative elite, erosion of the principle of careers open to talent became an important concern in the struggle of local elite groups.

The new hierarchy was justified on the basis of meritocracy. As with most of Bonaparte's claims, it held a degree of truth. Yet it was Napoleon who ultimately granted social status, and his conception of what constituted merit proved very narrow. True, no individual was formally excluded from a title on the basis of religious creed or lowly social birth, and there were some remarkable examples of the most common born rising to high places. Yet in granting honours on the basis of service to the state, Napoleon favoured certain groups. Military men gained by far the largest share of titles, with state officials and administrators coming in a distant second. Rewards to other contributors such as artists and entrepreneurs were relatively few in number but at least did exist. For the vast majority, however, there was simply no opportunity other than joining the ranks, and as usual there was no chance of honours for a woman on the basis of her own individual merit.

The elitist nature of Napoleonic society was fully apparent in regard to education. For women and the masses, Napoleon was content to leave what little education there was in the hands of the church – where he was for the most part correct in assuming emphasis would be placed on order, social deference and loyalty to the state, rather than self-betterment. More attention was given to the secondary level of education; in 1802 *lycées* were created, approximately one for every second department. Again, emphasis was placed on military-style regimentation, but the *lycées* were a crucial step towards entry into the administrative elite. Entry was determined through competition for scholarships, of which a percentage was set aside for the sons of military and state officials. By such means Bonaparte intended to assure a continuity within his elite which in effect would have become a self-perpetuating one.

Bonaparte's penchant for chain of command and preference of appointment over election were manifest in the Concordat of 1801 and his reorganization of the Catholic Church. The Concordat reestablished state and papal control over advancement in the upper ranks of the clergy and included abolition of the election of parish priests. Later Bonaparte would design clerical uniforms and create state-inspired catechisms. Yet while he might have been more thorough in his ordering of the church, Napoleon's Concordat bore a certain resemblance to the Civil Constitution of the Clergy of 1790. Once again the state would devote part of its budget to funding clergymen. The latter in turn were again to become agents of the state, preaching loyalty when it came to conscription and violating the sanctity of the confessional when the state's interests suggested it. If separation of church and state is a tenet of liberalism, then Napoleon certainly fails this part of the test. But then again so did the Revolutionaries of 1790; rather ironically it was during Thermidor (September 1794) that state subsidies to religions were terminated.

By the time of his return from exile on Elba (in March 1815), Bonaparte had come to regret certain aspects of his policy of elite fusion and recognized that apparent backsliding from the principle of equality had undermined his initial popularity. Thus during his remarkable 'Flight of the Eagle' he unleashed a torrent of rhetoric well attuned to the ears of former Jacobins and *sansculottes*. Although his primary target was the Bourbon dynasty, his chief means lay in associating the monarchy with the privileged orders of pre-1789 society. Should these nobles and clergymen not give up their pretensions to privilege, the great champion of the Revolution would hang them from the lamp posts.

While General Bonaparte may have overstated matters, the message was well received in certain quarters (most notably the 'cradle of the Revolution', the Parisian faubourgs of Saint-Antoine and Saint-Marcel). Indeed the way in which the subsequent Hundred Days reopened the wounds of the Revolution is notorious. A great deal of blame has been apportioned to Napoleon for this, though it is more just to recognize that ancien regime elements, including the Bourbons, had contributed greatly during the First Restoration. More to the point for our purposes, however, we should note that through this remarkable pirouette Bonaparte had succeeded in bringing his image back into line with the Revolution. Viewed from the standpoint of 1815, Bonaparte looks much more egalitarian than the Emperor of 1808.

Given that his attempt to build an homogeneous elite of notables had not been a resounding success, one well might ask whether the Napoleonic epoch had really changed much in French society. Indeed much of the literature of the debate between Marxist and liberal revisionist historians over the nature of the French Revolution has focused on socio-economic forces which evolve over long periods, and are not subject to the will of any one individual. However, much of the current literature on the Revolution has now shifted towards the field of political culture, and some echoes of this can be discerned in Napoleonic literature. Without being so bold as to predict what lines fuller investigation might take, one can suggest that Napoleon's militarization of society might still yield a great deal of insight into his impact.[9]

Recognizing that it served as a model for many of the social reforms enacted, one can hardly overemphasize the centrality of the Napoleonic army. In terms of military strategy, Bonaparte was in fact not a great innovator, though he was adept at applying the strategies developed by others. Certainly the carnage he wreaked had full Revolutionary precedents, and, according to at least one authority, the causes for war under Revolutionary governments did not differ greatly for those of Napoleon. Nor was the emphasis Bonaparte placed on military virtues entirely different from the heightened importance placed upon the army by Revolutionary governments once the war of 1792 had begun.[10]

Yet there is considerable debate as to whether Bonaparte changed the nature and ethos of the army, whether the citizen soldiers of the Revolution evolved into hardened professionals whose allegiance was not to Revolutionary ideals, but to the army itself and its commanders. It would indeed appear that the army was largely depoliticized under Bonaparte, in the sense that soldiers were hardly encouraged to act as citizens by joining political clubs. But this had occurred long before the *coup d'état* of Brumaire, and, of course, one could argue that society itself had been largely depoliticized by this time through repression of political associations beginning at least with the Terror.

A more central matter concerns whether Bonaparte altered value systems by substituting honour(s) for Revolutionary virtue. In theory, the latter meant that actions in the service of France (in which every soldier had a stake) were their own reward, requiring no awards such as medals and the like. They were not different in kind from the actions of any citizen. By way of contrast, Napoleon constantly used honours as a means of motivation, and there could be little doubt as to what types of action were deemed most valuable by the state. Moreover Napoleonic emphasis on loyalty to the commander (especially the Emperor) and *esprit de corps* had particularist qualities which went against the grain of Revolutionary patriotic *élan*. To what extent state policies affected the values of the common soldier is difficult to assess, but it is apparent that Bonaparte's intentions were significantly different from those of his predecessors. Certainly Napoleon himself commanded a personal loyalty which could threaten the values Revolutionaries had professed to hold dear, but it is instructive to note this loyalty was not easily transferred to other military figures after the second abdication. While society undoubtedly underwent militarization under his rule, Napoleon himself recognized that France would not submit to military dictatorship.

Nor did all men wish to enter the army. While promotion based on service and talent could bring social advance, entry into the prestigious officer corps from the ranks came about largely due to catastrophic casualty rates. Draft dodging and resistance remained major problems even in the heyday of the Empire. Yet this too was nothing new, and nor was the option for the wealthy to buy themselves out of military service. Moreover, when all is said and done, Bonaparte's ability to raise massive numbers of recruits in 1813 and 1815 remains impressive. Peasant resistance to conscription had always been a constant in history, yet D.M.G. Sutherland is surely correct in arguing that Napoleon had asked more of France by 1813–14 than had the Revolutionaries with their *levée en masse*. While he did not receive all the support he asked for, still, he received a great deal.[11]

Napoleon based his regime upon victory, and in doing so he encouraged a set of values and expectations which were going to pose problems for each successive nineteenth-century French regime. Concerns with the army would be a constant preoccupation, not just because of the spectre of *coup d'état*, but also because so much of society identified with military values. Moreover, by his very success, Napoleon fostered an association of glory with military victory which further confused notions of progress with imperialism. None of this was new in kind to France and one can argue that strong elements of militarization and imperialism could be found in the Revolution. Yet under Bonaparte France had clearly passed from defending her Revolution to imposing Napoleonic order abroad; the militarization of society that had helped accomplish this was intended to be permanent. Defeat in 1815 and in 1870–1 was going to be traumatic not so much because of the material and human losses entailed, but because the French had been taught to invest so much importance in military prowess.

NAPOLEON AND FRATERNITY

The third great watchword of the Revolution was perhaps the most elusive. What precisely it meant remains difficult to define. Certainly it had to do with the belief that all French people must unite in embarking on a revolution which would bring a better and more just future for all citizens. Yet from its origins the Revolution was highly divisive, became increasingly so as counter-revolution took on a mass base, and left France a legacy of bitter social tensions for the nineteenth and twentieth centuries.

To encourage fraternity, advocates of the Revolution had sought to spread patriotism through the use of festival and ceremonial. While the impact of festivals of liberty and reason as propaganda devices remains difficult to measure, it cannot be denied that the public ceremonies had a martial spirit from at least the federations of 1789 onwards. With his triumphal marches and military parades, Napoleon built on this use of spectacle, though, significantly, the opportunities for public participation were less.

If fraternity was ultimately the pursuit of unity and patriotism, not all of those invited to do their duty were granted the same liberty. In the initial phase of the Revolution, under the constitutional monarchy, women did not gain the right to vote, although a small number had been able to take part in the elections to the Estates General. They did, however, have some access to the public sphere in that women could form, or join, political clubs and petition the legislature; but even these rights were curtailed by Jacobin repression during the Terror and this was continued under the Thermidorean and Directorial regimes. Thus, if anything, Napoleon was continuing a Revolutionary tradition when he perpetuated the exclusion of women from the public sphere, where politics was concerned.

Feminist writers often point to the Napoleonic codes as a capstone of Revolutionary gender bias. There is a certain point to this. The civil code was patriarchal in character, consistently enhancing the legal status of the eldest male in a family, depriving married women of property rights, and creating a remarkable double standard when it came to matters such as divorce or acting as legal witness. But from an historical standpoint, one should make certain qualifications when interpreting the Napoleonic civil code as part and parcel of the Revolution. Bonaparte himself played a significant role in the drafting of laws; his interventions were almost always unfavourable to the rights of women, reversing or modifying more liberal Revolutionary legislation over matters such as cause for divorce. Even so, one could perhaps argue that Bonaparte's role was essentially that of consolidator – accepting certain changes rather than simply returning to ancien regime laws. Until thorough comparison is made with Revolutionary legislation and ancien regime law in regard to family and gender relations, whether the Napoleonic codes represented reaction or modest progress will remain unclear.

An interesting argument that springs from recent literature holds that while women could not hold public office under the ancien regime, aristocratic women exercised a great deal of indirect influence over those who held power. In part the Revolution constituted a backlash against the political influence of aristocratic women. Thus Jacobins not only repressed women who had organized in public associations, they also advocated theories of separate gender spheres which consigned women strictly to domesticity. Women not only gained little in their pleas for equal civil and political rights; effectively their influence through the private sphere was also curtailed. Napoleon, with his militarization of society and patriarchal codes, was true to Revolutionary gender bigotry. Not only did Bonaparte prevent Madame de Staël from publishing in France, he sent her packing from the boudoir.

One of the features of new lines of interpretation is that they put forward contentious arguments. To determine whether the Revolution checked the informal political influence of women will require substantial investigation of at least the Revolutionary, Napoleonic and Restoration periods. At present this has to be viewed as an open question, but given the importance of the informal exercise of power attempts to answer it could be highly revealing.[12]

Chauvinism takes a variety of forms. Among other Europeans the watchword of fraternity must have raised eyebrows, but this was probably no more the case under Napoleon than during the 1790s. True there was a degree of cosmopolitanism among the early Jacobin societies and the Convention did issue a decree of fraternity and help to foreign peoples in December 1792. Any expectations of independence thus raised were however soon dashed; like Belgian democrats, Dutch and German Jacobins were soon disillusioned by the way fraternity took a back seat to French national interests.

As Stuart Woolf has shown, there was an element of enlightened cosmopolitanism in the new administrative model by which Napoleon and his bureaucrats proposed to integrate Europe. In the eyes of Napoleonic administrators what constituted 'progress' for France must surely constitute progress for all. Yet there was a fair measure of chauvinism in this, often leaving Napoleonic officials no better equipped than their Jacobin predecessors to comprehend the peoples to whom they were bringing 'progress'. In the Kingdom of Italy all ministries other than those involved in foreign affairs may have been held by Italians, but the policies applied were essentially French. It can be argued that they therefore did more harm than good. And if Napoleon did not quite fuel nationalism in the way once thought, a key component of the particularist, regional or local rebellions against the Empire was Francophobia. Perhaps the main impact of the Revolution and Empire abroad was to encourage chauvinism.[13]

Part of the problem was that whatever good effects might have come from the new administrative model were undone by Bonaparte continuing the Revolutionary tradition of putting France first. This was nowhere more apparent than in the Continental System, which itself was a logical continuation of the economic policies of Revolutionary governments.

The Continental System was at one level a means of economic warfare designed to batter the British economy by preventing British merchants from trading on the continent. The disruption caused might produce a financial crisis severe enough to force Pitt and Co. to sue for peace on terms acceptable to France. Or it might produce enough distress in perfidious Albion to provoke revolution. One way or another, it was hoped that British financing of Austrian, Prussian or Russian revolts against an expanding French Empire would come to a halt.

While attractive in theory, the Continental System proved difficult to apply; the European coastline provided numerous opportunities for smuggling. Moreover, it was by no means clear to continental merchants why their trading patterns should be disrupted for the sake of Napoleon's warmongering; if British commercial prosperity partly depended on the continent, the reverse was also true. The sacrifice being asked was enormous, matched only by the resentment it incurred.

Yet the Continental System also had a more insidious purpose. Through manipulation of customs and tariffs, it was designed to substitute France for Britain as the industrial powerhouse of Europe. Italian textile manufacturers, for example, found themselves subjected to duties designed not just to hamper exports to France, but also to other parts of the Empire. Had the system lasted long enough, the Kingdom of Italy would have been reduced to an agricultural colony of France.[14]

The Continental System did not last long enough for this to transpire. Indeed, in seeking to apply it more fully, Napoleon made the crucial errors of intervening in first Portugal, then Spain, and ultimately Russia. By overstretching himself he brought his Empire crashing down. And by the time of the Fourth Coalition (1813–15) the Allies had learned their lesson, and Bonaparte's attempts to divide and conquer had failed him. French chauvinism had played its part in this; Napoleon's contribution, although massive in scale, had not been substantially different from that of the Revolutionaries.

In the *Mémorial* Bonaparte subsequently claimed that he had been an advocate of national sovereignty, not just for France, but for other peoples as well. Once again in his brief return in 1815 he had given a measure of credibility to this by promising to respect the boundaries of France's neighbours. It is of some interest to note that he made these promises not just to the Allied Powers, but also to the French public. The potentates and their representatives gathered at Vienna would, of course, have nothing to do with such promises, and thereby gave Bonaparte the opportunity to claim that he was going forth to war, once again, in defence of France.

It is difficult to see anything more than special pleading in Napoleon's claims regarding nationalism; when confronted by German nationalism in the form of a student who had attempted to assassinate him, the Emperor simply could not comprehend the student's motivation. Yet Bonaparte's ability to alter his image was subsequently apparent even in this regard. Half a century later his nephew Louis-Napoleon would claim to be the great friend of national independence and that this was part of his great uncle's legacy. In 1848 as Minister of Foreign Affairs Lamartine had made similar pronouncements on behalf of the government of the Second Republic. Much of the public in France was willing to entertain such claims. Other Europeans, including Italians to whom offers of French armed intervention were particularly aimed, were more sceptical. Their experience of French fraternity during both the Revolution and the Empire had taught them to be so.

EVOLVING NATURE OF BONAPARTISM

Contemporaries often attributed the many wars of the Napoleonic era to Bonaparte's lust for power. One need only note the number of Bonaparte family members who became rulers (though subject to the demands of their great patron) to realize there was some truth in such a belief. Yet it can also be argued that Bonaparte believed the key to assuring the durability of his dynasty lay in military victory. This was perhaps the main reason for his refusal to accept the peace conditions offered by the Allied Powers as the Empire crumbled in 1813–14.

Whether dictatorship was an inevitable result of Bonaparte's ego can be questioned; when the entire period of his rule is considered, his desire for eternal fame, both as military leader and legislator, appears the key to his character. That he linked his own personal fortunes to those of France is well known, but his actions during the Hundred Days suggest that he could compromise over power-sharing when circumstance necessitated. Dictatorship was perhaps not essential to the fame he cultivated.

Although there were certain continuities which were to give it consistency, Bonapartism was not static, reflecting Napoleon's own opportunism. In the aftermath of the Revolution, Bonapartism came increasingly to stand for order and national unity. At least in part, the onslaught on political liberty stemmed from Bonaparte's equation of political parties with factionalism – a force which had torn the nation apart, dividing France into bitterly hostile camps. The solution to this was to put an end to political division through repression when necessary, and through the more positive means of encouraging all to forget past allegiance and unite in opposition to hostile European states and, of course, loyal service to the rule of Napoleon Bonaparte.

Political antagonism had, at times, degenerated into simple crime and, indeed, in parts of France the two were very hard to differentiate. With a firm and not overly scrupulous hand, Bonaparte made dramatic progress during the Consulate in restoring order to regions that had fallen into virtual anarchy. In combination with his victories over foreign enemies, this earned him a gratitude reflected in the plebiscites elevating him first to Consul for life, and then hereditary monarch. Even when Lucien's fraudulent vote counting is taken into consideration, there can be little doubt that Bonaparte had quickly gained a measure of support not seen since 1789.

Napoleonic order was not simply a matter of re-establishing the state's ability to enforce its will; it also entailed the return of effective social and patriarchal hierarchy. The latter task was facilitated by past repression; the Montagnards themselves had made great strides in reducing the power of *sans-culotte* elements, a task which had been furthered by former Girondins after Thermidor. On the other side of the divide, Napoleon's negotiation of the Concordat helped to confirm his destruction of the mass base of counter-revolutionary opposition. Also, singular good fortune with grain harvests and a shrewd policy of public works helped keep lower-class agitation within bounds. In this regard the appalling casualty rates of battle served a twin purpose: work was usually plentiful. When economic fortunes were dampened by poor grain harvests, in May 1812 Bonaparte re-instituted the Maximum and introduced Rumford soup. If the Napoleonic regime was paternalistic, this did not mean ignoring the wishes of workers and artisans.

Yet order at the cost of liberty always depended on victory. Domestic opposition to Napoleon was never much of a threat, but restiveness became increasingly apparent as economic dislocation and military defeat set in. Bonaparte's call for a patriotic rallying in 1814 did not elicit a response similar to that of 1792, despite some favourable signs in parts of the east. Perhaps France was simply exhausted, yet it is apparent that much of the early enthusiasm for Bonaparte had gone. In certain rural areas conscription had made him hated, economic problems had cooled his support among the elite classes, and a longing for the restoration of political liberty was to some extent manifest. The circuitous route Bonaparte took towards his first exile is a well-known sign of how his fortunes had declined.

Yet within a year of the first abdication (April 1814) Bonaparte had returned in triumph to Paris (March 1815). Royalists and popular historians have subsequently attributed the 'Flight of the Eagle' to political conspiracy and misplaced loyalty on the part of an army misled by past glory. There was an element of conspiracy, though it was not nearly as widespread as purported. Interpreting the army as a sort of rogue element in French society constitutes a major misinterpretation – one which Restoration liberals and Jacobins did not subsequently make. It is instructive to note that while the highest ranks of the officer corps hesitated over how to react, there was no such hesitation among the rank-and-file. This in turn was complemented by an enormous outpouring of support both from peasants who accompanied Bonaparte along his route and urban workers who received him rapturously in cities such as Grenoble, Lyon and Paris.

Not all were pleased, but clearly Napoleon could still command a following which no one else could come close to approximating. Bourbon attempts to ward off the returning tyrant were pathetic at best. True, a royalist army led by Angoulême from Bourbon strongholds in Provence did manage to move as far forward as Valence, but this force was easily defeated. Perhaps its most impressive impact was the degree of spontaneous counter-mobilization it gave rise to in the old Dauphiné and points north. Thereafter royalist manifestations were largely held in check – either by troops of the line or by the federative movement. Attempts to reignite the Vendée and Britanny did enjoy some success, but the old fervour was largely gone. Bonaparte fell for a second time because he was defeated at the hands of the Allied Powers at Waterloo, not because of internal opposition.

Renewed support for Bonaparte was attributable to a number of causes. Defeat, occupation and having a ruler imposed by foreign potentates did not rest lightly on the shoulders of patriots, even those who had their qualms about Napoleon. During the First Restoration Bourbon government added fear to ignominy. Despite an apparent compromise with the Revolution embodied in the new constitution known as the Charter, the rule of Louis XVIII was very soon associated with ancien regime favouring of the nobility and Catholic Church. While Louis XVIII could perhaps not be blamed for the pretensions of intransigent returned émigrés, it was his government which gave former *chouans* plum posts in an army undergoing major cutbacks and insisted upon expiatory ceremonies for martyrs to the Revolution such as Marie-Antoinette. Nor did the Bourbon government object when ultra-royalists in the Chamber of Deputies lavished praise upon all those who had refused any compromise with the Revolution, while making provisions for the return of unsold nationalized lands. From the very beginning of Bourbon Restoration, the gains of the Revolution appeared to be under attack.

Napoleon learned from this. Always sensitive to the importance of propaganda and image, Bonaparte returned from Elba not as the great Imperial Charlemagne, but as the first general of the Revolution. The language he employed while addressing the 'citizens' of France was carefully calculated to rejuvenate support. So too were promises to respect the frontiers being established at Vienna. The warm response to such rhetoric at Lyon perhaps frightened him; certainly he toned it down once he had ensconced himself in Paris. Yet was it entirely a cynical device, meant to curry support in difficult circumstances, but to be discarded as soon as opportunity arose? This was a question for all contemporaries to consider; at the heart of it was Napoleon's relation to the Revolution.

During the Hundred Days non-royalist France enjoyed a degree of liberty far greater than under the Empire. The press gained a wide measure of freedom of expression and used it to ponder the true meaning of the Revolution and Napoleon's relation to it. Many found it difficult to reject his argument that he was the choice of the people, and some were willing to accept his revamped image. Across France federations were formed to combat royalist domestic intrigue and defend against Allied invasion. While it is difficult to determine precise numbers, *fédérés* were clearly numbered in the hundreds of thousands and their ranks were growing immediately prior to Waterloo. In supporting the federative movement, not without hesitation, Bonaparte tolerated a measure of freedom of association, thereby gaining the support of such Revolutionary luminaries as Joseph Cambon and Marc-Alexis Vadier. If inclusion of Fouché in the government said very little, the presence of Carnot, the great organizer of victory during the Terror, said a great deal. In calling on Benjamin Constant to revise the constitution of the Empire, the Emperor accepted that national sovereignty included at least a measure of political representation and power-sharing. Doubtless he did so reluctantly, and the *Acte Additionnel* garnered a great deal of criticism from those who wanted a wider franchise and a non-hereditary Senate. In its short existence the Chamber of Representatives exasperated Bonaparte, giving rise to suspicion that the old dictatorial habits were never far below the surface.

Yet in the crisis of June 1815, Bonaparte chose not to listen to the pleas of Parisian crowds asking for a signal to attack the Chamber. It is easy to attribute this simply to his dislike of the crowd, but it also resulted from his recognition that to succeed without disastrous civil war, he had to have broad-based support. This could not be gained by return to dictatorship, as his most trusted advisers constantly informed him. France had changed, could Bonaparte?[15]

If the essence of his character was desire for lasting fame, and if his greatest desire was to secure his dynasty, it follows that Bonaparte would have adapted to circumstance. Certainly this was the admittedly self-serving line he put forward from his second exile at St Helena. In 1799 France had needed order; he had given it by repressing those who had used liberty for licence. By 1815 France was ready for a restoration of at least limited liberty; although perhaps he had been slow to recognize this, he had done so by the Hundred Days. All along he had sought to consolidate what was good in the Revolution, while pruning away excesses. Through his plebiscites, he had always recognized the fundamental principle of national sovereignty.

Napoleon's interpretation of his own relation to the Revolution was fraught with consequence for the subsequent history of France. Under the Restoration liberals never did disassociate themselves from Bonapartists. The July Monarchy and most notably Adolphe Thiers sought to exploit the Napoleonic legend, apparently underestimating the power of it. Louis-Napoleon of course knew best how to use it, but more importantly, the evolution of his regime bore testimony to his belief in it. To the First Emperor's nephew, the Revolution and Bonapartism were intricately bound; the latter was a refinement of the former. Imperial dictatorship was not an end itself; it was a means to the end of saving what was good in the Revolution.

Ultimately, this assertion remains a half-truth. The Revolution itself stood for many things and can be seen as a forerunner of both authoritarian dictatorship and liberal democracy. For most of his reign Napoleon I built upon the former foundations; towards the end he shifted toward the latter. For his historical image he chose to emphasize the later liberal developments. Due to Allied intervention his sudden conversion to the early Revolution was never fully put to the test. Partly for this reason historians have long argued over Bonaparte's true relation to the Revolution, and doubtless will continue to do so. But, of more consequence for history, many French people chose to accept the Bonapartist line – that Napoleon was a true son of the French Revolution.

NOTES

1 Given the volume of works on the subject, one can only list a sampling. One way to start is by looking at J. Schulim, *Liberty, Equality and Fraternity: Studies on the Era of the French Revolution and Napoleon* (New York, 1989). The best work covering the two periods is D.M.G. Sutherland, *France 1789–1815. Revolution and Counter-Revolution* (London, 1985). Also of interest is L. Gershoy, *The French Revolution and Napoleon* (New York, 1964). For the Napoleonic epoch, P. Geyl, *Napoleon: For and Against* (London, 1976) offers a useful introduction to many of the classic authors and F. Kafker and J. Laux, *Napoleon and his Times: Selected Interpretations* (Malabar, Florida, 1989) has excerpts from the classic works. Those who wish to dig deeper can turn to G. Lefebvre, *Napoleon* (New York, 1969), J. Tulard, *Napoleon* (London, 1984), L. Bergeron, *France under Napoleon* (New Jersey, 1981) and R. Holtman, *The Napoleonic Revolution* (Baton Rouge, 1978). For those in a hurry, A. Stiles, *Napoleon, France and Europe* (London, 1993) and G. Ellis, *The Napoleonic Empire* (Atlantic Highlands, New Jersey, 1991) might well be the ticket. There is, of course, nothing quite like consulting the Great Man himself, even if it is through an amanuensis; see Comte Las Cases, *Le Mémorial de Sainte-Hélène*; there are many editions but I recommend the one with a preface by Jean Tulard (Paris, 1968).

2 The study of the Revolution referred to is W. Doyle, *The Oxford History of the French Revolution* (Oxford, 1989). A classic consideration of Bonapartism in English remains H.A.L. Fisher's *Bonapartism* (Oxford, 1908). The way in which Bonapartism shifted in 1815 has been superbly analysed in F. Bluche, *Le Bonapartisme* (Paris, 1980), to which I owed a great debt in R.S. Alexander, *Bonapartism and Revolutionary Tradition in France* (Cambridge, 1991).

3 Madame de Staël, *Considérations sur les principaux événemens de la Révolution Française* (3rd edn, Paris, 1820); I have kept the original spelling.

4 Among his many influential works, F. Furet's *Interpreting the French Revolution* (Cambridge, 1981) perhaps makes this view of the essential meaning of the Revolution most clear.

5 For recent discussions of the illiberal Revolutionary tradition see G. Mosse, 'Fascism and the French Revolution', *Journal of Contemporary History*, 24, n.1 (1989), and J. Leith, 'The French Revolution: the origins of modern liberal culture?', *Journal of the Canadian Historical Association*, 2 (1991). Where such a line of thought can lead can be seen in E. Presseisen, *Amiens and Munich: Comparisons in Appeasement* (The Hague, 1978), and D. Seward, *Napoleon and Hitler* (London, 1988). Concerns over Caesarism were of course expressed very early on by E. Burke in his *Reflections on the Revolution in France* (London, 1790).

A. de Tocqueville's fears were expressed in his *The Old Regime and the French Revolution* (New York, 1955, trs. Stuart Gilbert).
6 Despite its biases, J. Godechot, *La Grande Nation. L'expansion révolutionnaire de la France dans le monde 1789–1799* (Paris, 1956) remains a classic. R.R. Palmer, *The World of the French Revolution* (New York, 1971) is still a useful overview; for more detailed considerations see T.C.W. Blanning, *The French Revolution in Germany* (Oxford, 1983) and S. Schama, *Patriots and Liberators: Revolution in the Netherlands, 1780–1813* (London, 1977). For the Napoleonic period particularly see J. Tulard, *Le Grand Empire, 1804–1815* (Paris, 1982) and *L'Europe au temps de Napoléon* (Paris, n.d.). Owen Connelly's *Napoleon's Satellite Kingdoms* (Toronto, 1969) and *The Epoch of Napoleon* (Malabar, Florida, 1978) contain useful information and are agreeably written. The latter comments remain true also of F. Markham, *Napoleon and the Awakening of Europe* (London, 1954)
7 See S. Woolf, *Napoleon's Integration of Europe* (London, 1991); it is a fascinating study.
8 For an introduction to study of the notables, see G. Ellis, 'Rhine and Loire, Napoleonic elites and social order', in G. Lewis and C. Lucas (eds), *Beyond the Terror* (Cambridge, 1983).
9 The debate over the nature of the Revolution is discussed in brief form in T.C.W. Blanning, *The French Revolution: Aristocrats versus Bourgeois?* (London, 1988) and one can read a collection of articles on the subject in D. Johnson (ed.) *French Society and the Revolution* (Cambridge 1976). On political culture, see the three volumes edited by K.M. Baker, C. Lucas, F. Furet and M. Ozouf entitled *The French Revolution and the Creation of Modern Political Culture* (Oxford, 1987–9).
10 On the motivation for war, see T.C.W. Blanning, *The Origins of the French Revolutionary Wars* (London, 1986). On Bonaparte as commander, see D. Chandler, *The Campaigns of Napoleon* (London, 1966), G. Rothenberg, *The Art of Warfare in the Age of Napoleon* (Bloomington, Indiana, 1978) and O. Connelly, *Blundering to Glory* (Wilmington, Delaware, 1988).
11 Among many works on the nature of the army see J.P. Bertaud, *The Army of the French Revolution: From Citizen-soldiers to Instruments of Power* (Princeton, 1988), A. Forrest, *Soldiers of the French Revolution* (London, 1990), E. Arnold, 'Some observations on the French opposition to Napoleonic conscription, 1804–1806', *French Historical Studies*, IV (Fall 1966), and J. Lynn, 'Towards an army of honor: the moral evolution of the French Army, 1789–1815', *French Historical Studies*, XVI (Spring 1989), which is followed by a stimulating debate between Lynn and O. Connelly. D.M.G. Sutherland draws the conclusions alluded to in *France, op. cit.*, pp.423–5.
12 On Fraternity and festivals, the standard work is M. Ozouf, *Festivals and the French Revolution* (Cambridge, Mass., 1988). Many works have recently come forth on women's experience of the Revolution. Concerning the increasing division of gender spheres, a good starting point is J. Landes, *Women and the Public Sphere in the Age of the French Revolution* (Ithaca, 1988); see also S. Spencer (ed.) *French Women in the*

Age of the Enlightenment (Bloomington, Indiana, 1984), C. Goldberg Moses, *French Feminism in the Nineteenth Century* (Albany, 1984) and D. Goodman, 'Public sphere and private life: towards a synthesis of current historiographical approaches to the old regime', *History and Theory,* 31 (1992). More specific topics include J. Scott, 'French feminists and the Rights of Man: Olympe de Gouges's declarations' and E. Colwill, 'Just another citoyenne? Marie-Antoinette on trial, 1790–93', both in *History Workshop* (Autumn 1989) and S. Connor, 'Prostitution and the Jacobin agenda for social control', *Eighteenth-Century Life,* 12, n.1 (1988). On the Napoleonic Civil Code, see M. Garaud and R. Szramkiewicz, *La Révolution française et la famille* (Paris, 1978), of which there is a useful extract in Kafker and Laux, *Napoleon and his Times,* and B. Schwartz (ed.) *The Code Napoleon and the Common-Law World* (New York, 1956).

13 For the above two paragraphs, see the sources cited in notes 6 and 7; to these can be added S. Woolf, 'French civilization and ethnicity in the Napoleonic Empire', *Past and Present,* n.124 (August 1989), P. Morgan, 'Republicanism, identity and the new European order: Georg Forster's letters from Mainz and Paris, 1792–93', *Journal of European Studies,* XXII (March 1992) and M. Broers, 'Italy and the modern state: the experience of Napoleonic rule' in Furet and Ozouf (eds) *op. cit., The French Revolution and the Creation of Modern Political Culture,* vol.III.

14 The two main works on the Continental System are E. Heckscher, *The Continental System: An Economic Interpretation* (London, 1922) and G. Ellis, *Napoleon's Continental Blockade: The Case of Alsace* (Oxford, 1981). Also useful is F. Crouzet, 'Wars, blockade, and economic change in Europe, 1792–1815', *Journal of Economic History,* XXIV (1964).

15 On Napoleon's fall(s) and the Hundred Days see the sources cited in note 2 and to these may be added E. Le Gallo, *Les Cent Jours* (Paris, 1924) and especially H. Houssaye's *1814* (Paris, 1888) and *1815* (Paris, 1889–1905).

FURTHER READING

Alexander, R.S., *Bonapartism and Revolutionary Tradition* (Cambridge, 1991).

Bergeron, L., *France under Napoleon* (New Jersey, 1981).

Bertaud, J.P., *The Army of the French Revolution: From Citizen-soldiers to Instruments of Power* (Princeton, 1988).

Chandler, D., *The Campaigns of Napoleon* (London, 1966).

Connelly, O., *Blundering into Glory* (Wilmington, Delaware, 1988).

Ellis, G., *The Napoleonic Empire* (New Jersey, 1991).

Forrest, A., *Soldiers of the French Revolution* (London, 1990).

Holtman, R., *The Napoleonic Revolution* (Baton Rouge, 1978).

Lefebvre, G., *Napoleon* (New York, 1969).

Lynn, J., 'Towards an army of honor: the moral evolution of the French army, 1789–1815', *French Historical Studies,* XVI (1989).

Rothenberg, G., *The Art of Warfare in the Age of Napoleon* (Bloomington, Indiana, 1978).

Sutherland, D.M.G., *France 1789–1815. Revolution and Counter-Revolution* (London, 1985).

Tulard, J., *Napoleon. The Myth of the Saviour* (London, 1984).

Woolf, S., *Napoleon's Integration of Europe* (London, 1991).

Chapter 4

The eastern empires from the ancien regime to the challenge of the French wars, 1780–*c.*1806

Brendan Simms

Geographically, the scope of Chapters 4 and 5 is confined to the Prussian and Habsburg Monarchies and the European provinces of the Russian Empire. We shall call them the 'eastern empires' for convenience. Thematically, our remit is political developments and political conflict. For our purposes politics may be defined as being about power: personal power, state power and the power of intermediary bodies, what we might today call interest groups. Of course, politics can also be about socio-economic power, but that lies to a considerable extent outside our brief. We are therefore not concerned with 'society' as such or even with 'social power' itself, but rather with the interface between the state and the holders of social power, or those aspiring to it; in short, the political life of the state. This is distinct from the state as consumer and entrepreneur, or the state as patron of culture. Instead, our focus is the relationship of the state both to its politically significant component parts and to the other European states with which it was in constant competition. Foreign policy and war, political unrest and political reform: these are our centres of attention. The ordering principle here will be the primacy of foreign policy.[1] We shall see how the foreign–political needs of the state was the single most decisive factor in the transformation – or survival – of the political, governmental, military and ultimately social structures of all three eastern empires. For the most part, then, this chapter is concerned with politics at the highest level: it is self-consciously 'history from above'. By and large, the three states were not threatened by mass popular movements from below during our period; what matters is what the Austrian, Prussian and Russian governments did, or what was done to them by other governments.

There are several reasons why it is useful to consider the three eastern empires in comparative perspective. In the first place, there were, by comparison with western Europe, basic similarities in political and social structure. Second, throughout our period all three states focused on much the same foreign policy problems, especially Poland, the Balkans and the German Empire. Third, all three states bore the brunt of the challenge of Revolutionary France on the continent. In this respect, and in respect of their fundamental conservatism in domestic politics, the eastern empires were bound up in a community of fate which almost demands that their individual experiences be treated as a unified whole. Nor is the periodization a problem. Despite the apparent arbitrariness of our starting point at 1780 and the evident Franco-centricity of the prescribed terminating point of 1830, there *is* a plausible unity to the period under discussion. This unity will become abundantly clear in due course; for the present suffice it to say that the dividing line between the two chapters is the date at which the French danger ceased to be simply a foreign–political problem, but actually threatened the very survival of the eastern empires. In the case of Prussia the trauma of 1806 provides a neat halfway point. As for Austria, in the period 1801–5 the government responded to the problems thrown up by the French challenge with some substantially new policies. Finally, in the instance of Russia, the range of dates is wider still, but a plausible case can be made for seeing a – short-lived – new departure after 1802. In all three states, the resulting programmes of reform represented a fundamental change from the political developments of the previous two decades.

Any discussion of political conflict in the three eastern empires in the five decades preceding 1830 must begin with a survey of the political and socio-political structures as they existed in 1780. Many of these structures were to remain unchanged until 1848; they constitute at the same time both the permanent background to, and the frequent subject matter of, the political dramas to follow.

At the highest level, the similarity between Austria, Russia and Prussia was obvious. All three states were monarchies in which the sovereign had secured absolute power to direct foreign policy. In the case of Austria and Prussia, both monarchies had largely succeeded in emancipating themselves from the restrictions imposed by that larger German political commonwealth, the Holy Roman Empire. In the case of Russia, the customary traditional restraints on monarchic authority had hardly ever existed. The rulers all subscribed to some form of enlightened absolutism, Frederick the Great of Prussia and Catherine of Russia perhaps more so than Maria Theresa of Austria, whose enthusiasm for the Enlightenment lagged considerably behind that of her co-regent and son, Joseph. In concrete terms this involved movement towards legal and educational reforms; in all three cases it meant dealing with the problem of serfdom; in Russia it even meant consultation with the representatives of the townspeople, merchants, state peasants and nationalities about the feasibility of agrarian and local government reform (the Legislative Commission of 1767). However, these measures should not be seen as a move towards broader political participation. Catherine was aiming to extend the counsel and expertise available to her, not to share her power with others. Indeed, at first sight there were few restrictions on monarchical power: all three rulers had exclusive command over the armed forces. They possessed expanding bureaucracies eager to consolidate the grip of the state on society. There was no politically important middle class, either because, as in Russia, the level of urbanization was very low, or, as in Prussia and Austria, because the power of the cities had been all but eliminated by the seventeenth century.

All three monarchs were guided by the primacy of foreign policy. That is to say, they all regarded the defence and expansion of the state as their first priority. All considerations of domestic policy were subordinate to this aim. In one of his political testaments, Frederick the Great of Prussia wrote that, 'The first task of a prince is to survive, the second to expand.' The internal political consequences of this were clear: the state required a strong executive and a maximum of socio-political cohesion. To quote the words of Catherine in Russia, 'There is no better form of government than autocracy, for it combines the strength of law with the executive dispatch of a single authority.' Many of the internal reforms of the period were clearly motivated by this primacy of foreign policy. Perhaps the most striking example of this would be the Haugwitzian and Kaunitzian reforms of the 1750s and 1760s in the Habsburg Monarchy. Here the aim was to close the developmental gap between Prussia and Austria for the purposes of renewing the struggle for supremacy in Germany.

Conversely, internal reforms could be frustrated for foreign political reasons, such as when Catherine's Legislative Commission was shelved soon after the outbreak of the Russo–Turkish war of 1768.

Yet if the tendency was towards ever more absolute royal power, this did not mean that political conflict did not exist. It is true that the influence of the nobility *qua* nobility on state policy was limited outside the Habsburg Monarchy. Within the realm of 'high politics', however, there was almost infinite scope for the individual nobleman or bourgeois parvenu to fulfil his ambition as statesman, diplomat, soldier, administrator or courtier. Indeed, the capitals of the three eastern empires were riven by rivalry and intrigue, by the conflicts between a Potemkin and a Zavadovsky (Russia), a Hertzberg and an Eichel or a Prince Henry (Prussia), a Kaunitz and a Trauttmansdorf (Habsburg monarchy). These rivalries and high political alignments, it should be added, are not primarily explicable in terms of policy differences but rather in terms of irreconcilable personal ambitions. In Russia, for example, the divide between Potemkin and Panin/Vorontsov has often been portrayed as a conflict between middling nobility and 'aristocratic constitutionalists' respectively. In fact, as a recent study has shown,[2] such disputes were in the first instance personal in nature, with policy differences being instrumentalized and often intentionally polarized to achieve personal ends. A detailed treatment of this closed and arcane world lies beyond the remit of these chapters. Suffice it to say that the vagaries of high politics will be a constant accompaniment to political developments throughout our period, occasionally intervening as a *deus ex machina* to remove the one or the other player from the political chessboard.

As well as these similarities at the highest level of politics there were basic parallels in socio-political structure. A brief discussion of the question of noble–peasant relations is essential because it was on these relations that the politically significant crown–nobility relationship ultimately rested. In simple terms, what the three eastern empires had in common was this: all of them were characterized by a basic duality between monarchic power at the top and noble power at the lowest levels of political life. In return for military and state service, the aristocracy was permitted, and even encouraged, to retain and extend its hold on the non-privileged population in the countryside. The central features of this system were a noble monopoly of landownership and the institution of serfdom, a socio-legal concept involving varying degrees of personal bondage. It was this personal bondage which distinguished eastern and central Europe from the west. It was the contrast between *Grundherrschaft*, the western European and western German phenomenon by which the noble controlled only the property of the peasantry, and *Gutsherrschaft*, the dominant relationship in the east by which the lord also enjoyed a considerable degree of authority over the person of the peasant himself. In Russia, at least for the enserfed majority, this bondage was complete. The peasant was bound to the soil, was forbidden to possess property or to leave the village without the lord's consent. He could even be bought or sold. In Prussia personal bondage extended only to areas such as marriage, the practice of a trade or leaving the land; these activities all required the consent of the noble lord. In the Habsburg Monarchy the aristocracy enjoyed similar rights, though these tended to be less rigorously enforced. In all cases, the peasants were obliged to provide their overlords with either labour service or its cash equivalent, on which the agrarian economies still largely depended.

Indeed, the control of the nobility over the peasantry was not only socio-economic, but also politico-legal. Even in Prussia and the Habsburg Monarchy, where the civil service was expanding at the expense of the aristocracy, much of the administration was still entirely run by the nobility. Given the comparatively minuscule number of bureaucrats, it is hardly surprising that at local level government in all three states was in the hands of aristocratic assemblies. Most importantly, in all cases the nobility exercised patrimonial justice over their peasants. In Prussia and Russia, the relationship of noble to peasant was also central to the political economy and military structure of the three eastern empires. Whereas the peasantry – almost uniquely – was subject to direct taxation, the nobility was exempted by virtue of their service to the state. The Habsburg Monarchy was an exception, for here the nobility paid a land tax; in time this was to provide some of them with a lever with which to contest royal absolutism. In all three cases the levying of taxes in the countryside and the provision of conscripts for the army was entrusted to the nobility on behalf of the state. However, in both Austria and Prussia the state protected the peasant from absorption by noble landlords, in order to safeguard the flow of recruits. The term 'military agrarian complex', which has been coined to describe the relationship between state, peasant and lord in Prussia,[3] might equally be applied to all three eastern empires. Even if in some areas, especially in Russia, peasant lives were regulated by bailiffs, or some other kind of peasant intermediary, rather than by the resident aristocracy themselves, the underlying principle was still that of noble domination. In short, in rural areas the nobleman was employer, landlord, administrator, military superior, recruiting officer and judge all in one.

However, for all the similarities, there were also key differences in the political structures of the three eastern empires in 1780. First and foremost among them was the relationship between crown and nobility which was to be at the centre of internal political developments well beyond 1830.

In Prussia this relationship was relatively straightforward. In the seventeenth century an arrangement had been reached between prince and nobility by which the latter surrendered political power at the highest level in return for the socio-political privileges outlined above.[4] Under Frederick the Great, this governing compromise or *Herrschaftskompromiß*, was perfected. The crown undertook no longer to buy up noble land, recover alienated royal property or to tamper with noble–peasant relations. Noble land could not be sold to non-nobles while the state assisted in the setting up of rural credit institutes (1770s) which would both prop up struggling landowners and provide the capital for improvements. In return the nobility served the state as officers and bureaucrats. The only state intervention on the land was the rigorous enforcement of the laws protecting peasants from noble encroachments. This was known as *Bauernschutz* and its purpose was to ensure that each district was able to deliver the specified number of recruits. These arrangements were not subjected to closer scrutiny so long as they fulfilled the needs of the primacy of foreign policy, that is to say so long as they provided the monarchy with the internal cohesion essential to survive in the competitive world of power politics.

In Russia the situation was more problematic. Here, like Prussia, noble power had been linked to state service. Like Prussia, the state was a major landowner in its own right. But unlike Prussia, the link between state service and landownership was still a very direct one. Whereas the nobility in seventeenth-century Prussia had already held their land and titles before entering into the governing compromise with the prince, in Russia noble status and

landed property were often dependent on military or administrative service. To quote Richard Pipes, Russia was a 'proprietary
state' in which state power stemmed from ownership of the land.[5]
This had two main consequences. In the first place it impeded the
development of strong regional nobilities such as were to be found
in the Habsburg Monarchy. Even the largest Russian estates were
widely dispersed, with the lordship of a single village often being
shared among two or more nobles. Second, there was a rapid
turnover of property as the crown gave new grants of land in
return for service. According to some historians, about one-third
of land in a given region might change hands in the course of a
century. This was bound to inhibit the formation of possible
regional power concentrations.

All this was thrown into question, however, by the emancipation of the nobility from compulsory state service in 1762, under
Peter III, a measure which the young Catherine the Great endorsed. The old hierarchical system centred exclusively on the
Tsar was now replaced by a 'dyarchy'[6] in which the monarch ran
foreign policy, while the country itself was abandoned to the
nobility and the noble-dominated bureaucracy. Furthermore, the
control and possession of the peasantry by their lords was
formally recognized and certain peasant rights, such as the right
to invoke state protection against noble misconduct, were stripped
away (1767). The parallels to the Prussian situation are clear and
historians have not been slow to postulate the development of a
Russian *Herrschaftskompromiß* during the reign of Catherine.[7] On
the other hand it is possible to see the 'emancipation of the
nobility' as the 'final demobilization of the ruling class', as one
historian has described it.[8] Whatever the case may be, once
compulsory service had gone, the unchallenged justification for
noble privilege had gone with it. It should therefore come as no
surprise that almost immediately, as witnessed by the frame of
reference of the Legislative Commission of 1766/7, the whole
institution of serfdom became an issue. Quite apart from any
enlightened considerations, this noble privilege no longer seemed
to make any sense in terms of state efficiency.

By comparison with Russia and Prussia the nobility in the
Habsburg Monarchy were an obvious menace to state efficiency.
At the beginning of the eighteenth century, the uncontested rights
of the Emperor did not extend much beyond control of foreign
policy. Key areas such as taxation and conscription were subject

to the consent of 'estates', that is to say of representative assemblies of the nobility, clergy and, in some cases, towns. Unlike Russia or Prussia, the Habsburg Monarchy had to contend with regionally powerful nobilities. Families such as the Liechtensteins, Schwarzenbergs and Lobkowitz in Bohemia and Bathanyi, and the Szechenyi and Esterhazy in Hungary, were powerful political forces in their own right. In the decades preceding 1780 the Viennese authorities had been remarkably successful in suppressing the estates in the western half of the monarchy, but were entirely unsuccessful in Hungary. Here the problem was not so much the great magnates as the middling nobility who made up about one-third of the total and who found an outlet for their political energies in their representative institution, the Hungarian Diet. Collectively – there were about 20,000 of them – they packed a powerful punch. They exercised an iron grip on local administration, which they ran through their county assemblies (*congregationes*), and guarded their privileges jealously. In time they were to become the mainstay of Hungarian particularism and later nationalism. We shall be hearing more of them. For the time being trouble was avoided by the simple expediency of not summoning the Hungarian Diet after the Seven Years' War.

The second difference between the three eastern empires lay in their varying degrees of political stability. It would be difficult to imagine a more stable polity than Prussia: hardly a flicker of peasant unrest, not a trace of aristocratic *fronde*. The Habsburg Monarchy was less blessed: here some of the western estates had shown separatist tendencies as late as the 1740s while the Hungarian nobility still represented something of a state within a state; there was also considerable peasant unrest in Bohemia in the 1770s. But the most unstable polity of them all was clearly Russia. The sources of instability were twofold. In the first place, there was the ambiguity surrounding Catherine's claim to the throne, which she had ascended after having had her husband murdered. During the early years of her reign she was confronted with countless coup attempts on the part of army officers or courtiers with more or less plausible pretenders in tow. Second, there was the inherent explosiveness of the agrarian situation. Indeed, at one point in the early 1770s, the two elements combined to produce Pugachev's Rebellion (1773–4). This was no rural flash in the pan but a concerted challenge to Catherine's rule, made the more dangerous by the fact that its ringleader, Pugachev, claimed to be

Catherine's murdered husband, Peter III. After gathering together a dangerous cocktail of oppositional forces – Cossacks, Tartars, Old Believers and convicts – Pugachev then proceeded to offer to emancipate the serfs. He thus struck both at the socio-political basis of the existing order and at the legitimacy of the reigning monarch. The slender basis of social and political authority in Russia could not have been more cruelly exposed. Nearly a year was required to restore order.

Pugachev's revolt cast a long shadow over noble–peasant relations and Catherinian Russia as a whole. It made Catherine aware of her need for the nobility as an intermediary power to buttress autocracy. Whereas she had previously been sympathetic towards peasant emancipation, her first priority now was to strengthen the links between the state and the aristocracy. The Statute for Administration of 1775 was the first fruit of this new approach. This measure formally integrated the nobility into local government and shared out administrative tasks between government appointees and locally elected nobles. In addition the nobility were permitted to manage their corporate affairs in provincial assemblies. In the 1785 Charter to the Nobility Catherine spelt out her debt to the nobility in the preamble. In return she affirmed their privileges in army and bureaucracy, their right to be tried by their peers, their exemption from taxation, their exemption from compulsory service and many other rights. Above all, the relationship between serf and lord remained unchanged. When taken together, these measures amounted to a formidable – if not wholly intended – accretion of noble power. It is true that Catherine simultaneously issued a Charter to the Towns, which granted rights of urban self-government, but this hardly weighed in the balance.

It would be wrong, however, to assume that serf–noble or even noble–crown relations were the main centres of attention for the Prussian, Austrian and Russian governments in the period leading up to 1780. They conceived of domestic political structure not primarily as an end in itself but as a means to an end. This end was the preservation and expansion of the state. Internal affairs thus only moved to the top of the agenda either when, as in the case of Pugachev, unrest threatened the existence of government, or when, as in the case of the Habsburg Monarchy, existing internal political structures reduced the efficiency of the state to the extent of endangering foreign political success.

In terms of international relations, the decade which drew to a close in 1780 had been an unusually quiet one. The long lull in Germany which followed the end of the Seven Years' War had been broken only by the War of the Bavarian Succession (1777–8), a phony war which involved just enough serious campaigning to persuade the Austrians to abandon their designs on Bavaria. In Prussia Frederick the Great had long since forsworn further conquests and while Austro–Prussian dualism was still vibrant it was far from being as virulent as it had been in his early reign. Indeed, both Austria and Prussia began to show signs of a willingness to abide by the rules of good neighbourliness enjoined by the greater German political commonwealth to which they belonged: the Holy Roman Empire. Of all the eastern powers, by far the most active was Russia. To the west, a constant cold war was maintained against the hapless Poles, whose kingdom was partitioned in 1772 and whose rump state had sunk to the level of a Russian satellite by 1780. In Germany, Catherine had secured herself the role of guarantor of the German constitution at the Treaty of Teschen, a prestigious role, but one nullified by her subsequent behaviour. To the south, Catherine kept up the momentum generated by Peter the Great. A successful six-year struggle against the Turks (1768–74) brought Russia to the shores of the Black Sea, won her the right to send ships into the Mediterranean and gained her the status of protecting the power of the Balkan Christians. This latter clause was to provide a convenient excuse for future interventions. Her undisguised ultimate aim was control of Constantinople, a claim which was underlined when Catherine christened her new-born grandson Constantine in 1779.

The year 1780 marked a caesura in the history of the eastern empires, for the accession of Joseph II as sole ruler of the Habsburg Monarchy on the death of Maria Theresa set in motion a train of events which was to dominate the political life of all three states for the best part of the next decade.

Joseph II was the classic enlightened absolutist. He was bent both on regaining Habsburg supremacy in Germany and on acquiring a handsome slice of the Ottoman Empire's Balkan possessions. He was also determined to eradicate any internal barriers to his absolute rule. In so doing Joseph set both the internal Austrian and the European international agenda for the

1780s. First of all, because his aims coincided to a large degree with those of Catherine and thus enabled her to initiate her own campaign of expansion. Second, because his evident ambition demanded a Prussian response. Third, because his drive towards absolutism ran into serious internal resistance inside the Habsburg Monarchy which interacted with the international situation he had created.

The first victim of Joseph's depredations was the Holy Roman Empire of which he was the titular head. At first sight the *Reich*, an apparently motley collection of middling and minuscule princedoms, seemed an easy target. But when confronted by an obvious predator such as Joseph its defensive mechanisms, especially when harnessed to the dualist jealousies of Prussia, proved formidable.[9] An attempt to rationalize the episcopal boundaries and thus bring all the bishoprics under Habsburg control almost foundered on the resistance of Salzburg. Another attempt at securing Bavaria also failed when it encountered strong French opposition. Soon after, Frederick the Great succeeded in organizing the bulk of the more important German potentates into the *Fürstenbund* or League of Princes (1785) against Joseph. Frustrated, Joseph now turned his attention southwards. Having already secured Russian backing for his German designs through the treaty with Russia of 1781, he now rallied to Catherine's aid when the Ottoman Turks launched a pre-emptive strike designed to forestall imminent extinction. The Russians had already made good use of this treaty to annex the Crimea without opposition in 1783. By early 1788, it looked as if an Austro–Russian partition of Turkey would follow the rapid collapse of resistance.

In the meantime, not content with the havoc he had already caused, Joseph had simultaneously proceeded to assault all the internal barriers to his unfettered rule. To quote the words of one distinguished historian of the Habsburg Monarchy, the period 1780–90 was 'ten years of revolution (although Revolution from above)'.[10] The first to feel the cold wind from Vienna was the Catholic Church: the monasteries were suppressed, state control over the seminaries was imposed and civil marriage introduced. These religious policies especially came to be known as 'Josephinism', though the term could be applied to his reform programme as a whole. Much of what Joseph attempted was profoundly progressive, though premature. In 1787 he suspended the implementation of capital punishment. Even if this was not an all-time first – Tsarina Elizabeth had abolished the death penalty in the 1740s – it seems to have been more closely observed than the Russian measure. Already in 1781 he had grasped the nettle of peasant emancipation, by abolishing serfdom. Peasants were now permitted to migrate, take up a trade and marry without their lord's permission. Patrimonial justice was abolished. Labour services were to be transmuted into money payments. He earned little gratitude from the rural population, who found the new cash economy threatening and unfamiliar.

What finally brought Joseph down was a mixture of Prussian intervention and Hungarian obstruction. Ever since he had refused to have himself crowned king of Hungary it was clear that Joseph intended to bring the Hungarians to heel. In 1784 he decreed that German should replace Latin as the language of administration in Hungary. The following year he announced his intention to rationalize the administration of Hungary, which would largely devolve to royal commissioners, thus riding rough-shod over historic sensibilities and entrenched interests. A year later again he extended the abolition of serfdom and the imple-mentation of the new agrarian relationships to Hungary. He might have got away with all of this were it not for the fact that Prussia had mobilized with the obvious intention of setting limits to Joseph's ambitions in the Balkans, which, if realized, would drastically change the European balance to Prussia's disadvant-age. A clear primacy of foreign policy then came to govern Joseph's actions. In order to confront Prussia and prosecute the war against Turkey he needed men and money. Conscription was imposed on Hungary in 1786, and in order to fund his extensive foreign commitments Joseph had to turn to the Hungarian nobility in 1788 for financial assistance. The Magyar aristocracy, however, refused to cooperate and the result was a breakdown of Habsburg authority in Hungary. Indeed, by this stage, unrest had broken out all over the monarchy. In the Austrian Netherlands, the estates had been goaded into revolt by Joseph's administrative reforms and in November 1789 they deposed him. There were peasant risings in Hungary and unrest in Galicia, driven by hatred of conscription and bewilderment at the recent agrarian reforms. Joseph did not give up easily. He came back in 1789 with a scheme for a unified land tax across the monarchy. But in January 1790 he was finally forced to capitulate to the Hungarian nobility, an event which was to set the tone for much of the Habsburg Monarchy's subsequent history. Within two months, Joseph was dead.

It is thus easy to understand why in 1789, the year of the Revolution in France, all eyes were on the Balkans. At first, events in Paris elicited some interest and sympathy but certainly no sustained alarm. Russia and Austria were too involved in their attack on the Ottomans, and Prussia too preoccupied with possible Austrian gains, to pay any attention to the plight of the French monarch. In any case, at least one of the eastern powers had enough domestic problems of its own to worry about. Leopold II, who succeeded Joseph in mid-1790, inherited a state in deep crisis. The war with Turkey had dragged on for two years without conspicuous success; war with Prussia threatened. There was also the revolt in Belgium, the large-scale noble and urban obstructionism in Hungary, Galicia and the Italian possessions of the monarchy, not to mention widespread peasant turbulence. Like his brother, Leopold was himself a reformer, a radical even. But unlike his brother he recognized that the developments of the past decade had brought the monarchy to the very verge of disintegration. Leopold decided to cut his losses. Nearly all of the agrarian reforms were reversed; labour services and patrimonial justice were reintroduced. In Hungary, the language laws and the land tax were repealed.

The long-term consequences of the return to the status quo in domestic politics were only to become evident later; what was immediately obvious was the import of Leopold's new foreign policy. By July 1790 the Habsburg Monarchy had come to terms with Prussia at the Convention of Reichenbach. In it both parties agreed to honour the existing territorial order in central Europe and the Balkans. The net result of this was to refocus Austrian and Prussian energies on western Europe. Now that expansion elsewhere had been ruled out, the elaborate exchange plans which had been circulating in Berlin for some years, and which involved trading territory in the west for gains in the east, came into their own. Within two years the Austro–Prussian rapprochement had broadened into a defensive alliance. As yet, however, nothing definite had been undertaken. The Declaration of Pillnitz, issued in June 1791, in which Austria and Prussia expressed their concern at developments in France, was more in the nature of a face-saving exercise, for no concrete actions followed. Not even the plight of

Marie-Antoinette, an Austrian princess, was sufficient on its own to provoke intervention against Revolutionary France. The fact that war ultimately did break out was due to a combination of Austro–Prussian opportunism and a largely autonomous French domestic–political dynamic. For in April 1792, partly in response to genuine fears of an Austrian attack and partly in order to export the Revolution, the French National Assembly declared war on the Habsburg Monarchy. This activated the Austro–Prussian defensive alliance and within a month Prussia, too, was at war with Revolutionary France.

In the eastern empires, the ancien regime did not crumble at the first revolutionary fanfare from France. Nor was the Revolution itself seen as an immediate threat to the established order. Indeed, both the Austrian and Prussian governments initially adopted a positive stance. Joseph II regarded the early Revolution as an imitation of his own efforts at reform. It is true that in Berlin, Frederick William II, who had succeeded Frederick the Great in 1786, was hostile, but many of his ministers were not. The foreign secretary, Ewald von Hertzberg, even went so far as to say that Prussia need have no fear of revolution as she was already sufficiently enlightened to make radical change superfluous. It should not surprise us that this conceit was widespread among statesmen of the eastern powers; they had after all been ruled by enlightened absolutists for the best part of three decades. Nor was this confidence misplaced. Subversive activity was very limited and often blown out of all proportion by the authorities. The only Jacobin experiment to get off the ground in Germany was the Republic of Mainz, and that only in the wake of, and under the protection of, the victorious French armies.[11] In Austria proper and Hungary there was a ludicrously exaggerated Jacobin scare in the mid-1790s. Prussia faced no serious Jacobin problem. Admittedly, there was a marked move away from the Enlightenment in the late 1780s and early 1790s, but it had already begun *before* 1789 with the obscurantist policies of Woellner, and the old Fredericians such as Hertzberg continued to exist more or less uneasily with the new king's favourites, such as Woellner and Bischoffwerder. Of course, secret societies such as freemasonry and the Rosicrucians were widespread, in Berlin and Vienna as well as St Petersburg. But these were almost too commonplace to be of real political significance; in any case, at least as many members were anti-Revolutionary as were inclined towards radical change.

In short, no copycat Austrian, Prussian and Russian revolutions followed the French example. Why this should have been so has long puzzled historians.[12] In the case of Russia the obvious answer is the complete absence of all the preconditions for a successful revolution, let alone the absence of any revolutionary situation, in the 1790s, once the turbulence associated with Pugachev's revolt had settled. The Prussian and Habsburg cases are more problematic, not least because of the total lack of consensus about the factors leading to revolution in France. If we are inclined to see the middle classes as the agents of radical change, we should look to the political passivity of artisans, professionals and merchants throughout most of central and eastern Europe. If we are minded to attach weight to the force of ideas, we should look to the way in which the spread of enlightened ideas tended to confirm rather than challenge the existing order. A good example of this phenomenon would be Kant, who was sympathetic to the French Revolution, yet enjoined obedience to the Prussian state. As for the peasants, it appears that the grip of the 'military agrarian complex' in all three states was too strong to permit much turbulence – there was of course some unrest, most notably in Silesia (1794). To those for whom the 'revolt of the nobles' was the decisive event in France, the quiescence of the aristocracy in Prussia, Russia and Austria throughout the Revolutionary period would be the key to the stability of the ancien regime. In the Prussian and Russian cases the nobility were too intimately bound up and too obviously beneficiaries of the existing order to think of challenging it. In the Habsburg Monarchy, on the other hand, the relationship of the aristocracy to the state was often ambiguous but both found sufficient common ground against radicalism to bury the hatchet – for the time being – on the basis of the status quo. Besides, the awful fate of the French crown was a very persuasive argument in favour of noble moderation towards a beleaguered monarch. Finally, and relatedly, there is a sense in which the revolutionary situation had already passed in the Habsburg Monarchy. Her experience of the full gamut of noble revolt, regional separatism and peasant unrest had *preceded* and – with the exception of Belgium – was entirely distinct from the French Revolution.

One should not be deceived by the fire-breathing and reactionary manifesto issued by the Duke of Brunswick from Mainz in the summer of 1792. The War of the First Coalition, which pitted first Prussia and Austria and then Britain against Revolutionary France was not therefore a war of ideology.[13] Rather it was an opportunist war of aggression. Despite her aversion to the Revolution, Catherine took no part in the operation. Her attention was elsewhere, partly on Poland, where the activities of the reforming Diet of 1788 were giving cause for concern, but largely still on the Balkans. After some time she resumed her drive south. Ottoman resistance, which had held up very well over the previous two years, began to crumble. The following year, in the Ochakov crisis, so called after the name of the Black Sea town at issue, Britain was unable to force Catherine to surrender her gains. These were consolidated in the Russo–Turkish peace treaty of 1792.

In the meantime the war in the west was going badly. Initial successes were followed by defeat at Valmy and the subsequent invasion of Germany. The international situation in Europe was about to be fundamentally transformed. Before 1806 the French threat was to spawn three coalitions and was to remain at the centre of Great Power attention until 1815. By 1795 Prussia, defeated and bankrupted, had dropped out of the First Coalition. Austria soldiered on, not without success, until forced to come to terms with France at Campó Formio in 1797. For both states the brush with Revolutionary French power had been a bruising experience. Austria lost Belgium, though she gained Venetia. Prussia lost her western possessions and abandoned the whole left bank of the Rhine to the French. Austria, this time joined by Russia, made another concerted attempt to face down French power. Once again, after initial successes, the coalition disintegrated and led to further losses at the Treaty of Lunéville in 1801.

The main reason for the failure of the eastern empires to come to grips with the resurgence of French power was that they were deeply divided among themselves. Throughout the 1790s Prussia was still too blinkered by her old dualist obsession with Austria to make a serious stand against France. This applies to an even greater extent to Russia, entirely fixated on issues nearer home until the close of the 1790s. When she finally did join battle, in the War of the Second Coalition, she soon fell out with her allies. Indeed, within a year Russia had formed the second Armed Neutrality *against* Britain. In all of these cases we see a clear primacy of foreign policy at work. Once one had accepted in Berlin, Vienna and St Petersburg that ideological grounds alone were an insufficient basis for a coalition against France, it was but a short step to the contention that concerns about the resurgence of French power, or about the spread of revolutionary radicalism, should be subordinated to the prosecution of long-standing rivalries and policies. Indeed, two of the eastern powers were quite prepared to make common cause both with Revolutionary France, and with subversive movements in rival states. Thus in 1788, Catherine the Great was happy to deal with Finnish separatists to embarrass the Swedes. In 1788–90 the Prussians encouraged the Belgian, Hungarian and Galician rebels to annoy Joseph.

At first sight, the final partitions of Poland (1793 and 1795), after which that country disappeared for more than a century, would seem to contradict this picture. After all, could it not be argued that the three reactionary eastern powers were acting in unison to forestall the revolutionary danger of the refoming Diet which had been sitting since 1788? In fact, what was objectionable about the new constitution of 1791 was not its radical but its absolutist elements. In it the role of the Polish king was immeasurably strengthened by the abolition of the *liberum veto* (individual right of veto) of the gentry in the Diet. This unnerved the Russians in particular, for it threatened both the loss of a client state and the rise of a new power centre on her western border. As Catherine herself commented, 'No sooner did the Polish king raise the spectre of another partition than they [the Diet] conferred on him arbitrary power.' It was renewed monarchic power that she feared in Poland, not anti-monarchic revolution. Despite her enlightened sympathies, Catherine had no hesitation in stamping out the stirrings of reform in Poland, nor did her role as protector of the orthodox population of Poland interfere with her backing of the fiercely Catholic and intolerant Confederation of Bar under Ignaz Potocki to bring down the constitution. Finally, as far as Austria and especially Prussia were concerned, a key motivating factor was the desire to make good territorial losses in the west. In the Polish case, as ever, considerations of foreign policy were paramount.

Towards the end of the decade it was becoming clear that the Revolutionary Wars had exposed several weaknesses in the ancien regimes of the eastern powers. This was most obvious in the military field, where the old line armies struggled against the *élan*, tactics and numbers of the French juggernaut. The Austrian, Russian and Prussian response was sluggish, partly because the existing military structure was too intimately bound up with the internal socio-political structure of the state and partly because there still remained a considerable residual confidence in the strength of the three armies. Another area in which deficiencies became apparent was that of finance. Shortage of funds had been one of the prime reasons for Prussia's exit from the First Coalition, while the Habsburgs, unable to tap their entire potential because of noble resistance, were chronically impecunious. In the Prussian case the financial problems were all the more striking for the fact that she had begun the campaign with an ample war chest collected by Frederick the Great. Clearly, the new war could not be fought with the financial structures of the old regime. Here again, however, the forces of inertia were too strong to permit any reform before the end of the decade. Last but not least, the challenge of Revolutionary France, and later of Napoleon, cruelly laid bare the inadequacy of the decision-making structures of the eastern empires. These were too involved and cluttered with historic anomalies to allow the rapid responses required by the exigencies of the international situation.

Increased censorship and anti-revolutionary vigilance apart, domestic politics in the three eastern empires in the 1790s proceeded as if 1789 and the explosion of French power had never happened. In Austria, Leopold II and Francis I (after 1792) were content simply to restore the *status quo ante* after the turbulences of the Josephine years. Catherine's domestic policy remained unchanged and much the same could be said for Prussia, where the enlightened reform projects launched by Frederick the Great were beginning to bear fruit, despite the cool obscurantist wind blowing from the royal palace. These led to the *Allgemeines Landrecht* or basic law of 1794. At root, the basic law confirmed the old division of society into estates and the existing relationships on the land. The political implications of the measure were thus far from 'progressive'. This is not to say that no serious attempts at reform were made. Almost immediately after his accession to the throne in 1797, Frederick William III set up reform commissions and extended his patronage to reform-minded bureaucrats. One notable achievement was the emancipation of the peasantry on the royal domains. But the main task, that of a thoroughgoing overhaul of state and society, was not attempted.

Surprisingly, it was only in Russia where Paul I succeeded

Catherine as Tsar in 1796 that a broad programme of reform was initiated before the decade was out. But Paul fell into the Josephinist trap of attempting too much at once. His main target was the aristocracy. He repudiated the Charter to the Nobility and subjected them to the same disciplinary measures, including corporal punishment, as the serfs. In 1797 he imposed a land tax on the nobility. Measures for the alleviation of serfdom were also introduced. He purged the military and sacked almost 3,000 officers. What had taken Joseph a whole ten years, Paul achieved in four. Friendless, justly paranoid and possibly unhinged, the Tsar found himself isolated among nobles, bureaucrats and military men. In 1801 a high political intrigue in St Petersburg led to his murder and replacement by his son, Alexander I.

To sum up: by the turn of the century the impact of the French Revolutionary Wars on the society and the internal political structure of the three eastern empires was still minimal. What had radically changed was the world around them. Both Prussia and Austria had made significant territorial losses and gains. Russia had continued to advance at the expense of Poland and the Ottomans. In the west the old order had been altered beyond recognition. Belgium, Holland, northern Italy and much of the Holy Roman Empire were now firmly in the French orbit. By 1804 the Habsburgs had seen the writing on the wall and proclaimed a separate Austrian imperial title. The old *Reich* was now on the verge of collapse. For the smaller western German states this meant extinction; for the middling states it meant a chance to free themselves from Austro–Prussian control as they scrambled for the territorial scraps tossed to them by Napoleon. The wave of secularizations and acquisitions which followed the new territorial arrangements of the Congress of Rastatt and the Final Recess (*Reichsdeputationshauptschlüss*) of 1803 set a new domestic political agenda which was to carry them well into the nineteenth century. Around 1800 the same could not yet be said of the eastern empires. For all three states the decisive challenge of the age and the responses it engendered still lay ahead.

ACKNOWLEDGEMENTS

I would like to thank Tim Blanning, Simon Dixon, Anita Bunyan and my editors for their help in writing this and the following chapter.

NOTES

1   For the classic Rankean statement on the primacy of foreign policy see the translations in T.H. von Laue (ed.) *Leopold von Ranke: The Formative Years* (Princeton, 1950), p.169.
2   David L. Ransel, *The Politics of Catherinian Russia: The Panin Party* (New Haven and London, 1973).
3   Hanna Schissler, 'The social and political power of the Prussian Junkers', in Ralph Gibson and Martin Blinkhorn (eds) *Landownership and Power in Modern Europe* (London, 1991), p.103.
4   The classic statement of this thesis would be Hans Rosenberg, *Bureaucracy, Aristocracy and Autocracy. The Prussian Experience 1660–1815* (Cambridge, Mass., 1958).
5   Richard Pipes, *Russia under the Old Regime* (London, 1974).
6   Pipes, *op. cit.*, p.137; see also Paul Dukes, *Catherine the Great and the Russian Nobility. A Study based on the Materials of the Legislative Commission of 1767* (Cambridge, Mass., 1967), p.149.
7   There is a useful discussion of this in Isabel de Madariaga, *Russia in the Age of Catherine the Great* (New Haven and London, 1981), p.585.
8   John P. Le Donne, *Ruling Russia. Politics and Administration in the Age of Absolutism 1762–1796* (Princeton, 1984), p.53.
9   The best account of this in English is John G. Gagliardo, *Reich and Nation. The Holy Roman Empire as Idea and Reality, 1763–1806* (Bloomington and London, 1980), pp.66–98.
10 C.A. Macartney, *The Habsburg Empire 1790–1918* (London, 1968), p.2.
11 See T.C.W. Blanning, *Reform and Revolution in Mainz, 1743–1803* (Cambridge, 1974).
12 See for example the sub-section entitled 'Revolutionskriege und Reformabsolutismus: warum gab es keine deutsche Revolution?', in Hans-Ulrich Wehler, *Deutsche Gesellschaftsgeschichte*, vol.I (Munich, 1987), pp.353–62.
13 Macartney, *op. cit.*, p.157 describes it as such.

FURTHER READING

See end of Chapter 5.

Chapter 5

The eastern empires from the challenge of Napoleon to the Restoration, *c.*1806–30

Brendan Simms

If the eighteenth century had closed with the débâcle of the Second Coalition, the nineteenth century opened with a series of near mortal blows against all three eastern powers, inflicted by Napoleon. In a way that had never been true of the Revolutionary French behemoth, this man now became the central figure of political life in Austria, Prussia and Russia. Fear of Napoleon ruled foreign policy; the example of Napoleon dominated domestic affairs. For the statesmen of Berlin, Vienna and St Petersburg this was a challenge they had genuinely hoped to avoid. At first they had greeted Napoleon with relief as the tamer of the Revolution. Peaceful coexistence seemed possible. The Prussians clung to the neutrality policy they had pursued ever since leaving the War of the First Coalition. Austria desperately needed time to recuperate after the lost wars of the previous decade. As for the new Tsar, Alexander I, he too was not ill disposed to an accommodation with France. In any case all three eastern powers had made substantial 'compensatory' territorial gains out of recent settlements which they were loath to lose in a general restorationist crusade. Only Britain, suspect to all of the eastern empires by virtue of her maritime policies, continued to press for a renewal of conflict against France. Yet it was not the persuasive powers of British diplomacy or even British gold, let alone ideological considerations, which finally motivated the Austrians, Prussians and Russians to restart the struggle. It was solely the lack of any obvious limit to Napoleonic ambition, as manifested in his relentless advance in Germany and Italy, that led to the War of the Third Coalition. The result was disaster. Crushing defeats for Austria and Prussia were followed by the precipitate retreat of the Tsar's armies from central Europe and the destruction of the Holy

Roman Empire in 1806. Yet despite the fact that defeat had been universal, the experience of defeat was to lead to quite distinct responses. Prussia, so far in many ways the least dynamic and important of the eastern powers, was now to take centre-stage.

In October 1806 the Prussian army was decisively beaten by Napoleon at the battles of Auerstedt and Jena. Within weeks, resistance across the monarchy had all but collapsed as well-defended fortresses capitulated without so much as firing a shot. At the end of the year, only a tiny tip of the country in the north-east was still in government hands; by the middle of the following year Napoleon had been victorious here also. In the ensuing Treaty of Tilsit (June 1807), Prussia lost all her western possessions and her Polish gains, thus effectively relegating her to the status of a second-rate power. A French army of occupation was imposed. Prussia was also saddled with an immense war indemnity. The response of Prussian statesmen and administrators to this crisis is known as the Era of Prussian Reform. Their short-term aim was the payment of the indemnity and the withdrawal of French troops; their long-term aim was the re-establishment of Prussia as a great power. The pursuit of these aims was ultimately to bring the state into conflict with the established socio-political structures outlined at the beginning of the last chapter. But this was a price the Prussian state was prepared to pay. There followed a systematic policy of what one bureaucrat described as 'revolution from above', a term which has found much resonance among historians.[1] But this revolution, a 'revolution in the good sense' to use the words of Hardenberg, the leading reforming statesman, bore little resemblance to the ideas of the French Revolution. Nor was the aim of remoulding state and society an end in itself. Rather, all of the military, governmental, economic and societal reforms of the next ten years or so were undertaken in accordance with the primacy of foreign policy.

This was most evident in the field of military reform. Here tactics were revised, corporal punishment abolished and the officer corps opened to non-nobles. Most importantly, conscription was introduced and a militia, the *Landwehr*, was set up. It was only, as the military reformer, Scharnhorst, wrote, 'by arming the whole mass of the people that a small nation could achieve any kind of parity with a larger nation waging a war of conquest'. Another way in which the smaller nation could survive in a world of predatory neighbours was by streamlining its decision-making process. This was the thinking behind the *Staatsreform* begun in 1807. Out went the old *Kabinetssystem* (of government through shadowy royal favourites) and the antiquated administrative structures, in came responsible ministries. Some historians have seen in this a 'dictatorship of the bureaucracy'[2] or a 'bureaucratic Revolution'. In fact the aim and result of these changes was the strenghtening of the monarchic executive and thus of the state as a whole. Ultimate power still rested with Frederick William III, so long as he chose to exercise it.

Finally, there were the economic and societal reforms, intended to bolster the internal cohesion and efficiency of the state. Here the key figures were Stein and Hardenberg whose names would henceforth be inseparable from the whole Prussian Reform Movement. They recognized that if Prussia was to stay afloat in a competitive world she must modernize. The core of their reform programme lay in the emancipation of the peasants (1807). This measure lifted all restrictions on landownership, on the free movement of the rural population, and on the practice of a trade. It also lifted the traditional protection which the state offered against noble absorption of peasant holdings; the consequences of this were to be serious. Three years later there followed a financial and economic reform. Guild restrictions were abolished and monopolies ended. Noble privileges of brewing and distilling in the countryside were taken away. Taxation levels were harmonized across the monarchy. The reformers hoped for great things from these measures. In this they were at first to be disappointed, but in time the developments they had instituted were to pay dividends.

In Russia the omens for a successful reform movement seemed good. The new Tsar, Alexander, was known to be in favour of change. His closest confidants, Czartoryski, Stroganov and Novosiltsev were all either radical or reformist in outlook. Moreover, at Catherine's insistence, Alexander had received an enlightened education and this had a profound influence on his early political views. In 1797 he had written to his tutor that he wanted 'the best sort of Revolution as it would be undertaken by a legal authority which would cease to exist as soon as the constitution was finished and the nation had chosen its representatives'. Nor did Alexander renege on his promises once in power. Almost immediately after his accession he set up the so-called unofficial committee of confidants, including the three intimates listed above, which was to guide Russian policy for the coming years. Their first move was the establishment of formal ministries in 1802 headed by responsible ministers. These replaced the old inefficient collegiate administrative structures. In 1810 there followed a Council of State which satisfied the bureaucracy's demand for formalized decision-making structures. Yet here too it would be wrong to see a resurgent self-confident bureaucracy asserting its power over the Tsar. Alexander remained in full control of the executive. As in Prussia, the aim of the reform was primarily to strengthen the state in the struggle against Napoleon.

Exactly the same motivation underlay the activities of Alexander's most prominent reformer, Michael Speransky. A man of modest background, Speransky rose to become the dominant force in domestic politics between 1808 and 1812. Yet even he, a man often seen as a Russian liberal, was essentially a conservative interested in order and efficiency. Speransky aimed at turning Russia into a *Rechtsstaat*, a monarchy based on the rule of law,[3] very like Prussia in fact. It may be true that he did envisage involving wider groups in government,[4] but the overall thrust of his plans tended towards cohesion not participation, decision not discussion. It is no coincidence that in his famous and often misunderstood 'Introduction to the Codification of State Laws' of 1809, the Tsar retained sole control over foreign policy, the army and the right to declare a state of emergency.

Yet another example of the effect of foreign–political exigencies on Russian domestic politics was the establishment of a militia in November 1806 and the creation of the 'military colonies'. The militia was intended to supplement the line army in the event of foreign invasion. As for the military colonies, these were first introduced in the period of armed peace after 1810. Their function was fourfold. In the first place they were to provide a regular supply of troops for service abroad. Second, those planted in border areas were to perform a policing role. Third, they were to act as model agricultural producers by disseminating new techniques among the peasantry. Fourth, they were intended to colonize marginal lands. Ultimately, Alexander wanted to turn all state peasants, who made up nearly half the total rural population, into military colonists. As it was, there were soon three-quarters of a million people involved out of about forty million Russians. In this way the French threat profoundly affected Russian society long before the first soldier of Napoleon's *Grande Armée* set foot on Russian soil. After 1815 the colonies were given a new boost with the question of how to reintegrate the bulk of the one million strong army in Europe back into civilian life. Hence the military colonies were first a response to the Napoleonic challenge and thereafter an answer to the problems of demobilization.

The Napoleonic threat also engendered a reform movement in the Habsburg Monarchy. A rationalization of the cumbersome decision-making structure was the first step. This produced the ministerial reform of 1801 which set up separate ministries in place of the old colleges. Much-needed military reforms were introduced under Archduke Charles: better tactics, reduced terms of service and improved equipment. After 1805, the defeats of the Third Coalition gave an urgent new impulse to the work of the reformers. As in Prussia, old and incompetent generals were weeded out. In 1809 the military power of the monarchy was considerably strengthened by the creation of a militia, the *Landwehr*, based on compulsory universal military service. Once again, the main aim of reform was to strengthen the foreign–political position of the state.

Clearly, the primacy of foreign policy underpinned the reform programmes of all three eastern powers. In the face of the Napoleonic threat they moved almost simultaneously to create national militias, responsible ministries and conscript armies. But that was not all: a 'revolution from above' was also attempted, though as we shall see with varying success. It is not hard to see a similar intent behind Alexander's 'best sort of Revolution' and Hardenberg's 'revolution in the good sense'. This was not, as has often been claimed, a case of things having to change so that they could remain the same. The aim of the reformers was not the preservation of the essence of the old social order. Rather, they wished to refashion society and government in accordance with the extraordinary foreign–political demands of the time. In the pursuit of this 'revolution' the state did not spare the vested interests of the nobility. 'Better three battles of Jena than one emancipation edict' exclaimed one exasperated Junker; 'one defends feudal society against the revolution, but what is to be gained from this struggle if it requires that revolution to be introduced into society?' asked one Austrian conservative. To this extent the reform programmes were simply the culmination of the drive for state efficiency implicit in enlightened absolutism. Indeed, one historian, Otto Hintze, has argued that what happened in Prussia after 1806 was in many cases just the implementation of programmes circulating well before the defeats of Auerstedt and Jena.[5]

Were the reforms about 'modernization'? If we take the Weberian definition, in which modernization means the development of capitalism, of classes, of rationalization, the nation state and bureaucracy, then we can see many elements of this in the Prussian experience. It is much less applicable, however, to the Russian and Habsburg cases. If, however, we take the rather narrower conception of Barbara Vogel, for whom modernization denotes 'a process of conscious and planned development to raise the capability of social systems', then the activities of the eastern reformers can be seen as 'modernizing'.[6]

Of course reform did not take place in a vacuum, but was directed towards and interacted with the international situation. It is to the dramatic events of the first two decades of the nineteenth century that we must now turn.

Contrary to what one might think, there was no direct or necessary link between support for reform and hostility to France. In Russia, Speransky was broadly pro-French in foreign policy orientation while other reformers such as Stroganov, Novosiltsev and Czartoryski were violently Francophobe. In Prussia Scharnhorst and Stein pressed for an immediate breach with France, while Hardenberg adopted a more circumspect policy. Similarly, in the Habsburg Monarchy, Stadion steered towards confrontation with France whereas the more cautious Zinzendorf and the Archduke Charles hoped to use the period of peace to complete their reforms. To a considerable extent these were differences of strategy, not of principle. Generally speaking it is true that the ultimate aim of the reformers was almost always the destruction of French hegemony. The central question for all Austrian, Prussian and Russian statesmen – and not just the reformers – remained how to cope with Napoleon.

Throughout the first decade, French power dominated the political life of central and eastern Europe. In Germany, outside of Prussia and Austria, Napoleon's writ ran unchallenged. In the *Rheinbund*, or Confederation of the Rhine, he had assembled nearly all of the middling princes under his overlordship. Further east he had reconstituted a satellite Polish state, the Grand Duchy of Warsaw, which threatened both Prussia and Russia. To make matters worse, Napoleon vigorously enforced adherence to his

Continental System, the collection of decrees by which he hoped to exclude British trade from the European mainland and thus strangle his last remaining adversary. It seemed as if nothing could stop the 'hegemonic integration' of Europe under the supremacy of France.

Of all the eastern powers, Russia preserved by far the greatest freedom of action under the new dispensation. Indeed, she was allied to Napoleon by the terms of the Treaty of Tilsit. During the next five years or so Russia used the cover of the French alliance to renew her drive south, which by 1812 had wrested Bessarabia from the Ottomans. The Prussians by contrast kept their heads firmly down, partly so as not to endanger their reform programme and partly because the international situation seemed entirely unfavourable to a new war against France. This was not an analysis shared in Vienna. Here the bellicose policy of Stadion, encouraged by French reverses in Spain, prevailed over the wiser counsels of the Archduke Charles. The resulting war of 1809 saw some initial Austrian successes but was otherwise an unmitigated disaster. Prussia remained strictly neutral while Russia honoured her obligation towards France sufficiently to tie down bodies of troops badly needed elsewhere. She also used the opportunity to annex Finland and some Austrian territory. Never did the prospect of monarchic solidarity against Napoleon seem more remote. In the wake of the recriminations at Vienna Count Metternich rose to be the dominant minister and henceforth emulated the Prussian policy of fulfilment, that is, of alliance with France. Now that the great liberating effort had misfired, the reform policy petered out.

The year 1809 was also a milestone in the development of German nationalism, for in appealing to the patriotism of his subjects and indeed to all Germans, the Austrian Emperor hoped to channel nationalist enthusiasm into the struggle against Napoleon. He was to be disappointed. Despite the steady growth of Francophobia arising out of the experience of occupation, despite the heartening example of the Spanish rebellion and despite the entirely novel development of nationalist associations such as the *Turnvereine* (gymnastic associations) and the *Tugendbund* (League of Virtue), national feeling in Germany had yet to become politically important. The year 1809 saw only a few isolated risings in northern Germany; the highly successful Tyrolean revolt bore too many characteristics of a pre-modern religious and particularist movement to be rated as truly nationalist in the modern sense.

More importantly, the government refused to be stampeded into precipitate action by nationalist hotheads straining at the leash. For the time being, therefore, nationalism was of little political consequence.

It was clear that, unaided, neither Austria nor Prussia had much hope of emancipating themselves from Napoleonic domination. Their best policy lay in awaiting the inevitable showdown between Russia and France. It was not long in coming. Both empires entertained mutually incompatible ambitions in Poland and Turkey, not to mention French fury at Alexander's inability or unwillingness to enforce the economic blockade against Britain. After a two-year cold war, Napoleon invaded Russia in the summer of 1812. By the end of the year the decimated French army had withdrawn into central Europe. Once the Tsar had taken the crucial decision to carry the war beyond the Russian border, it became feasible for Austria and Prussia to think of shaking off the French yoke. In December 1812, the Prussian corps under General York von Wartenburg, notionally allied to Napoleon, defected to the Russians. This set in train a process by which eventually, though by no means inevitably, both the Berlin and the Viennese governments declared against France. Nationalism played no role in their considerations. Frederick William of Prussia's call upon the people to rise up against the French was purely tactical. This has not prevented his declaration being interpreted as a nationalist clarion call. In fact, however, the ensuing *Befreiungskriege*, or 'wars of liberation', were at least as much wars of states and cabinets as they were national wars.

After many tribulations Napoleon was defeated and exiled, initially to Elba and then to St Helena. His legacy, however, was not so easily banished. This legacy was twofold. First of all, there remained the deep-seated fear of single-power hegemony. Second, he left behind a complex tangle of internal political changes which had either been wrought directly by Napoleon, or were undertaken by the eastern powers themselves in their attempt to survive.

The Vienna settlement of 1815 was an attempt to address these problems. Now that the French had been ejected from central Europe, Austrian, Prussian and Russian foreign policy aims diverged radically. Naturally, all the eastern powers were agreed on the suppression of France, but that was about the limit of the consensus. Of the three, Prussia's ambitions were the most extensive: she wished to annex the whole of the former Napoleonic satellite of Saxony. Russia aimed to absorb Poland; here it was the size of the accretion that was at issue. As for the Austrians, they were especially anxious not to see French hegemony simply replaced by Russian hegemony. They were also concerned to integrate the British into future European security arrangements. Within a few months foreign political disagreements had dissipated the fleeting monarchical solidarity of the final coalition against Napoleon. Talleyrand, the French negotiator, skilfully exploited these differences, and it was only the brief return of the Napoleonic nightmare during the 'Hundred Days' that refocused the three empires on the problem of French power.

The upshot of all this was an arrangement which was designed to keep the Russians out, the British in and the French down. To the east, the Russians retained the larger share of Poland and dropped all further claims. To the south, the Austrians regained and extended their hold on Italy. France was reduced to her ancien regime borders. A system of congresses was instituted. This was primarily intended to coordinate the coalition powers against a possible French resurgence. But the core of the settlement was the new dispensation in Germany. As a sop to old *Reich* patriotism and the growing German national consciousness, the federal bonds between the German states, which Napoleon had destroyed, were reforged by the creation of the *Bund*, or German Federation. Its function was the defence of German territory against outside aggression, but its military muscle, though impressive on paper, was even less formidable than that of the old *Reich* had been. The presidency of the Federation was held by Austria, a fact which underlined her supremacy in Germany in the immediate post-1815 period. Significantly, however, the Prussians were made the guardian of the gate. For instead of coveted Saxony, of which she only received the northern half, Prussia was awarded the Rhineland. In thus raising her up as the barrier to French aggression, the diplomats at Vienna injected two fundamentally new elements into Prussian political life. First of all, Prussia became a major western power almost overnight, thus reversing the eastward orientation of the previous four decades. Second, with the Rhineland Prussia acquired two things which were to be of crucial political importance in the future: coal and Catholics.

Meanwhile, the reform programmes spawned by the Napoleonic threat had run into difficulties in all three eastern empires.

In Austria, the lost war of 1809 had effectively put an end to reform. By 1812 all hopes of financial reform had been frustrated by the obstruction of the Hungarian Diet. In Prussia, the landed Junker elite had fought back successfully. They furiously rejected the contention that Prussian backwardness had been to blame for the disaster of 1806. By 1815 they had warded off the threat to patrimonial justice and in the following year they succeeded in severely reducing the number of peasants able to avail themselves of the emancipation edict. There were also the unintended by-products of reform, for by lifting the traditional state protection of the peasantry, the nobility were able to rationalize their estates at peasant expense practically unchecked. Because of their greater access to capital through the rural credit institutes they were also in a much better position to exploit the new market in land. As for the projected local government reforms, these had got nowhere. Administration at the lowest level remained in the hands of representatives of the nobility, a *Landrat* chosen from the ranks of the local aristocracy.

Of course, none of this was achieved without a bitter struggle with the state and especially the reforming bureaucracy. The ringleader of the Junker opposition, Friedrich August von der Marwitz, was even thrown into jail. It is certainly not true to say, as Hanna Schissler does, that during the reform period the old governing compromise was revitalized at the expense of the rural workers.[7] In fact the compromise was unilaterally redefined by the state and refashioned to suit the new criteria of efficiency. If the government backed down on agrarian reform, it was not primarily because it was so dependent on the nobility that it could not do otherwise. Rather, it was because with the elimination of the Napoleonic threat after 1815 there was no longer the same pressing need for reform. The primacy of foreign policy had ceased to operate.

In Russia, peasant emancipation had never really got off the ground. What Alexander did do was to discontinue the practice of giving away state peasants to the nobility. At the beginning of his reign he also passed a law allowing the purchase of unused land by non-nobles, including free peasants. Thereafter, Alexander moved with the greatest circumspection in matters relating to the socio-political situation in the countryside. Mindful of his father's – and his grandfather's – fate, Alexander had confirmed the Charter to the Nobility on acceding to the throne. In any case he was soon to be distracted from internal reform by the demands of foreign policy after 1804. Under Speransky the whole serf question was briefly reopened, but he was removed by a high political intrigue in 1812. Towards the end of the decade, Alexander took another long look at the peasant problem, but undertook nothing beyond the emancipation of the Baltic serfs, a measure designed at least as much to irritate the local German aristocracy as to be progressive in intent.

Continuity rather than change thus characterized the politics of all three eastern rural societies which emerged from the Napoleonic Wars. The gentry continued to control most of the economic, social and judicial structures of peasant life. In Prussia the peasantry merely exchanged the old politico-legal domination of the nobility for a socio-economic one. Indeed, after emancipation, the number of free peasant holdings actually seems to have declined. In Austria the agrarian compromises – emancipation, but the persistence of patrimonial justice and forced labour dues (the *robot*) – rescued by Leopold in the 1790s from the Josephine wreck remained more or less unchanged until 1848. As for Russia, here too not much had changed since the outbreak of the Revolutionary Wars.

A similar fate befell constitutional reform. In southern Germany constitutions were granted in the five years after 1815 in order to assimilate the extremely diverse gains of the Napoleonic period. This was a case of integration through representation. But for the Prussian, Austrian and Russian governments the problem was of a rather different nature. Here the notion of introducing a participatory element into political life threatened the power of the monarchy and thus the very basis upon which the whole political structure of all three eastern empires rested. In any case the chief justification for a constitution and a representative body was the need to secure the financial reforms which the Napoleonic challenge had necessitated. In 1810, on the occasion of his momentous financial reform, Hardenberg had envisaged the need for a representative assembly to sanction his taxation plans. Partly with this in mind and partly to encourage the population to support the state against Napoleon, Frederick William had somewhat rashly promised a constitution in 1815. But the Napoleonic challenge had now passed and the promise was never kept. The financial difficulties of the state were mastered without a representative assembly. The fall of the reform party in Prussia was now not far off. In 1819, the principal military reformer, Boyen, took his leave after an unsuccessful attempt to prevent the independence of the *Landwehr* being curtailed. That same year Humboldt, another prominent reformer, also resigned. Hardenberg hung on until his death in 1822. As a sop provincial assemblies, manned by representatives of the nobility, townspeople and peasantry, and elected in accordance with a stiff property qualification, were set up throughout Prussia in 1823. In so far as no such representative bodies had existed in Prussia, apart from Cleves-Mark, since the seventeenth century, the provincial assemblies (*Provinzialland-stände*) were a radically new development. However, they were competent to deal with local affairs only, though they did enjoy some wider consultative rights in discussing new legal proposals. Above all, they had no control over the state budget and thus fell far short of what the reformers had envisaged.

As for Austria, Metternich gave some consideration to the creation of a *Reichsrat*, which would involve certain regional notables in the higher affairs of state. But given the fact that Austria's financial difficulties were largely *due* to representative institutions, namely the Hungarian Diet, it is not surprising that these deliberations came to nothing. In Russia, too, plans for an all-Russian national representation came to naught, though Alexander did experiment with constitutions in Finland and Poland. In all three eastern empires the period of reform engendered by the Napoleonic threat was now over.

The restoration period brought new problems. In the Russian case, the Tsar had to contend with the constitutional demands of the Finns and Poles. For the time being, the former were relatively passive; in 1809 Alexander had exempted the Finns from serfdom and conscription and the Diet did not meet for another fifty years. The major headache was Poland. Here one of the most progressive constitutions had been granted in November 1815. According to its terms, the Poles were guaranteed civil rights such as *habeas corpus* and religious toleration. Freedom of the press was introduced. Polish was made the language of government and administration. A bi-cameral parliament elected on a broad franchise was set up. It met every two years. The Poles were allowed their own army; they were even encouraged to believe that eastern lands taken away in the eighteenth century might be returned. Foreign policy, of course, remained under the direct control of the Tsar.

All this was not enough to satisfy the fiercely independent-minded Poles; by the end of our period (1830–1) they had risen in revolt and the experiment came to an abrupt end. Very soon, Poland was holding down almost two-thirds of the Russian army.

Austria was afflicted by Italy, which for foreign and domestic–political reasons frequently became the centre of attention after 1815. Here Napoleonic rule had left behind a tradition of political radicalism. In Italy more than anywhere else, except perhaps Hungary, antipathy towards Austrian rule and institutions was most widespread. Indeed, for much of the next fifty years, the larger part of the Habsburg army was to be concentrated there.[8] This fact also reflected the great strategic importance of the Italian peninsula, from which the Austrians sought to exclude the French. During the next decades Austria was also to intervene against revolutionary manifestations outside her own Italian possessions, most notably in Piedmont and Naples in 1821. Prussia too had inherited a brace of new problems at Vienna. Her Polish subjects looked wistfully to the autonomy their Tsarist cousins enjoyed and despite an initially liberal government policy after 1815 they were never truly reconciled to rule from Berlin. Further west, the Prussian state soon found itself embroiled in a prolonged cold war with the Catholic inhabitants of the new Rhine province. Here again the Napoleonic legacy was decisive, for it proved impossible to reverse the rights granted during the occupation. Specifically, progressive French legal codes and communal institutions were retained and by 1818 the Prussians had been forced to shelve their plans for the introduction of standard Prussian law.

The twin threats of nationalism and constitutionalism were also to be found outside peripheral areas such as Italy and Poland. In fact, it was in Germany itself where the two phenomena first became a matter of grave concern. In the aftermath of the raised and then disappointed expectations of the Wars of Liberation against Napoleon, political nationalism had taken on a distinctly radical hue throughout the territory of the German Federation. Indeed, the emergence of clubs and associations had added a completely new element to politics. These clubs articulated an entirely novel claim to broader popular political participation. The movement gathered pace. Radical *Burschenschaften*, or student leagues, sprang up all over Germany, and also in Prussia. Many of them, such as the *Schwarzen*, 'the black ones', in Gießen, made no secret of their desire to forge a Germany that would be both united and free. Other clubs, with seemingly innocuous names such as *Schillerverein* or *Lutherverein*, were often merely fronts for similar activities. The backbone of these groups seems to have been academic youth. Many of them were idealists; others belonged to what Lenore O'Boyle has termed the 'excess of educated men' which the shortage of jobs in the civil services had created.[9] In 1817 there was a nationalist and radical rally on the Wartburg, at which Luther and the victories of the Wars of Liberation were commemorated. In the following year a pan-German student association, the *Allgemeine Deutsche Burschenschaft*, was set up which linked the individual associations nationally. A year later, the hated reactionary playwright and Russian spy, August von Kotzebue, was murdered by a radical student.

For Metternich, the murder of Kotzebue was the last straw. It also simplified his task of gaining active Prussian and tacit Russian backing for concerted action against the nationalist and constitutionalist threat. In 1815 such support could not have been taken for granted but a lot had changed in the meantime. The Prussian government had retreated both from its supposed national mission and its promise of a constitution. Alexander, who had for long toyed with the idea of becoming the hero of liberal Europe, was now beginning to reincarnate himself as a reactionary. The result was the Karlsbad Decrees of 1819. Prominent nationalists, such as the pioneer of the Prussian gymnastics clubs, Jahn, were arrested. The universities were purged, student associations banned and suspect professors sacked. Pre-censorship of the press was introduced. A central investigative commission was set up at Mainz with the purpose of weeding out radicals. Nor was this all. In order to counteract the bad example of southern German constitutionalism, Metternich ensured that the final act of the Vienna Congress (1820) stipulated that the internal government of all German states should be governed by the 'monarchic principle' rather than constitutions. All over the eastern empires, the hatches were now being battened down. In Austria, the revived political police under Count Sedlnitzky ran a very tight ship. As for Russia, Alexander banned foreign societies in 1822 while his successor, Nicholas I, founded the political police in 1826.

Despite appearances, the main political threat to at least two of the eastern empires did not emanate from popular radicalism and nationalism but from the long-standing conflict between crown and nobility. This was particularly true of the Habsburg Monarchy, for now the compromises of the 1790s came back to haunt the government in Vienna. Hungary had succeeded in preserving a separate taxation and customs system. The political and financial power of the Hungarian nobility had remained unbroken. To make matters worse, a great Magyar cultural revival was in progress; one political consequence of this was the demand for the use of the Hungarian language in government and administration. Throughout the Napoleonic period, the Hungarian Diet had only grudgingly and inadequately supported the Austrian war effort against France. Almost every financial measure also affecting Hungary was either rejected or altered beyond recognition; when in 1818 Francis took up the Josephine idea of an equal land tax he wisely exempted Hungary. After 1815, rather like after 1763, the Viennese government hoped that peace would remove the need to summon the Diet. It was not to be. In 1820, the intervention against Naples and Piedmont necessitated increased taxation and recruitment. Once again the impact of foreign political events produced an internal crisis for the empire. The result was the Diet of 1825 at which the Hungarians under Szechenyi faced down the Habsburgs. Neither side achieved their aims: the Austrians were sent away empty handed; the Diet failed to have Hungarian adopted as the official language. However, it was beyond doubt the most serious domestic political crisis of the decade.

Even in Prussia there were Junker separatists, mostly pietists who kept up the struggle against royal power and the advance of the bureaucracy.[10] But it was in the Russian Empire that the nobility mounted the most decisive challenge of all: the Decembrist rising of 1825 was nothing if not a revolt of the nobility to which nearly all of the conspirators belonged. It was also a military coup, liberal revolution and nationalist rising all in one, for the final campaigns against Napoleon had brought the Russian army into the heart of Europe and exposed junior officers to radical ideas. Very soon afterwards (1816) the Union of Salvation was set up on the lines of the Prussian patriotic and revolutionary associations. Five years later the Union split in two. The southern and more radical branch aimed to abolish serfdom, crush Polish aspirations for the return of their eastern lands, and establish the rule of law and a strong central government. The northern and more moderate branch was more gradualist in approach; they also favoured looser federal bonds between the provinces of the empire. For the first time, Russia was about to witness a bid for power which went beyond the narrow intrigues of eighteenth-century court politics. The coup itself, which was hurriedly mounted to take advantage of the succession crisis following Alexander's death, was a complete fiasco. Nevertheless, a new factor, that of attempted radical change through revolutionary means, had appeared on the political scene.

Finally, it is worth noting that in Russia and Austria the era of reaction also extended to areas of economic and commercial policy. Reformers such as Speransky, who had begun to return to grace from 1819 onwards, were powerless to prevent Alexander from strengthening state protection of the guilds, very much a retrograde step. In Austria, a central directory, *Kommerzdirektorium*, was set up in 1816 to plan economic growth and development. Very soon, however, it ran out of steam and in 1824 it had to be shut down. Furthermore, despite fitful attempts to break their grip on trades, the guilds continued to flourish. Prussia was the exception: here political reaction took place without economic implications. In 1818 a taxation and custom law made Prussia a unitary tax area; this was something the Habsburgs never achieved. By 1822 the budget had been balanced and all debts paid off, another achievement well beyond the capacity of the shambolic impoverished Austrian and Russian Empires.

Despite considerable differences of approach in the early restoration period, by the 1820s all three eastern empires were united in their opposition to radicalism. This hostility led to a novel degree of cooperation on internal matters. To Metternich, the international nature of the revolutionary threat – which he believed to be centrally orchestrated by a mysterious *Comité directeur* based in Paris – demanded an international response. In the Austrian and Prussian cases this coordination took place through the institutions of the German Federation. In the case of Russia there was an exchange of information between the police chiefs of Vienna and St Petersburg. At Great Power level the anti-revolutionary consensus was expressed through the 'congress system'. These were what would now be called multilateral summits at which the three eastern powers and France reaffirmed their hostility to radicalism and, if necessary, authorized intervention against local revolutionary manifestations. This system for the maintenance of monarchic principles and the suppression of revolutionary nationalism has come to be known as the 'Metternich system', though Metternich himself denied that any such thing existed. Yet the image of reactionary solidarity is deceptive. Once the initial harmonious phase had passed, none of the three powers allowed the common front against revolution to override narrower considerations of state interest.

Metternich himself was one of the greatest offenders in this respect. As Paul Schroeder has pointed out, far from being a far-sighted statesman, whose 'true fatherland' was Europe, Metternich's actions betray him as no more than an Austrian diplomat bent on fulfilling narrowly Austrian state interests.[11] Metternich once claimed that after 1815 he had to devote himself 'to propping up rotten buildings', yet in the case of Spain he attempted – unsuccessfully – to sabotage a French intervention for the simple reason that he considered the consequent boost to French power more dangerous than the Iberian revolutionaries themselves. It was not long before Russia also began to pursue her foreign political interests at the expense of monarchic solidarity. For many years Alexander had kept out of the Greek revolt on the grounds that insurgency should not be encouraged. Among other things, this had enraged the liberal and nationalist sympathies of the Decembrist conspirators for whom the orthodox Greeks were a kindred people. Under Nicholas I, the policy of non-intervention was abandoned. The protective rights over the Balkan Christians secured at Kutchuk Kainardjii were invoked and the Russian armies resumed their drive south. By 1829 they were threatening Constantinople and thus on the verge of realizing Catherine's dream. Even the Prussians, after 1819 the faithful allies in reaction of Austria, began to go their own way. A clear shift in policy can be identified in 1825. That date marked the emergence or re-emergence of a non-ideological, that is anti-Austrian, approach. The old dualism, briefly dormant after the Congress of Vienna, was reasserting itself. At first this only found expression in the aggressive economic and customs policies of Berlin, policies which may at least in part have been a sublimation of deeper political differences.

It is against this background that the events of 1830 must be seen. As far as internal politics were concerned the revolutions of that year were a non-event for Austria and Prussia, though there were successful revolts in some of the smaller German states. Only in Poland was there a major challenge to an eastern power and here the motivating force was not so much the classic liberalism driving many of the other European revolutions as old-style noble separatism, reincarnated as early nationalism. What was important about 1830 was what did *not* happen. In the east, there was only one attempted revolution and no successful revolution on the French model. Much more importantly, the eastern powers produced no coordinated response to the wave of radicalism across Europe, with the exception of Prussia closing her eastern border to the rebels in Russian Poland. Despite promising noises from the Tsar, Metternich was unable to drum up support for a counter-revolutionary crusade against France. All that he could muster was a meaningless statement of counter-revolutionary principle by all three eastern powers. This *Chiffon* of Karlsbad, as it came to be known, bore an uncanny resemblance to the Declaration of Pillnitz some forty years earlier. The sense of *déjà vu* is increased by the fact that once again revolts in Belgium and France found the eastern powers divided. Indeed, Prussia sabotaged Austrian attempts to mount a concerted effort against the Belgian revolution and the disturbances in the smaller German states. Her reason for so doing was the old dualist suspicion of Austrian power. But here the resemblance ends, for unlike 1792–3 the French government did not carry the revolution into Europe. This time Austria, Prussia and Russia escaped direct confrontation with the main force of the revolution. In short, once again foreign political factors were decisive in the political development of all three eastern empires.

We have now reached the end of our period. If we look back at the political structures outlined at the beginning of the preceding chapter, we find that very little has changed, despite fifty years of active political life. All three states retained their monarchical character and the primary object of politics remained the pursuit of state interests on the international scene. Where substantial – if problematic – change had taken place, as in Prussia, this was principally the response to a foreign–political imperative. But by and large the persistence of the old power relationships was unmistakable. Even in Prussia the old elites had adapted themselves successfully to the new situation. After warding off the reformist threat engendered by the Napoleonic Wars, the Austrian, Russian and Prussian nobility continued to dominate army and bureaucracy every bit as much as they had in 1780.

Very soon, however, the conservative order in all three states was to come under renewed attack, for the year 1830 marked the beginning of a fresh phase in the history of the eastern empires. The decade ahead was to see a whole range of fundamentally new political developments. In Austria the Hungarian Diet succeeded in claiming its first pound of flesh from the monarchy, with the introduction of the use of the Hungarian language in government and administration (1830); this was but a foretaste of what was in store. In Russia the principle of 'official nationality', the beginning of large-scale state-sponsored nationalism, and of state-tolerated anti-semitism lay just around the corner (1833). Polish nationalism had already made its presence felt in 1830; the nationalism of the Ukrainians, Czechs and Croats was gestating. A new explosive charge, quite as deadly as Polish and Hungarian noble separatism had ever been, was about to be placed under the Habsburg Empire and ultimately under Tsarist Russia as well.

But it was particularly in Germany and Prussia that a new departure took place after 1830. A surge of liberal and nationalist activity was about to assail the old order. In the authoritative words of James Sheehan, 'The revolution of 1830 marked a significant turning point in the evolution of German political life,'[12] for it was from then on that political participation really began to take shape. Another expert, Thomas Nipperdey, dates the emergence of German political parties from 1830.[13] Hence, just a few years after the close of our period, it is already clear that political life has fundamentally changed. The Hambacher Fest, a kind of nationalist and democratic jamboree attended by more than 20,000 people, took place in 1832. In 1834 the Prussians made a bid for economic supremacy with the creation of the customs union, the *Zollverein*, which the Austrians refused to join. That same year Rotteck and Welcker published their multi-volume *Staatslexikon*, which was to become a point of reference for liberal politics. But the forces of reaction were also mobilizing. The launch of Hengstenberg's *Evangelische Kirchenzeitung* in 1827 and of the *Berliner Politische Wochenblatt* in 1831 were milestones in the development of organized conservative party politics. Time was to expose the weakness of liberalism. However, the other three forces of Prussian state interest, Junker conservatism and German nationalism, were to make for a heady political cocktail in the years to come.

NOTES

1 See the discussion in Hans-Ulrich Wehler, *Deutsche Gesellschafts-geschichte 1700–1815* (Munich, 1987), pp.397ff.
2 Eckhart Kehr, 'Zur Genesis der preußischen Bürokratie und des Rechtsstaats', in Hans-Ulrich Wehler (ed.) *Der Primat der Innenpolitik. Gesammelte Aufsätze zur preußisch-deutschen Sozialgeschichte im 19. und 20. Jahrhundert* (Frankfurt, Berlin and Vienna, 1976), pp.31–52.
3 See Marc Raeff, *Michael Speransky: Statesman of Imperial Russia 1772–1839* (The Hague, 1957).
4 David Saunders, *Russia in the Age of Reaction and Reform 1801–1881* (London and New York, 1992), p.65.
5 This was the theme of his pioneering 'Preußische Reformbestre-bungen vor 1806', in Gerhard Oestreich (ed.) *Regierung und Verwaltung. Gesammelte Abhandlungen zur Staats-, Rechts und Sozialgeschichte Preussens* (Göttingen, 1967), pp.504–29.
6 See Barbara Vogel, *Allgemeine Gewerbefreiheit. Die Reformpolitik des preußischen Staatskanzlers Hardenberg (1810–1820)* (Göttingen, 1983).
7 Hanna Schissler, 'The social and political power of the Prussian Junkers', in Ralph Gibson and Martin Blinkhorn (eds) *Landownership and Power in Modern Europe* (London, 1991).
8 A.J.P. Taylor, *The Habsburg Monarchy 1809–1918. A History of the Austrian Empire and Austria-Hungary* (London, 1948), p.40.
9 Lenore O'Boyle, 'The problem of an excess of educated men in western Europe, 1800–1850', *Journal of Modern History*, 42 (1972), pp.471–95.
10 The political importance of these groups is only just being recognized. See Christopher Munro Clark, 'The politics of revival. Pietists, aristocrats and the state church in early nineteenth-century Prussia', in Larry E. Jones and J.N. Retallack (eds) *Between Reform, Reaction and Resistance* (Providence, Rhode Island and Oxford, 1993).
11 Paul Schroeder, *Metternich's Diplomacy at its Zenith: Austria and the Congresses of Troppau, Laibach and Verona* (Austin, Texas, 1962).
12 James Sheehan, *German History 1770–1866* (Oxford, 1989), p.604
13 Thomas Nipperdey, *Deutsche Geschichte 1800–1866. Bürgerwelt und starker Staat* (Munich, 1983), p.337.

FURTHER READING

This includes reading for Chapter 4.

A good start for Austria and Prussia would be the following general surveys: James J. Sheehan, *German History 1770–1866* (Oxford, 1989), J.G. Gagliardo, *Germany under the Old Regime 1600–1790* (London and New York, 1991) and Charles Ingrao, *The Habsburg Monarchy 1618–1815* (Cambridge, 1994). T.C.W. Blanning's *Joseph II* (London, 1994) was published in June 1994. For eighteenth-century Russia see Paul Dukes, *The Making of Russian Absolutism 1613–1801* (2nd edn, London and New

York, 1990) and Isabel de Madariaga, *Russia in the Age of Catherine the Great* (New Haven and London, 1981). For early nineteenth-century Russia, David Saunders, *Russia in the Age of Reaction and Reform 1801–1881* (London and New York, 1992) is excellent. Just published is Janet Hartley, *Alexander I* (London, 1994).

The structure of socio-political power in the countryside is described in R.M. Berdahl, *The Politics of the Prussian Nobility 1770–1848* (Princeton, New Jersey, 1988); F.L. Carsten, *A History of the Prussian Junkers* (Aldershot, 1989); Richard Pipes, *Russia under the Old Regime* (London, 1990; first published in 1974); Jerome K. Blum, *Lord and Peasant in Russia from the Ninth to the Nineteenh Century* (Princeton, New Jersey, 1961). There is no direct equivalent for Austria, but all the necessary information can be gleaned from the extremely detailed first one hundred pages of C.A. Macartney, *The Habsburg Empire 1790–1918* (London, 1968). Specifically for the nineteenth century see Dominic Lieven, *The Aristocracy in Europe 1815–1914* (Basingstoke, 1992) and Ralph Gibson and Martin Blinkhorn (eds) *Landownership and Power in Modern Europe* (London, 1991).

There are numerous publications on politics and government. The articles by R.J.W. Evans, H.M. Scott and T.C.W. Blanning in H.M. Scott, *Enlightened Absolutism. Reform and Reformers in Later Eighteenth-century Europe* (London, 1990) are very useful; Hans Rosenberg, *Bureaucracy, Aristocracy and Autocracy. The Prussian Experience 1660–1815* (Cambridge, Mass., 1958) is suggestive if wrong-headed; John P. Le Donne, *Ruling Russia. Politics and Administration in the Age of Absolutism 1762–1796* (Princeton, New Jersey, 1984). On Joseph II the literature is legion. Unfortunately, Derek Beales, *Joseph II. Volume I: In the Shadow of Maria Theresa, 1741–1780* (Cambridge, 1987) ends before our period begins, but provides useful background knowledge. Specifically for the nineteenth century see Walter M. Simon, *The Failure of the Prussian Reform Movement 1807–1819* (Cornell, 1955) and R.C. Raack, *The Fall of Stein* (Cambridge, Mass., 1965); Marion W. Gray, *Prussia in Transition: Society and Politics under the Stein Ministry of 1808* (Philadelphia, 1986). Daniel T. Orlovsky, *The Limits of Reform. The Ministry of Internal Affairs in Imperial Russia* (Cambridge, Mass., 1981); Marc Raeff, *Michael Speransky: Statesman of Imperial Russia 1772–1839* (The Hague, 1969); Walter C. Langsam, *The Napoleonic Wars and German Nationalism in Austria* (New York, 1930); Karl A. Roider, 'The Habsburg foreign ministry and political reform, 1801–1805', *Central European History,* 22(2) (1989); Alan Sked, *The Decline of the Habsburg Empire 1815–1918* (London and New York, 1989).

By contrast the crucial area of foreign policy is not so well served by specialist studies in English. A good general overview of the predatory world of international affairs in which the political life of all three states took place is H.M. Scott and Derek McKay, *The Rise of the Great Powers, 1648–1815* (London and New York, 1983). Indispensable for the diplomatic context of the 1780s and 1790s is T.C.W. Blanning's excellent *The Origins of the French Revolutionary Wars* (London, 1986). Worthy of mention is Karl Roider, *Austria's Eastern Question 1700–1790* (Princeton, 1982). For the later period see the good surveys by Alan Sked (ed.) *Europe's Balance of Power 1815–1848* (London and Basingstoke, 1979) and F.R.

Bridge and Roger Bullen, *The Great Powers and the European States System, 1815–1914* (London and New York, 1980) which put everything in context. The following are also worth a look: Lawrence J. Baack, *Christian Bernstorff and Prussia. Diplomacy and Reform Conservatism 1818–1832* (New Brunswick, New Jersey, 1980) and Paul Schroeder, *Metternich's Diplomacy at its Zenith: Austria and the Congresses of Troppau, Laibach and Verona* (Austin, Texas, 1962). Finally, Paul Schroeder's *The Transformation of European Politics 1763–1848* (Oxford, 1994), should be the definitive account of international relations throughout the period.

The best recent books on nationalism are Hagen Schulze, *The Course of German Nationalism, 1763–1867* (Cambridge, 1991) and John Breuilly (ed.) *The State of Germany. The National Idea in the Making, Unmaking and Remaking of a Modern Nation State* (London and New York, 1992).

Chapter 6

The 'Restoration' of western Europe, 1814–15

Pamela M. Pilbeam

The restoration of a pre-war Europe and the elimination of Napoleon was not a constant preoccupation of France's enemies. If it had been, France would have fallen long before the battle of Waterloo. This chapter will consider how far what was created in the Catholic western states of Europe, in France and the Italian and Iberian peninsulas at and after the peace settlements of 1814 and 1815 was a conscious attempt to restore pre-war institutions. We shall ask to what degree post-war conservatism was a product of the Romantic imagination or an opportunistic or radical response to the impact of a quarter-century of revolutionary change and war. We shall focus on the new monarchies and their institutions of government, their ruling elites and the Catholic Church.

Napoleon was defeated by an alliance of Great Britain, Russia, Austria and Prussia in March 1814 after a mere year of campaigning, following the alliance signed in 1813. Previously each of Napoleon's enemies had believed that they could do better in separate deals and individual campaigns against the French. The invasion of Russia convinced them of the need for cooperation and Napoleon's bedraggled withdrawal from Moscow, overcome by the weather and land made desolate by the retreating, but undefeated Russian armies, offered them the opportunity of engagement with a weakened enemy. The Allied alliance was specifically directed, for the first time in the war, not merely to the defeat of France, but also to the removal of Napoleon as Emperor.

The Allies were conscious that the French would only accept the removal of the Emperor if military defeat was incontrovertible. For nearly two decades Napoleon seemed to embody and guarantee significant elements of the Revolution for many of its enthusiasts, maintaining order at home and relatively cheap and glorious conquest abroad. Within France there was little support for a royal cause of any kind during the Empire. Among the victors there was considerable conflict about whom should replace Napoleon. The Allied governments were in accord that it should be a monarch, but the return of the Bourbons was far from clear-cut. At £20,000 a year the heir presumptive, the comte de Provence, had been an expensive luxury for the British government and they would be glad to be rid of him.[1] His relative moderation seemed to offer some guarantees, but his heir, his brother, the comte d'Artois was a strident anti-revolutionary ultra-royalist, little inclined for the compromise with Bonapartists which would be required if a restoration was to succeed. The alternatives discussed included the younger branch of the Bourbons in the guise of Louis-Philippe, duke of Orleans, son of the regicide, Philippe Egalité. The duke of Orleans wanted the opportunity to recover his very extensive properties in France, but was convinced that his best chance was as a loyal subject of his cousin. Alexander I of Russia favoured Napoleon's turncoat general Bernadotte, now established as ruler of Sweden and fighting for the Allies, and there was some talk of a minor, temporarily dispossessed German princeling.

Expediency was more prominent a consideration than principles of legitimacy. A fairly restrained rising in favour of the Bourbons in Bordeaux in 1814 and soundings among Napoleon's senior officials convinced the British, paymasters of the Grand Alliance against Napoleon, that their own costly guests had the best chances of success and would be the most tractable of the options. To maintain the new king securely in place the Allies agreed to allow the French themselves to negotiate the Restoration settlement. Napoleon was deposed by his own Senate, who invited the comte de Provence to return as king of the French people on condition that he accepted a short written constitution.

What were the objectives of the peacemakers, Britain, Russia, Prussia and Austria, who met in congress in Vienna in the autumn of 1814? France's enemies were imbued with two main considerations. The first of these was to ensure that France was permanently contained, unable to launch future large-scale war. The Allies were persuaded, in part by the eloquence of former Napoleonic servants like Talleyrand and Fouché and also by their own mutual jealousy, that the borders of old regime France should be left intact to guard against civil war in France. The terms offered to the French were relatively generous, considering that France had engaged her enemies in war for a generation. The first Treaty of Paris did no more than take France back to the 1792 borders, although Britain acquired some of her few surviving colonies. Only Martinique, Guadeloupe and some Pacific islands remained and France's world trade was left in tatters due to the British blockade. There was to be no army of occupation, no indemnity.

The massive conquered Empire had to be renounced. We speak of a 'restored' Europe, but this was barely perceptible on a map. The frontiers of post-war Europe bore little relation to those of 1792. Above all, there was no attempt to restore the Holy Roman Empire. Even in 1792, its existence had been hard to justify, and even harder to retain. The Bonapartist constructs, the Confederation of the Rhine, the Grand Duchy of Warsaw, Napoleon's relatives neatly ensconced in Italian states, all disappeared. Instead the continental Allies took the opportunity to partition Europe, rather as they had done Poland during the eighteenth century. The only visible principles behind their actions were those of an opportunistic balancing act, to ensure that none acquired appreciably more territory than the other. Their decisions were graced with the epithet 'legitimacy', but deposed monarchs were only restored where convenient for the Allies. Thus the victorious Quadruple Alliance tried to create a ring of effective neighbours to ensure the containment of France. Hence an enlarged kingdom of the Netherlands, the consolidation of the Rhineland provinces under Prussian control and the strengthening of Piedmont-Sardinia on the south-eastern border.

The second major aim of each of the Allies was to grab as much territory as they could, without offending each other and risking renewed war. Russia, already in possession of Bessarabia and Finland, acquired most of the Napoleonic Grand Duchy of Warsaw, which consolidated her Polish territories and upset the Prussians, who had ambitions in the same direction. In compensation the Prussians were granted the Rhenish provinces, which they did not want, considering them as foreign in comparison with Polish lands and as a liability, given their close proximity to the recently belligerent France. The enormous economic potential of the coal and iron therein was as yet untapped and even scarcely appreciated. For the moment the Prussians could only see that their territories were even more scattered and that they had independent-minded provinces which were reluctant to accede to Prussian suzerainty. The acquisition of half of Saxony was some compensation for their disappointments.

Austria's gains were a mixed bag. Her chancellor, Metternich, was an important and charismatic figure at the peace negotiations, appearing to embody the ideals of the old order in a clever and flexible mind.[2] The Holy Roman Empire could not be rebuilt. Austria was a victor, but had contributed less than the others to France's defeat and her claims were sustained by the British determination to prevent Russia becoming too powerful. The Habsburgs had to accept that they now ruled an Austro-Hungarian Monarchy, including not only the dominant minority German elite but also Magyars and Italians, together with Czechs, Croats and huge numbers of other varied Slav inhabitants. The valuable Italian province of Lombardy remained an integral part of the Empire to which was added Venetia. Austrian princes continued to rule the semi-autonomous provinces of Tuscany, Parma and Modena. The whole Italian peninsula was to be regarded as an Austrian sphere of influence. The Catholic Austrian ruler would watch over the Italian frontier to contain the French, would protect the Pope and the restored rulers of Piedmont, Naples and Sicily. In addition, as compensation for the elimination of Austria's overseeing role in the Holy Roman Empire, her ruler was declared head of a German Confederation.

The German Confederation was a curious construct, initially designed to salve Austrian pride, but also to unite the now thirty-nine instead of nearly four hundred German states. They were meant to band together and form a common army, to defend them should France attack again. In reality the federal army was never formed and the Confederation never consisted of more than meetings in Frankfurt of ambassadors from the various states. Less tangible, a traditional respect for the Habsburgs and the Viennese sphere of influence remained, fanned by Metternich. This was felt in the form of a conservative influence on the members of the Confederation, who in the years after 1815 were persuaded to abandon constitutional innovations and pursue reactionary policies.

If defence against France and equal shares for the victors were the main 'principles' of the settlement, there was also the over-riding determination to do away with the new-fangled principles of the Revolution. The French revolutionaries had talked of liberal ideas and patriotic and national sentiments. The peacemakers wanted none of either. To protect themselves they wanted to construct a *cordon sanitaire* to prevent seepage of such ideas out of France. The German Confederation was not meant as a nation-state in embryo. However, huge provinces of the two biggest of the thirty-nine states, Austria and Prussia, were specifically excluded from the Confederation, because they were not German-speaking. This was a move which may have corresponded to traditional ideas on the old Holy Roman Empire, but was dangerous in that it tacitly accepted that ethnicity mattered. However, the Confederation had no political authority or decision-making machinery. It was set up to control the French, and the failure to create a confederate army ensured that it would serve little purpose in that direction. Instead, the fact that a German Confederation existed as a line on a map encouraged those who dreamt of uniting the German *volk* into a single state.

The peacemakers consciously destroyed Napoleon's kingdom of Italy, which had pretended to involve some notion of the peninsula incorporating a distinct nation, while in reality signifying nothing more than France's success in dominating the area. In 1814 the peninsula was once more split into half-a-dozen states, none of which stood for ideals of nationalism. Victor Emmanuel I, head of the House of Savoy and the old ruler of Sardinia was 'restored' to a kingdom which included not only Piedmont but also Genoa, thus creating a stronger block in case of future French aggression. The sentiments of the Piedmontese were ignored and so too were those of the Genoese for whom their Sardinian masters were feudal barbarians. The Spanish Bourbon family, former rulers in the south, were handed Naples and Sicily to be run, in considerable and predictable disharmony, as the kingdom of the Two Sicilies. In northern Europe the aspirations of the Belgians were also disregarded for the sake of containing France, and their provinces were absorbed into the kingdom of the Netherlands. Europe was to be a continent of absolutist kingdoms, in the hands of 'legitimate' rulers, only if their claims corresponded to the ambitions of the Allies.

The arrangements of 1814 were temporarily challenged in less than a year. In March 1815 Napoleon escaped from his imprisonment on Elba and made his way to Marseille and a triumphant return to France. He was obliged to accept the constitutional arrangements made by the Bourbons and even had the cheek to say that only the determination of the Allies to fight France had prevented him setting up a liberal constitution earlier. Many of his old officials and army returned to him, indicating that the Restoration was far from welcome in France. But the French were in no position to resume the war with any hope of success and the Allies would not tolerate Napoleon.

After a Hundred Day rule, in which a number of formerly unreconciled revolutionaries joined the Emperor in defensive federations against both the Bourbons and the Allies,[3] Napoleon was again defeated, and the battle of Waterloo signified the end of the Empire. Napoleon was moved to a secure exile in the middle of the Atlantic on the island of St Helena. The Bourbons once more returned to Paris, accompanied by an assertive and vindictive movement of ultra-royalist anti-revolutionaries, who had been kept in check during the first Restoration.[4] The peace settlement was now more punitive. The second Treaty of Paris in 1815 left the Allied armies, 1,200,000-strong at the outset, in occupation of half of France. The French had to foot a bill of 250 million francs a year for this army of occupation until they had paid an indemnity of 700 million francs. In addition France was reduced to her 1789 borders, which trimmed a little from her eastern frontiers. Final meetings of the Congress of Vienna (1815) formalized all the territorial changes made. The four Allies additionally agreed on meeting regularly to try to maintain a conservative peace in Europe. Alexander I persuaded the rest to sign a 'Holy Alliance' of sovereigns. In 1818, when the indemnity was paid, they met at Aix-la-Chapelle and there France joined them, as a conservative and peaceable power and a member of the Alliance.

What did the arrangements of 1814–15 restore? There was some superficial appearance of restoration but coercion and sometimes bribery were as visible as consent. Allied armies of occupation were dotted throughout the old Empire, including Sicily. Ruling dynasties, dispossessed during the wars, were returned like undelivered packages. There is little evidence that their return was popular. In France an aristocratic secret organization, the *chevaliers de la foi*, formed in 1810 and confined to the south, had only begun to make contact with the Bourbon claimant after Napoleon's failures in Russia. Popular revolts against conscription at this time were quite separate from conspiratorial aristocratic yearnings. The imminence of defeat in March–April 1814 sparked a little interest in the royalist cause in Bordeaux and Marseille. In the Italian peninsula popular protest against French occupation was localized and unrelated to 'national' sentiment. Conspirational formations run by the elite were far more numerous than in France, but here too they were totally divorced from popular protest. British agents encouraged them to hope that a single Italian constitutional regime might replace that of Napoleon.[5] In April 1814 Murat tried offering a similar bait in order to retain his throne after the fall of his master, but there was too much discord among Italians for such a project. Thus Austrian princes returned to the north and Ferdinand IV to Naples.

The rulers may have been the same, preserved in amber by the tedium and unreality of exile, but their countries were often much changed. The power of the state had been greatly enhanced. In France, above all, a completely new framework of institutions had been created. Any attempt to destroy it would have aroused ire among the French, as well as opposition from their enemies who did not want to resume the war. In institutional terms the Bourbon Restoration was the Empire without Napoleon. A wise restored ruler, such as Louis XVIII in France, was aware that the changes accomplished in his absence could be used to advantage. Louis inherited a centralized system of civil, judicial, military, educational, fiscal and financial institutions. Superficially this itself may have seemed in some ways a restoration, since, as de Tocqueville observed in his famous study of the 1789 Revolution written in the 1850s,[6] France was already a centralized state before the Revolution. But the degree of control available to the centre far exceeded that of the old regime.

At the apex of these new institutions was the Council of State, a body of experts on government appointed by the ruler. They drafted legislation at his behest and trained their subordinates for prefectoral and lesser posts. All official appointments, however minor, were made from Paris. The restored Bourbons thus had the potential for unrivalled control. Their revolutionary and Bonapartist predecessors had hoped that the new systems would eliminate privilege and exalt the principle of career open to talent. The training provided in the Council of State and in the senior institutions of higher education, the *grandes écoles* like the *école polytechnique*, in part fufilled this objective and the Restoration sustained it. However, increasingly after 1814, noble background counted for more than professional training. The expectation that privileged corporative institutions would cease to challenge the centralized state was never realized. Centralization existed on paper. In reality local notables divided power among themselves and corporate and professional bodies demanded that the state recognize their integrity, in effect their autonomy. Lawyers more than any other groups resisted attempts to mould them into the centralized system, stressing Montesquieu's demands for the separation of powers within the state, behind which they protected the privileges of their profession.

France had codes of law which decreed equality before the law (not for women) and a rational and centralized system of courts. But they were staffed by the offspring of members of the independent parlements, the old regime's courts of appeal. Traditions of independence were rewritten as tests of professional standards and competence. The authority of the professions, defined by internally judged competence and high entry fees replaced that of venal hereditary office, and amounted to an even more effective block on centralized power. Successive regimes in nineteenth-century France were obliged to compromise both with local elites and independent judiciaries. The myriad of separate corporations and venal office-holding of the old regime could not be restored, but the bases of both had survived the Revolution. Norms triumphed over institutions.

In two very important respects, their armies and their tax systems, restored monarchies headed states incomparably more powerful than those of the old regime. In France a single system of direct taxation was thankfully inherited from the Revolution, which together with far less welcome indirect taxes effectively financed the rapidly expanding functions of the modern state. The principle of uniform direct taxes was never again disputed, although an actual income tax was not introduced for more than a century. The main direct tax was on the value of land and corresponded roughly to a 16 per cent levy on revenue. In addition there was a charge on industrial and commercial activity, which was much lighter, taxing the value of the property, not profits. Indirect taxes, then as now, were a source of constant grievance. *Droits réunis*, paid by the producers of wine, salt and tobacco were resented, but the income raised was so valuable that Napoleon's reimposition of these hated old regime taxes was eagerly continued by the Bourbons.

The standing professional army created by the 1789 Revolution was maintained and conscription was retained with some reluctance. The army was reduced to just over a third of a million men and 14,000 officers were retired, but the principle of a national army was not contested. The Bourbons tried to counter its strong Bonapartist ethos, but three-quarters of its officers were still of Imperial vintage (and probably sympathies) in the mid-1820s.[7] In the absence of an effective civil police force and seconded by a civilian militia (the National Guard founded in 1789, which still thought of itself as the symbol of the Revolution), the army was a vital instrument of political control. However the inevitable continuity of personnel with the far more glorious Imperial period lessened its usefulness for the Bourbons.

Restored dynasties elsewhere frequently found it desirable to retain innovations imposed during the Napoleonic conquest. The Austrian arch-duchess of Parma, Marie-Louise, second wife of Napoleon, used the French codes as a model for her new kingdom. Tuscany kept the Napoleonic centralized administrative system intact. In Lombardy and Venetia Napoleonic financial and judicial institutions were preserved. Ferdinand, king of the new combined kingdom of the Two Sicilies, introduced Neapolitan (i.e. Napoleonic) administrative and judicial structures together with the law codes throughout his state, although rivalry between the ruling groups of Naples and Sicily made consensus tricky.[8]

Not only did the institutions survive, so too did the wartime personnel. Bonaparte's bureaucrats were retained to run the institutions he had created in Lombardy and Venetia. Until the escape from Elba and the Hundred Day rule made continuity inappropriate, Louis XVIII used the bulk of the former Imperial officials. These included 76 per cent of Napoleon's corps and more than half of his prefects. Even where the king made new appointments, he often chose Imperial servants. Two-thirds of his prefects, pivotal officials in the centralized system, had worked for Napoleon. However, at the second Restoration those officials who had twice changed their allegiance were dismissed in perpetuity and émigrés secured the appointments they had craved unsuccessfully a year earlier.

In some areas there was no attempt to compromise, even in the spring of 1814. The papacy, restored as ruler of most of central Italy, reversed the Napoleonic codes. Sales of church lands were recognized, but former owners received an indemnity. In the new kingdom of Piedmont-Sardinia pre-Napoleonic systems were revived to the disgust of the Piedmontese elite which had profited from and staffed the Napoleonic system.

Old regime monarchies were supposed to have divine sanction over subjects. Restored monarchies made agreements with their citizens. In 1814 monarchy was effectively a matter of appointment. Louis was invited to be king of the French people and the 1814 constitution was clearly a matter of negotiation. However there was ambiguity. Louis accepted the crown from the Napoleonic Senate and agreed to their draft constitution, all of which sounded like a shadow of the old Bourbon monarchy, but the intervention of his ultra-royalist brother appeared to add old-style pomp. The constitution was revamped by a new committee in which the three royal nominees had more of a voice. It became a constitutional 'charter', which was rather like saying that 'the dark is light'. The preamble insisted that the constitution was indeed a charter, in the tradition of old regime pronouncements by divinely appointed rulers to loyal subject peoples. It was not negotiated with equal 'citizens', but was 'octroyée', a grace-and-favour grant from above.

The preamble was little more than the misguided flutterings of the ultra-royalist imagination, although its inclusion caused much resentment among former revolutionaries and Bonapartists. There was no old regime written constitution to restore and build on in 1814. The committee's models were the British constitution and to a degree the abortive constitution of 1791. The basis of Louis XVIII's power lay in the main body of the document, which was clearly a new agreement, not a restoration. The monarch was indeed to be an hereditary 'king of France' and head of the executive. But legislative power was to be shared with a bicameral assembly. The Chamber of Deputies was to be elected by a wealthy elite of men who paid 300 francs a year in direct taxes (mainly the land tax). The right to be a candidate was restricted to an even smaller group of about 15,000 who paid at least 1,000 francs a year in tax. The king could not impose taxation without the consent of this body. The Chamber of Peers was an hereditary assembly of nobles appointed by the king. Initially it was actually the Imperial Senate given a new name. Only thirty-seven of Napoleon's senators failed to find a place in the Chamber of Peers. The Restoration thus included the principle of representative constitutional government which had been sought in 1789 but subsequently lost in the upheaval of the Revolution.

In this important respect the new regime was neither the restoration of 1789 nor the continuation of the Empire. It was a carefully crafted compromise, in which the leading liberal thinker, Benjamin Constant, had a major role. The constitution created representative, but not parliamentary government. The king chose his own ministers, whom the constitution said were 'responsible'. The failure to say to whom they were responsible was deliberate. The former revolutionaries, now usually termed liberals, or *doctrinaires*, a jibe at their fondness for the written constitution, assumed that ministers were responsible to parliament. Royalists, and especially ultras, would not have welcomed the bald statement of parliamentary power. The ambiguity was quickly resolved in practice, for a government which did not have the confidence of parliament could not legislate. Only in an emergency, it was stated, could the king issue decree law on his authority alone.

The French constitution was an important innovation, blending radical political concepts with the institutionalized dominance of wealthy elites. Apart from intransigent ultras, most royalists appreciated the attractions of a constitutional regime. They were convinced that the electoral principle could give increased sanction and legitimacy to the power of the rich, if the electorate was restricted. In 1820, after the next in line to the throne beyond Artois, the duc de Berri, was murdered, the ultras claimed by a liberal hand, the suffrage was narrowed. The richest quarter of the enfranchised were given a second vote in special departmental electoral colleges. Thus the wealthiest would control the Chamber and conservatives believed that this would be a guarantee of a stable and conservative France. The success of the right in the election of 1824 seemed to confirm that conservatism had triumphed by adapting and using the erstwhile revolutionary concept of elections and parliaments.[9]

The idea that constitutionalism could be an ally of conservatism made some modest progress elsewhere. In Milan and Venice Francis I created congregations, central and local assemblies composed of nominated local notables, which were consulted over taxation and legislation. In Spain, the restored Ferdinand VII who had swept aside the 1812 constitution and brought back the Inquisition, was challenged in 1822 by a liberal constitutional revolt which was only thwarted by French intervention. In both Naples and Piedmont attempts were made during the 1820s to persuade the rulers to agree to modest power-sharing, but, as we shall see, these concepts were still seen as too radical.

If the institutions of government were often in reality very different from pre-revolutionary ones, what of the composition of the ruling elites? In France, the Italian states and elsewhere, dominant aristocratic families who had gone into exile during the Napoleonic era returned to repossess estates protected for them by their land agents. The French constitution was careful to establish that the land settlement of the Revolution was permanent. There was no question of returning land which had been sold to the former owners, which caused some resentment among those émigrés who did not come back to France until 1814. However, any unsold land could be reclaimed. The issue remained explosive and former émigrés continued to demand compensation. In 1825 a law of indemnification was passed which raised a state loan to pay compensation to those who lost land in the Revolution. Former revolutionaries, especially those who had bought *biens nationaux*, were shocked both by the payment and by the underlying assumption that the initial sequestration had been wrong.

It used to be thought that the landed aristocracies were substantially deprived of property and status during the Revolution and the Napoleonic years. The apologists of the nobility certainly emphasized the sufferings of émigré families. In reality the French nobility lost at most 5 per cent of its property, emerging in 1814 in possession of about 20 per cent of the land and remaining the largest single group of property-owners. Land was, if anything, enhanced as a desirable commodity. The right to vote depended on the land tax and recurring economic crises made speculative commercial and industrial ventures risky. The social status of nobility remained pre-eminent, to the extent that an aspiring individual undecorated by either the Bourbons or Napoleon would invent a title.

What of the political power of the elites? In the last quarter-century revisionist historians have been anxious to show that Marxists got it wrong when they said that the 1789 Revolution began the process of unpicking a feudal aristocratic landowning elite and replacing it with a bourgeois entrepreneurial model. Long before the Revolution the nobility had shared political power with a wealthy bourgeois elite; 1789 temporarily displaced the noble element and exalted the bourgeois. Napoleon, as we have seen, tried to enlist noble support, while retaining that of the revolutionaries. Louis XVIII attempted to continue the compromise, although this was marred by the Hundred Days. His ultra-royalist supporters dreamt a Romantic myth of a totally aristocratic elite. Many of these ultras had been émigrés, whose passion for a monarchy squarely backed by Catholic Church and nobility, had been fostered by absence and anti-revolutionary venom. The comte d'Artois, Charles X from 1824, consciously sought to fill official posts with members of the nobility, of as ancient lineage as possible. Revolutionary institutions such as the prefectoral corps and the Council of State, as well as the church hierarchy and the army officer corps, were packed with scions of old noble households as never before. The gap between the norms of these new officials and the institutions they operated was substantial. The ultras' experiment in socio-political engineering created an inexperienced administrative corps, contributed to the July Days and did not survive the 1830 Revolution.

The Catholic Church, harried, insulted and deprived of its lands by anti-clericals during the revolutionary years, was named in new-style constitutions, such as the French Constitutional Charter of 1814 and the Spanish constitution of 1837 as the state church. Pius VII was released from imprisonment and the papacy was restored to its extensive domains in central Italy, as well as to its position as the head of an international church. Conservative writers like de Maistre and de Bonald asserted the role of Christianity and the hierarchy of the Catholic Church as an antidote to the demonic influence of the 1789 Revolution. However they sought a restoration not of the old regime but of an idealized medieval church, purified and exalted as a senior corporation in a pyramid of traditional political and social as well as spiritual power. Restoration had to be accompanied by purification.[10]

Throughout Europe a religious revival, which encompassed all branches of Christianity, gave renewed authority and status to religion, particularly after 1814. In France the extensive nation-wide evangelical revival was fervently pursued in every commune by young, recently trained priests. It put women in particular on their knees to seek divine forgiveness for the sins of the 1789 Revolution.[11] While there was no specific attempt to attract the less well-off, we do find in the nineteenth century a development of the cult of the 'Sacred Heart', a greater veneration of Mary, and a spate of 'visions' mainly by young girls, which together with female canonizations and popular pilgrimages were presumably designed to appeal both to women and to the less educated.

The restoration of the Catholic Church as an educator of the young was to become a contentious issue after 1814. Church-run schools expanded rapidly at all levels to fill the practical and perceived spiritual gap left by the 1789 Revolution. Religious orders were welcomed back in both France and Italy. In France the Christian Brothers set up cheap, ubiquitous 'little seminaries', ostensibly to train priests, but whose clientèle was in reality broader. Even more alarming to supporters of the anti-clericalist policies of the Revolution was the takeover of secondary education after 1814. Bishops often participated in the running of royal colleges. Even the state-run *lycées* were challenged, especially by the expensive, and therefore socially very exclusive, private boarding schools founded by religious orders such as the Marists and the Assumptionists and (however contested their triumphs) by the Jesuits too.

In 1822 a senior cleric, Mgr de Frayssinous, was made Grand Master of the University, administrative heart of the state-run secondary system. Priests gained ground as anti-clerical professors such as Guizot and Victor Cousin were ousted from the faculties. Although there was no question of the return of church lands confiscated and sold during the 1790s as 'national lands', individuals could once more donate land, which permitted the revival of teaching orders.

In France and in other Catholic states the church recovered its political role as prop of the restored monarchies. There was a close association with ultra-royalist politics, particularly after the accession of Charles X in 1824. Bishops and *curés* ordered their congregations to vote for ultra candidates in elections. Caricatures often portrayed the king in clerical dress. A number of senior clerics were openly ultra-royalist. Ultra-royalism, with its anachronistic and romantic vision of French society harmoniously headed by king, church and the nobility, had a heady attraction for the churchmen. Senior clerics like the archbishop of Paris were known ultras and both the rumour and reality of the power of the *Congrégation*, a 'secret' ultra and Catholic organization, caused alarm to former revolutionaries. The high point of the influence of the *Congrégation* was the law against sacrilege, passed by parliament in 1825.

However, although ultras cherished the ideal of a state run by king, church and aristocracy in a pyramid of restored harmony, the reality was somewhat different. In France clerics were civil servants. Before the Revolution the king had had to negotiate with the recalcitrant and independent Assembly of the Clergy to persuade them to pay tax. The Revolution had reversed this position and neither of the restored Bourbons wanted to change this aspect of their authority. A reflection of the subservience of the Restored church was that the senior noble families no longer sent younger sons to be bishops. The Martignac government of 1828 underlined the power of the state by demanding that the Jesuits leave France.

The restoration of the social and political role of the French Catholic Church was short-lived. Anti-clericalism was far more muted among the educated than a generation earlier, but popular anti-clerical riots, particularly against the new missionary crosses and newer religious orders such as the Christian Brothers, accompanied the 1830 Revolution in France. Catholicism was reduced from being the official doctrine of the state after July 1830 to serving merely as the 'religion of the majority'. In 1833 legislation provided for the creation of lay primary schools in all communes, and thus stimulated a renewed rift between church and state.

Even in the Italian lands the Catholic Church did not resume its former dominance. After Napoleon's defeat the restored rulers throughout the peninsula valued the church as a conservative ally, but even in the Papal States there was no question of giving land back. Francis I confirmed the sale of church lands in Lombardy and Venetia. The Napoleonic Concordat was upheld in Parma. In Tuscany also land sales were maintained and the Jesuits were denied entry. Elsewhere in the peninsula the church regained more influence. In Piedmont the Jesuits regained control of education and a concordat provided for the reconstitution of ecclesiastical courts. Pius VII, martyr after his captivity, regained most of his territory, despite Austrian demands.[12] In Spain the church's status had been raised by its championship of resistance to Napoleonic rule. Liberal reformers within the Spanish church were pushed aside after 1814 and the sale of church property did not begin until 1840.[13] In Spain and Italy the church remained a major corporation, the senior echelons of its hierarchy still staffed by old and rich noble families. Unlike France there had been little challenge to its control of education. The absence of parliaments meant that clerics were not asked to fulfil the contentious and demeaning task of unpaid election agent.

If Restoration institutions were substantively different from the pre-war originals, those who worked within them claimed to be conservative. What did this imply? Conservative was a fluid chameleon term, which had several meanings. One covered the romantics or ultra-conservatives; another referred to the broad centre, made up of monarchists. Reforming or liberal elements believed they too were conservative, although their ultra opponents did not.

The ultra-conservatives, or ultra-royalists or merely ultras, as individuals were called by contemporaries, were conservatives on the defensive against revolutionary change. They represented a dynamic conservatism, typified by writers such as de Maistre and de Bonald in France. Their leaders had been exiles, often self-imposed émigrés from their own countries during the revolutionary and wartime years. They were unbendingly, and usually uncomprehendingly hostile to the changes which had taken place in their absence. However they were part of the Romanticism of the age, with a passion for history, because they believed that the study of the Middle Ages could reveal the wrong steps taken by those who had intended to conserve as well as by revolutionaries who for them were Anti-Christ. For ultras, as for revolutionary sympathizers, history was the study, not merely of kings and battles, but of peoples. The 'people' for ultras were not individuals in search of constitutions, but an organic whole, a *volk* for German writers, in search of their identity through the understanding of a common history, culture and language, even where, as in eastern Europe and the Italian peninsula aspects of these had to be invented. This was a generation brought up on the novels of Sir Walter Scott, the most popular writer in Europe in the 1820s and 1830s, who eulogized medieval Scotland, France and the Italian states.

Ultras believed that modern society was misguided. The 1789 Revolution was demonic, but the revolutionaries were merely the tools of almighty justice, punishing wayward peoples. The sin lay not just in 1789, but also in the centralizing, absolutist tendencies of recent old regime monarchs, who had disregarded the traditions of provinces, estates and corporate bodies. De Maistre's solution was an idealized, hierarchical society and government. The crown, clergy and nobility should form a united trinity to restore order and tranquillity to a troubled people.

Such a united trinity had never existed. Before the Revolution crown, clergy and nobility had been constantly bickering and divided within themselves at all levels. The counter-revolutionaries, who found de Maistre to their taste, invented the notion that old regime France already had a traditional monarchist constitution which had been neglected and ignored. Once this was rediscovered, they argued, France's problems would be solved. How absolute should the ruler be? Although these counter-revolutionaries came to be called ultra-royalists, more royalist than the king, in reality many wanted to curb the king's power. Within the 'traditional' constitution they dreamt of were layers of noble power, dormant in the regional assemblies of the estates, which had often fallen into decay in old regime France. Counter-revolutionaries wanted to restore these traditional spheres of influence of the nobility to counteract what they claimed had been an upstart tendency of royal ministers to overcentralize France in the century or so before the Revolution. Behind the ultras lay the Fronde. Before them stood the comte d'Artois, a reformed dissolute fop, anxious to fulfil a royal destiny if he had the chance.

Centrist conservatives tried to find a middle ground of compromise between the Revolution and the ultras. In France Louis XVIII epitomized this attempt. He could see the benefits which the Revolution had brought him in greater centralization and tried to resist pressure from the right. The ultimate failure of the Restoration by 1830 was not due to the collapse of this search for a *juste milieu*, but to the temporary ascendancy of counter-revolutionaries during the reign of Charles X. To their activities, which allowed former left-wingers to present themselves by contrast as men of relative moderation, we will now turn.

NOTES

1 J.M. Sherwig, *Guineas and Gunpowder. British Foreign Aid in the Wars with France 1793–1815* (London, 1969).
2 A. Sked (ed.) *Europe's Balance of Power, 1815–1848* (London, 1979).
3 R.S. Alexander explores *Bonapartism and the Revolutionary Tradition in France. The Fédérés of 1815* (Cambridge, 1991).
4 J. Roberts, *The Counter-Revolution in France 1787–1830* (London, 1990).
5 S. Woolf, *History of Italy* (London, 1979), p.224.
6 A. de Tocqueville, *The Old Régime and the French Revolution* (New York, 1955, trs. S. Gilbert).
7 R. Holyrood, 'The Bourbon army 1815–30', *Historical Journal* xiv (3) (1971).

8   S. Woolf, *A History of Italy 1700–1860. The Social Constraints of Political Change* (London, 1979).
9   An accessible survey of France in A. Jardin and A.J. Tudesq, *Restoration and Reaction 1815–48* (Cambridge, 1983).
10 J. de Maistre, *Considerations sur la France* (Geneva, 1796).
11 R. Gibson, *A Social History of French Catholicism 1789–1914* (London, 1989).
12 S. Woolf, *A History of Italy 1700–1860. The Social Constraints of Political Change* (London, 1979), pp.202–3, 212, 243.
13 A. Shubert, *A Social History of Modern Spain* (London, 1990), pp.146–7.

FURTHER READING

A. Sked (ed.) *Europe's Balance of Power, 1815–1848* (London, 1979) deals effectively with the diplomacy of the period.

A useful survey of France in these years can be gained from A. Jardin and A.J. Tudesq, *Restoration and Reaction 1815–48* (Cambridge, 1983) and R. Magraw, *France 1814–1914. The Bourgeois Century* (London, 1983). J. Roberts, *The Counter-Revolution in France 1787–1830* (London, 1990) offers a masterly brief survey of the right wing.

The affairs of the Italian peninsula are well documented in S. Woolf, *A History of Italy 1700–1860. The Social Constraints of Political Change* (London, 1979), H. Hearder, *Italy in the Age of the Risorgimento 1790–1870* (Harlow, 1986) and L. Riall, *The Italian Risorgimento. State, Society and National Unification* (London, 1994). J.A. Davies, *Conflict and Control. Law and Order in Nineteenth Century Italy* (London, 1988) offers a valuable new perspective.

Portugal has attracted the least attention, but W.C. Atkinson, *A History of Spain and Portugal* (London, 1960) gives the basic outline and further information can be obtained from A.H. Oliveira Marques, *A History of Portugal* (New York, 1972). Spain is well served in J. Lynch, *Bourbon Spain* (Oxford, 1989), R. Carr, *Spain 1808–1939* (Oxford, 1975) and the illuminating *Social History of Modern Spain* by A. Shubert (London, 1990). Major aspects of her history are explored in W.J. Callahan, *Church, Politics and Society in Spain, 1750–1874* (Cambridge, Mass., 1984).

For works on Austria, the German states and Russia, see the notes on Further Reading attached to Chapter 5.

Chapter 7

Revolutionary movements in western Europe, 1814–30

Pamela M. Pilbeam

What constituted a revolution and who were the revolutionaries in these years? Revolutions were largely concerned with liberal or national objectives and directed to the substitution of one narrow political elite by another. The 'successful' revolutions of this period illustrate these aspirations. The 1830 Revolution in France preserved constitutional government, the Belgian and Greek revolts secured national independence. The victors in each case were well-heeled members of the educated middle class. However, the upheavals which created opportunities for ambitious politicians had few connections with liberal or national concepts but were the product of the economic grievances of urban artisans. Popular demonstrations contributed to revolutionary takeover in areas where the legacy of the 1789 Revolution, subsequent wars and military conquest left governments and their armies nervous and irresolute.

The upheaval of the 1790s in France and Europe had shown that change through force was possible and could be legitimated and made permanent by successful insurgents. However, the intervention of artisans and peasants in that process and the scale of popular upheaval at intervals during the 1790s had convinced most property-owners that force was a danger rather than an opportunity. After 1814 those who had gained from the initial Revolution were anxious to defend and protect the achievements of the 1790s: a lay state, the confirmation of revolutionary land sales, codes of law, new judicial structures, above all their own jobs. They also sought a constitution to replace absolutism, an objective attempted but not realized in the upheaval of the initial Revolution. In other words, by 1814 and within their own terms of reference, the adherents of 1789 were somewhat conservative.

A minority were more radical and aimed at more democratic, not merely constitutional, government. They were also inclined to be more attentive to the many socio-economic problems of these years and to favour humanitarian measures. The term liberal came to be used to describe those who thus sought personal and constitutional liberties, but in reality the liberties they wanted were for an educated elite and liberalism tended to be defined more by negatives than agreed programmes of a positive kind.

In the years up to 1830 nationalism was also becoming an issue, although less specific even than liberalism. Like liberal ideas, nationalism was not a 'popular' sentiment, but part of romantic, cultural dreams of uniting 'peoples' as counterweights to the traditional absolutist authority of rulers. Encouraged by the new conglomerate states Napoleon had created in the German, Polish and Italian lands, some thinkers and writers spun liberal and patriotic concepts together. For the moment these were rooted in history, language and culture. In the Italian peninsula the experience of French conquest gave rise to the idea of a 'Risorgimento' or rebirth of Italy. The defeat of Napoleon resulted in the renewed subdivision of the peninsula, with the Austrian Empire resuming the traditional position of dominant foreign power, part overlord, part overseer. Rebirth for the moment was literary, but also insurrectionary and conspiratorial on a small scale, awakening regional rather than united national sentiments and lacking any sense of common military or political objectives.

Italian literary patriots could look back to the early modern period for a past which may have been glorious in terms of culture and commerce, but had hardly been marked by unity. Unfortunately, they had also to look back in different languages, Italian being little used outside Tuscany. The Romantic novelist Manzoni set the tone for future attempts at mutual comprehension and harmony with the first novel in Italian, *I promessi sposi*. The author glorified Italian patriotism in a love story set in the Lombardy of the 1630s.[1] But even this much prized step to a common language had to be rewritten from the Lombardian dialect into Tuscan Italian.

In post-war Europe revolution lay as much in the nightmares of the conservative observer as in insurrectionary activity itself. The desire for revolutionary change was a fluid concept, whose definition depended on the perceptions of the onlooker. The terms used by contemporaries indicate the subjective and elusive quality of our subject matter. At their most objective, authors of the numerous biographical political dictionaries simply divided politicians into gradations of right and left. Those on the left tended to be called liberals, and these were split into sub-categories whose names varied from country to country but roughly corresponded to moderate and radical. Sometimes 'democrat' was preferred for the latter, but the precise word used depended, then as now, on whether insult or compliment was intended. All supporters of the changes of 1789, whether moderate or radical liberals, were dangerous subversives to traditional supporters of the restored governments, who would call them names like Jacobin or revolutionary and imagine vast international conspiracies. In reality moderate liberals were also appalled by the extremism of the radicals and believed that they were a threat to the social as well as the political fabric. Wealthy notables and a majority of other middle-class property-owners regarded those members of the lower middle class, artisans and peasants who from time to time engaged in popular demonstrations as revolutionaries, however limited and economically conservative the objectives of these latter groups may have been.

After 1814 conflict within the elites centred on who should run the state. The demands of liberals tended to weaken its centralized structures. Economic change and periodic crises led to a constant undercurrent of popular protest and to peaks of unrest. The grievances of the political elites and these 'popular classes' were quite distinct, but there were overlaps, both in what they sought and in the membership of some organizations. In this chapter elite and popular movements will be assessed separately but also comparatively.

In 1814 in France the first Restoration seemed tolerable to those who had gained from the 1789 Revolution, partly because of the shock of Napoleon's total defeat and the extent of the collapse of the Empire, but equally because the Restoration settlement was a compromise. Napoleonic elites often remained intact and Bonapartist systems still in force. It was the experience of the Hundred Days which reversed the situation by giving the excuse for a counter-revolutionary backlash to the changes of the Revolutionary years. Napoleon's escape in March 1815 had encouraged his former supporters to believe that the Bourbons could be eliminated. The revived Empire was strengthened by Napoleon's adoption of a liberal constitution and the assumption of revolutionaries that, if a deal could be struck with the Allies, Napoleon could be obliged to retain elected institutions. In France the federations which were rapidly created to fight the Allies and keep out the Bourbons stimulated new alignments between Bonapartists and previously unreconciled revolutionaries, especially former Jacobins.

The events of the second Restoration brought an end to hopes of a peaceful compromise between former revolutionaries and supporters of the monarchy. Royalists, particularly ultra-royalists, launched a White Terror against those who had supported Napoleon in the Hundred Days, notably the members of federations. Bonapartists were persecuted, imprisoned, even put to death. Waves of lawless revenge spread through southern France from June 1815. In Marseille fifty died and two hundred were injured. In Toulouse the moderate royalist leader of the National Guard was killed, as were thirty-seven Protestant notables in Languedoc. As well as unlicensed persecution, 6,000 Bonapartists were put on trial, including seventeen army officers summoned to appear before military courts. Among the latter some fled, some were condemned to perpetual exile and two were executed. Marshal Ney, a popular patriotic figure, was put to death.

Large numbers of officials who had twice changed their loyalties were permanently excluded from office for the whole of the Restoration. These fickle and self-seeking bureaucrats left the king with little choice but to remove them if his own regime was to be credible. A growing preference for noble candidates convinced the discarded Bonapartist elite that they were in the midst of an assault on revolutionary principles. Elections for a Chamber of Deputies produced the ultra-royalist *Chambre Introuvable*. Louis XVIII wisely dissolved this body within the year and the next Assembly was more moderate.

The circumstances of the second Restoration ensured that in France and elsewhere the lines of conflict and the personnel of elite resistance to restored regimes had been created. In France's former Empire opposition to restored regimes was even more rapid because of the lack of any compromise. In 1814 in Naples and Piedmont the Spanish Bourbon Ferdinand IV and the House of Savoy led by Victor Emmanuel I made no pretence of considering the constitutional aspirations of their landed aristocratic elites, some of whom had worked with Napoleon while others had formed conspiratorial groups to oppose him. In Spain liberals were optimistic that the defeat of France would finally permit the implementation of their constitution of 1812, drawn up by a hastily elected liberal *Cortes* during the French occupation. Since this was to be the model and ideal for Spanish liberals and for liberal groups elsewhere throughout the nineteenth century, its details should be briefly considered.

In 1808 Napoleon's brother Joseph, who was trying to gain control of the peninsula and acceptance as king of Spain while both Bourbon contenders were incarcerated in France, had called a *Cortes* to legitimate his authority. Joseph issued a liberal constitution, which was never applied. Beleaguered Spanish liberals set out their terms for constitutional government. An elected assembly was to meet for three to four months a year, choosing a small Deputation to function during its recess. In addition a small second chamber, a Council of State, was to be chosen by the king from a list of names prepared by the assembly. A uniform income tax and a centralized administrative structure was provided for, although it was not clear whether the new officials were to be locally elected or centrally appointed. Monastic lands were to be sold and a direct and simple system of property titles drawn up. Surviving feudal institutions were to be abolished and common lands sold. Half of this property was to be reserved for war veterans and the landless, to try to prevent established property-owners seizing the lot, as had happened in France. A single rational judicial system would ensure the abolition of seigneurial justice, much resented by peasants. Thus the privileges of traditional corporate bodies – the Catholic Church, the guilds, the aristocracy – were to be curbed, with the intention, as in France, of asserting the power of the professional middle classes. It is somewhat ironical, in view of the resentment of French conquest, that the constitution-makers were strongly influenced by what their occupiers themselves had tried to do in France in the 1790s and only partly achieved.[2]

The 1812 constitution remained a liberal dream. The French only tinkered with modernization and the dispossession of the church in contrast to their radical approach elsewhere, because their own control of the peninsula was constantly challenged by the British armies. A modern administrative system, based on the French prefectoral model, was created. The church successfully resisted inroads into its power. In March 1814, Ferdinand VII was released from French imprisonment and promised to observe the

1812 constitution. However, the support of the army and some popular demonstrations in Madrid allowed him to defy the liberals and ignore the constitution.

Thus in Spain liberals were disillusioned with the Restoration. Some critics were themselves forced into exile. Ferdinand tried to re-establish the reformed absolutism he had known in 1808, but the desperate financial problems of the monarchy were exacerbated by the cost of trying to contain the continuing rebellion of Spain's South American Empire. Not entirely surprisingly it was within the army that criticism of the disastrous royal policy grew. The failure to recapture the colonies and their wealth forced severe retrenchments within the army, and rebels were typically men whose career or retirement prospects were thwarted. Between 1814 and 1820 a series of *pronunciamientos* was made by groups of officers, usually in concert with civilian liberal opponents of the king, including an attempt in 1816 to murder Ferdinand. These *pronunciamientos* set the trend for a form of nineteenth-century liberalism which was unique to Spain and had some roots in eighteenth-century practice. Such *pronunciamientos* by sections of the army became the frequent, typical, rapidly stylized and usually disastrous means of liberal revolt in Spain during the nineteenth century. Small groups of officers would hold discussions within the army and with civilian conspirators to try to effect liberal change. Both groups operated within masonic structures. Military lodges were particularly significant and the younger adherents had been stirred by contact with British masons during the war years. Civilian liberals were also grouped in masonic lodges, which in a country of the Inquisition were more directly crucibles of liberal politics than elsewhere.[3]

After 1815 small, secret conspiratorial formations developed in France and the Italian states, notably in Piedmont and the kingdom of the Two Sicilies. In these countries also radical groups owed their structure and to some degree their spiritual roots to freemasonry. Their initiation ceremonies, hierarchal chain of membership, secret symbols and codes, were closely related. The groups themselves were sometimes direct offshoots of masonic lodges, or even lodges themselves, although masonry existed separately from political formations and in France the Grand Orient and Scottish lodges were not only tolerated, but organized and led by members of the royalist governing elite.[4]

Why was opposition secret? In France formal political organizations of more than twenty members were banned by Article 291 of the code and elsewhere persecution was the norm. Political formations had to be secret to survive. Radical secret groups were also a way of counteracting equally covert right-wing formations. The *Chevaliers de la foi* were formed in France in 1810 to promote the royalist cause. To them were added the *Congrégation*, which was apparently a public Catholic charitable body, but had secret ramifications and links with the *Chevaliers*. Both were the spearhead of ultra politics, of the various manifestations of counter- or anti-revolution. They continued to grow after 1814, under the protection of the comte d'Artois, heir to the throne, because ultra-royalists found the king too prepared to compromise with former revolutionaries. The Catholic Church, the main target for the 1789 revolutionaries, was a natural focus for the suspicions of the left. Within the church itself, religious orders like the Jesuits were traditionally regarded as secret and powerful papal forces. After 1815 the Jesuits unofficially re-established themselves in France and in other Catholic states, to the alarm of moderate Catholic opinion as well as sympathizers with 1789.

After 1815 left-wing groups committed to opposing the ultra political and religious claims began to appear. In 1816 Joseph Rey, a lawyer in Grenoble, set up the republican *Union* and tried to seize power in the town together with 4,000 Bonapartist veterans. Government repression was swift; six were killed in the fighting and twenty-five conspirators were tried and executed. A year later there was a Bonapartist rising in Lyon and in 1819 a branch of the *Union* was set up in Paris under the patronage of leading left-wingers like the veteran revolutionary Lafayette. An organization began in Saumur whose name directly echoed that of the ultra group, the *Chevaliers de la liberté*; and in Paris leading radicals formed the influential radical masonic lodge, the *Amis de la Verité*.[5]

In the Italian peninsula similar groups already existed, often as reconstructions of wartime committees. The secret elite formations which had flowered during the Napoleonic occupation, when they had been encouraged by British agents and cash, resumed their activities. The British presence had encouraged groups like the *carbonari*, which had spread from its roots in Sicily to Naples, to expect constitutional government, perhaps on the British model and perhaps for the whole of Italy. There were a number of such organizations, including the *adelfia*, started in Geneva by Buonarroti, Babeuf's partner in the neo-Jacobin

'Conspiracy of the Equals' of 1796, which liked to publicize their links and conspiratorial powers.[6] Buonarroti, for instance, was in contact with Rey in Grenoble.[7] The *adelfia* gained ground in northern Italy.[8]

The settlement of 1814 was a disappointment, with its restoration of deposed rulers who yearned for absolute power. The constitution agreed by the Bourbon ruler of Sicily in 1812, under the impetus of the British occupiers, was forgotten by Ferdinand IV in his new kingdom of the Two Sicilies. In Piedmont elite Bonapartist bureaucrats and secret groups which had conspired with the Allies against Napoleon were aggrieved when they not only failed to obtain a promised liberal constitution but also found that Napoleonic institutions themselves were being abolished. An absolutist Sardinian-dominated regime was imposed by Victor Emmanuel, now ruler of the enlarged combined kingdom. Small secret groups of conspirators grew throughout the Papal States and the Austrian Duchies and independently organized *carbonari* formations, initially set up in Naples to fight Murat, were now used against the restored Bourbons. In Spain, established and ambitious members of the revolutionary political elite were appalled when the 1812 constitution was abandoned after Napoleon's defeat, and their counterparts in Lisbon were shaken when Portugal's modest reforming programme was reversed.

The leaders of these small groups included both former anti-Bonapartist conspirators and deposed Bonapartist officials in Italy, and former Napoleonic officials as well as forcibly retired or currently serving officers and soldiers in France. In Piedmont the liberals included Balbo and other members of the tiny aristocratic elite excluded from power by Victor Emmanuel, who was determined not to employ those who had served the Emperor. This discarded and discontented group were army officers who had been able to identify with Napoleonic glory much better than with the restored king. They treasured an ideal of the Piedmontese military elite spearheading national liberation.[9]

Within France many Bonapartist sympathizers were still serving officers and conspiracy tended to centre, as in Saumur, on garrison towns and military schools. In addition the secret groups attracted the large numbers of former Bonapartist civilian officials who were dismissed at the second Restoration. Many, but not all, who joined were middle class. They felt that the elevation of young, inexperienced members of old noble families to official positions was a counter-revolutionary threat to the achievements of 1789. The Revolution was increasingly revered as a 'bourgeois' liberal triumph, even by sympathizers who were themselves noble.

In addition to the grumbles of recently unseated elites, opposition groups attracted their offspring, who deplored the reactionary, pro-Catholic atmosphere of the post-war world. In the universities, faculties and Napoleonic *grandes écoles* at which they were students, liberal lecturers who mounted unrestrained campaigns in support of enlightened philosophy and the ideas of 1789 were increasingly silenced. Guizot, Cousin and others were dismissed. Faculties were closed and and then reopened, now staffed with clerics or clerical sympathizers who denied rationalism and asserted the traditional doctrines of Catholic submission and obedience to authority.[10] A generation raised in the Napoleonic *lycées*, in France and elsewhere, was appalled by this retreat, which seemed to cheat them. In Spain and the Italian states also, the universities became the centre of liberal debate and, as in the case of France, were persecuted and closed.

It was not only intellectual doors which seemed impenetrable. Actual opportunities of employment shrank in the post-war world. There was the obvious, if rather ambiguous, elimination of the opportunity for fame and social advancement through war itself, publicized after 1830 by Stendhal's hero Julien Sorel, in *Le Rouge et le Noir*. In addition career promotions in the legal and medical professions were checked, whether by reduced peacetime needs, or the preference given to right-wing candidates, or government intervention in the organization of the professions. In the emergencies of the war, Napoleon had encouraged the development of less qualified, rapidly trained army medical men, *officiers de santé*; and the attractions of fast and therefore much cheaper training meant that the numbers of *officiers* continued to grow in peacetime. The legal profession still smarted under the reorganization of the Revolutionary and Imperial years which sought, with some success, to reduce the judiciary's privileged independence from the state. There was also, in these years, an actual surplus of young men qualified for these professions. It is no coincidence that many of those who joined left-wing groups were law and medical students as well as qualified members of those professions.

What did the conspirators hope for? In the early years of the

Restoration the French were primarily Bonapartist. In Piedmont and Naples they demanded constitutional rule; and there the French constitution of 1814 attracted less emulation than the Spanish constitution of 1812, on which their Spanish counterparts also focused their own endeavours.

Portuguese liberalism was somewhat exceptional, as was Portugal itself. In 1814 it was ruled from Brazil by the Regent John (the queen Maria was permanently insane). The country had undergone some modernization in the previous half-century, under the dictatorial control of the king's minister, Pombal, who is traditionally included by historians among the enlightened despots. The power of the church, including the influential Inquisition, had been checked, and the Jesuits expelled. Some educational reform had been undertaken and Pombal had done battle with the dominant landed aristocratic elite. However in 1777, on the death of king Joseph and the succession of his daughter, Maria, Pombal had been forcibly retired by resurgent noble families who re-established their control. In 1792, when Maria retreated into insanity on the death of her husband, her son John took control. When Murat had led French troops into the peninsula in 1807, John moved the government of the Empire to Rio de Janeiro, reducing mainland Portugal almost to colonial status. He was reluctant to return in 1814.

In 1820, encouraged by unrest elsewhere, liberals in the Oporto garrison mutinied, but swore to join John if he would accept a liberal constitution. A *Cortes* was elected and a constitution on the Spanish model approved. The powers of the nobility and of the Catholic Church were reduced, including those of the Inquisition. John returned and promised to abide by the constitution, but two years later the entry of the French into Spain encouraged conservatives to push it aside. Liberal army officers turned to John's son, Dom Miquel, who promised to restore a constitutional regime. In Brazil John's elder son, Peter, agreed to head an independent Brazil as a constitutional king. The situation became more complicated when Peter returned to Portugal. By 1830 Portugal was in the midst of civil war between the rival royal factions.[11]

The economic climate of post-war western Europe added a popular dimension to criticism of newly restored regimes. Three interlinked factors can be noted. Short-term commercial and industrial setbacks were a direct consequence of the ending of the war and the absence of government strategies. Production declined in key industries such as textiles and the metallurgical trades as fewer uniforms and weapons were required. Large numbers of demobilized soldiers searched for jobs in a shrinking market. These problems were accompanied by harvest failures in 1816 and 1817, the accidental consequences of bad weather. To these short-term factors should be added the impact of long-term structural change. The onslaught on surviving feudal institutions which had been intensified by the French Revolutionary armies and their allies in conquered territory not only 'liberated' peasants from the payment of feudal dues (often rewritten into new leases later), but also, in the name of liberty, with the enthusiastic connivance of the richer peasants, assaulted communal rights and property. The right to pasture animals on land owned by the local commune, to gather timber from communal forests for a multitude of vital uses, was reduced and often eliminated as the richer peasants competed to buy communal land. The Revolution, vaunted as a triumph for the peasant, turned into a disaster for the majority of the rural poor.

The less well-off artisans, rural and urban, likewise suffered as Revolutionary 'liberal' legislation continued to erode guild structures and obliged workers to carry a work book. Technical changes were even more damaging for the independence of the artisanate. Factory developments were few, but technological progress eroded independence. In the silk industry the Jacquard loom (1808), which wove the elaborate brocaded silks fashionable in these years, was not only beyond the resources of most master weavers in silk towns like Lyon, but necessitated workshops with high ceilings, very different from the traditional locations in central Lyon between the two main rivers. Weavers had to borrow from silk merchants to buy the machines and rent new lodgings in the suburb of Croix Rousse. Merchants took on the role of protocapitalists, increasingly able to dictate not only the price of the raw silk they sold the craftsmen, but also the price they were prepared to pay him for the finished goods.[12]

Similar phenomena were present in other trades, though less visible than in the silk industry where production was concentrated in one of the four large cities of France. In the cotton industry the number of rural weavers had increased for more than a generation as technical change in weaving machines had been much slower than in accompanying spinning activities. Spinning became concentrated in factories, while rural domestic weaving had expanded. In these post-war years weaving machines began to be installed in factories too and hand loom weavers joined those who suffered from the impact of the early industrial revolution. Like the silk weavers of Lyon, they did not accept their loss of livelihood quietly. Tailors were another group prone to demonstrate. For them the problem centred around the growth of the 'ready-made' side of the trade. Garments were cut out in the traditional craft workshop, but the sewing was 'put-out' to less skilled and lowly paid women workers. Both the pride and the pocket of the journeymen tailors were hurt and they became an important element in Parisian unrest in particular.[13]

The coincidence of short- and long-term factors provoked widespread popular protest in 1816 and 1817 as shortages and high food prices were accompanied by reduced rates of pay and hours and by actual unemployment. Governments responded by protectionist commercial strategies, refused to abolish indirect taxes and continued to encourage the erosion of communal rights, which did not help. They also used troops to control demonstrations, which did not add to their own popularity. We know little about the motives of marchers and demonstrators. Sometimes the official who wrote the gendarmerie report or kept the record of a trial would note cries of 'Long live Napoleon' or 'Long live the Republic' or attach a subversive, scrawled, handwritten poster to his report. It would depend on what angle would serve his own career prospects best when the report was read by a superior in Paris. There were only limited direct links between elite and popular grievances. In larger towns like Lyon, artisans took an interest in political issues and popular Bonapartism grew. However in general the legacy of the 1790s was to make the elites suspicious and fearful of popular demonstrations, rural and urban.

It was the success of the ultras in France which provoked the growth and unity of elite liberal opposition. In February 1820 the duc de Berri, designated to succeed the already elderly comte d'Artois to the throne, was murdered. At the time of his death he was childless, which would have called into question the survival of the dynasty. Fortunately, at the end of the year but within a respectable number of months, his widow produced Henri, the miracle child as he was called by enthusiasts. Ultras blamed liberals for de Berri's death and urged a tightening of the political system. Since it was generally assumed that the very wealthy were the most conservative, a law of the double vote was passed. The richest quarter of voters were given a second vote in parliamentary elections in special departmental electoral colleges, two for each department.

The first reaction of liberals was to retreat into conspiracy. A number of the *Amis de la Verité* lodge fled to Naples after their violent protest against the law of the double vote. Two of their leading members, Buchez and Joubert, returned with the idea of forming *carbonari* cells in France. The French *charbonnerie*, as it was called, quickly grew, absorbing the *Chevaliers de la liberté*, and attracting up to 60,000 supporters in sixty departments, especially in the east. Its membership was similar to that of earlier conspiratorial groups and its structure labyrinthine and masonic. Members committed themselves to an altruistic primitive Christianity and expressed a romantic, subversive loyalty to Napoleon, and after his death to vaguely republican sentiments. Members had to provide themselves with weapons for a future seizure of power. Between 1820 and 1822 *charbonnerie* groups in a number of key garrison towns, where junior officers had been drawn into membership, tried to launch rebellions. These were invariably stillborn, partly because of the number of members who were fifth-columnist government spies.[14]

If it were not documented that substantial numbers of the local liberal elites supported the *charbonnerie*, it would be tempting to assume that the organization was mainly the product of the frenzied anti-revolutionary persecution mania of the ultras. Yet it did exist, and was the crucible for many future republicans and socialists, as well as Orleanists. Towards the end of 1822, however, its activities were much reduced, perhaps because of government intervention and persecution; the leaders of several abortive *charbonnerie* military conspiracies were tried and executed. In addition the bored soldiery were found something to do, ironically suppressing liberal aspirations in Spain. More positively, liberal opinion began to focus on legal means to express disgust with the Restoration. Former members of the French *charbonnerie* were attracted to Saint-Simon's ideas for the reorganization of the state. Some became journalists writing for the successful liberal papers. Many began to concentrate on parliament, besieged by renewed ultra attacks.

Alarmed by the scale of popular protest during the economic

crisis, restored regimes feared that popular and elite protest were linked. In 1820 there were revolts to try to restore constitutions eliminated in 1814 in Spain, Portugal and the kingdom of the Two Sicilies. In 1821 there were risings in Piedmont and Greece too. The restored rulers had no intention of sharing power through elected assemblies with deposed elites, but in both Italy and Spain they generally lacked adequate loyal troops to re-establish their authority. The Great Powers had promised to maintain the settlement of 1814. They responded by gathering in congress at Troppau (1820) where Metternich successfully urged joint intervention and sanction for anti-revolutionary measures. At Laibach (1821) they supported Austrian intervention to prop up the conservative regime of the kingdom of the Two Sicilies. A year later at Verona they were to sanction French intervention to suppress the liberal rising in Spain which began in 1820.

In January 1820 a tiny group of junior officers in Andalusia, in concert with others, led by Colonel Quiroga and Major Riego, 'pronounced' in favour of the 1812 constitution. This time they were successful, partly because so many junior officers were reluctant to fight the hopeless battle to recapture the Americas. However they remained a small group. Their temporary triumph was mainly due to the failure of the monarchy to suppress scattered liberal military risings in Galicia and elsewhere in the following weeks, at a time when the vast majority of the army remained loyal to the regime. In March a 'junta' in Madrid, dominated by Riego, obliged the king to appoint a constitutional government, although the military had little respect for civilian liberals. Other 'juntas' sprang up. Until the summer of 1820, when the *Cortes* finally met, Spain was in the hands of these ad hoc provincial committees.

The basic lines of conflict within Spanish liberalism, between moderates and radicals, were familiar Europe-wide. Spanish liberals were divided by provincial and ideological loyalties. Richer property-owners wanted a moderate strategy, urban radicals favoured democracy. The moderates were Catholics who were aware of the power of the church and cautious in their dealings with it, while the radicals were anti-clericals keen to expel the religious orders.[15] The moderates were mostly exiles or men imprisoned at the Restoration. There were two main groups among the moderates. Those who had helped to make the 1812 constitution believed that they had limited the king too much and hoped that Ferdinand could be conciliated by some modest extension of his powers. They were strongly influenced by the British example. Others, with basically not dissimilar moderate views, had collaborated with the French, in the hope of thus protecting Spain, and of course their careers. They were regarded as traitors after 1814 by other moderates. The radicals, on the other hand, were kept out of office because they would not compromise on the 1812 constitution. They tried to enlist popular support by backing such issues as the abolition of indirect taxes, which were spontaneously declared illegal in 1820.

The success of the 1820 liberal revolt was seriously jeopardized by conflict between moderates and radicals, while the king manoeuvred to try to defeat both groups. During 1821 the radicals were in the ascendant in provincial risings in areas like Galicia which were unwilling to accept dictates from Madrid. The radicals secured a majority in the newly elected *Cortes*, while the king appointed moderate ministers.

In July 1822 the Royal Guard regiments in Madrid attempted to seize power, apparently with the blessing of the king, though this was not entirely clear. By now the king was a disappointment to royalists as well as to liberals and a thoroughly anarchic situation had developed in the provinces where the troops and the civilian militia were engaged in rooting out royalists. The king was obliged to change his moderate ministers for radicals, freemasons and military men, and the government effectively became a military dictatorship. Royalists were even more divided than liberals. Some wanted to dispose of Ferdinand and make the heir to the throne, his brother Don Carlos, king. The majority dreamt of a king in tandem with Spain's 'ancient constitution'; like counter-revolutionaries in France they thus hoped to dispose of the liberals and those monarchists who wanted royal despotism. Others were inclined to welcome French intervention to restore royal power, perhaps with a constitution like that of Bourbon France.

In the early months of 1823 the last solution seemed the most likely. Ferdinand, expecting the arrival of French troops, dismissed his radical ministers. He then found that these, with the popular backing which they always courted, were able to depose him and set up a Regency. In April French troops arrived and liberal army officers were quick to join them to protect their own careers. Ferdinand was restored as an absolute despot by the

French occupying forces. The army was virtually dissolved, but liberals were retained as bureaucrats to supervise an expanding economy, which however failed to solve the crown's persistent poverty. It was royalists more than liberals who were disillusioned with the restoration of royal power and plots to replace the king with his brother continued. The first Carlist revolt, undertaken without Don Carlos's support, occurred in Catalonia in 1827.[16]

In the Italian peninsula the years 1820–1 witnessed a series of revolts, which usually centred on the *carbonari* or similar secret formations. These risings habitually involved a section of the elite, sometimes within the army, men who had either served the Napoleonic regime and lost their jobs in 1814 and/or those who had conspired against Napoleon. These representatives of the landed elite were anxious to oblige rulers imposed in 1814 to grant constitutions. Their ideal was sometimes either the 1812 constitution in Naples or Spain, or the French Bourbon constitution of 1814. These liberal elites were internally divided between moderates and democrats, sometimes called radicals, who sought popular elections and humanitarian measures to help the impoverished. The poor, both artisans and peasants, were the real shock troops. The mainspring of their repeated popular protests during much of the nineteenth century was economic and defensive. Peasants sought to protect their livelihood by trying to preserve communal institutions under attack in the sale of communal land.

In Naples the 1820 liberal revolt was launched in July by military and civilian *carbonari* units led by a priest. A section of the army, under the command of General Pepe, a former officer in Murat's army, deserted. There was widespread support for the movement, including the landowning middle class, peasants and urban artisans. In less than a week the king had adopted a constitution and named his son Francis regent. The constitution was modelled on that of Spain. The salt tax, universally detested, was abolished, decentralization decreed and universal suffrage declared. As in Spain, liberals were divided between democrats, who had the upper hand at first, and moderates, including former members of Murat's ruling elite, who actually headed the new government. Popular demonstrations and floods of reform petitions reinforced the democratic position, but the Murattians, backed by the landowning elite, controlled the bureaucracy and the army and had a powerful voice in the new assembly. They were nervous of popular intervention and preferred the centralized system that had operated under Napoleon. On the other hand there was strong humanitarian pressure within the assembly from middle-class deputies, including landowners, professional men, merchants and civil servants. These middle-class landowners spoke up in favour of peasant demands for the preservation of communal rights, the main motive force in peasant support for the liberal movement. Despite their obvious divisions, the liberals were convinced that the monarchy would respect the constitution which had been adopted and took few precautions for its military defence. There was no attempt to reinforce and develop the army, despite threats of Austrian intervention to restore the king's full powers. In March 1821 General Pepe was easily defeated by an Austrian army and the liberal revolt collapsed.

A fortnight after the revolt in Naples in 1820, there was a spontaneous rising in Palermo, whose shock-troops were artisans and whose beneficiaries were the local nobility. The latter were anxious to profit from conflict in Naples by asserting their separatist claims for Sicilian independence. They had no interest in Italian nationalism. Divisions within the movement were obvious from the outset. The provisional government included barons and middle-class separatists, men who had led the attempt to introduce a constitution in 1812–14. The artisans, organized in seventy-two still-influential guild corporations, demanded the adoption of the Spanish, not the Sicilian constitution of 1812, as well as the ending of conscription and a veto for the guilds in future decisions. The witch's brew of rival liberal claims was even more explosively contradictory than elsewhere: independence from Naples with not one but two constitutional proposals, the defence of the traditional corporate guild privileges, and popular demands for the abolition of indirect taxes, which led to tax offices being burnt. There was little support in the rest of Sicily for the Palermo revolt. The liberals in the capital tried to force other areas to join them. Unsurprisingly, when the Neapolitan government sent troops to the island, they found more allies than enemies.

The Piedmontese liberal revolt of 1820 was preoccupied with Italian as well as constitutional issues, but cripplingly divided between moderates and radicals. Moderates like Balbo hoped to persuade the king of the wisdom of granting a constitution. Others, including a group of young noble army officers who had been active in the Napoleonic regime, preferred to press the claims of the heir to the throne, Charles Albert, himself a veteran of the Bonapartist administration. Victor Emmanuel was persuaded to grant a constitution, but the situation was distorted by the proximity of Austrian troops and the constant threat of invasion to restore the king's full powers. Liberal nobles in the army urged a *pronunciamiento* reminiscent of Spain, and support for a Spanish-rather than a French-style constitution grew. The violent suppression of a harmless student demonstration by aristocratic officers widened the gap between democrats and those who wanted an elitist constitution as a prelude to Piedmont leading a movement to unify Italy.

In March 1821 democratic army and civilian *carbonari* units in Alessandria formed a provisional government and proclaimed the 'Spanish' constitution. An almost exclusively military insurrection spread to the main towns of Piedmont, although some sections in the army remained loyal to the king. Victor Emmanuel resigned, appointing Charles Albert regent for the new king, Charles Felix. Although some of the *carbonari* units talked of a popular uprising, there was very little mass support. Divisions within the army grew and Austrian troops were able to squash the constitutional pretensions of the rebels with the loss of only ten men.

The intensity of subsequent repression varied from state to state. In Lombardy there were four mass trials of over ninety members of the *carbonari* and other secret groups. Some notable leaders were arrested, others fled abroad. Nearly half of those charged received death sentences and although these were commuted, the resulting jail sentences were prolonged. A similar show trial was organized in Piedmont. The accused were wealthy notables and most fled abroad. Death sentences totalled ninety-seven, but ninety of these were passed *in absentia*. In the Papal States *carbonari* plots had not matured in 1820, but 500 members were arrested. In Naples there was a purge in all departments of government, including the army and judiciary, which seriously weakened royal control. The *carbonari* split up and took on new forms, often allying with brigand gangs to avoid persecution. Many of the better-off members fled into exile. Over 1,000 Italians, mostly Neapolitans, but including some Piedmontese, joined Spanish liberals to fight for their constitution in 1823.

In France too the right seemed to be in the ascendant. Charles X came to the throne in 1824. The 1824 Chamber of Deputies was overwhelmingly royalist, including more than a hundred members of the ultra *Congrégation* and no more than forty liberals, only nine of whom had been elected in the special double vote constituencies. The right, itself divided over many issues, began to believe that constitutional government could be used to its advantage. A law was quickly passed which abolished annual elections in favour of a general election every seven years. To the disgust of the liberals the triumphant royalist chamber also protected its own future by insisting that the statute could be applied retrospectively. A law of indemnification followed in 1825 which offered compensation for those whose lands had been sequestrated and sold during their emigration in the 1790s. A statute about sacrilege was also passed which made profanation of the host and other anti-clerical outrages in churches punishable by death. Finally in 1825 Charles was crowned with amazing and anachronistic Romantic splendour in Rheims cathedral. There seemed to be no end to the ultra-royalist revival.

Until this wave of ultra-inspired legislation, liberals (or doctrinaires as they were often called) were a diffuse and divided element. They were enthusiasts for the 1814 constitution, but so too were the majority of centrist royalists. The liberals were sympathetic towards the 1789 Revolution, although they were in disagreement about what it had signified. However, the resurgence of ultra-royalism provided liberals with unity and a platform. The defence of parliament became a major issue. Previously their minority position in the Chamber had made parliamentary opposition to legislation which nibbled away at the 1814 constitution ineffective. Liberals had doubted the impartiality of prefects in elections. They began to accumulate incontrovertible proof that prefects were cheating on a large scale. Many liberals were being left off electoral lists. The electorate fell from around 110,000 in 1817 to less than 79,000 ten years later. It was assumed that the Paris-appointed prefects would favour royalist candidates, but liberals discovered that these officials were doing so to the point of dishonestly returning royalists as deputies and forging election results.[17]

The realization that such deception was nation-wide eventually provoked liberals to unite. In 1827 they formed *Aide-toi, le ciel t'aidera*, under the leadership of the renowned academic François Guizot. Its aim was to inform prospective electors of how to ensure that their names appeared on electoral lists and how to oblige prefects to conduct elections fairly and return accurate results.

With a steering committee in Paris, small *Aide-toi* committees were formed throughout France. The prospect of a general election only once in seven years made regular and proper checks on electoral lists necessary. Royalists also were alarmed at the scale of corruption and fudging. In 1827 legislation was passed to provide for the regular annual revision of electoral lists. *Aide-toi* published short, informative pamphlets explaining how to furnish the prefect with evidence of eligibility and ensure that one's name appeared on the list. In some departments lists grew by 40 per cent as a direct consequence and nationally reached over 90,000 within the year. *Aide-toi* also checked election results and took prefects to court if irregularity was suspected. Ten prefects were successfully prosecuted and elections annulled after the 1827 election.

Aide-toi did not break the law, it affirmed it. Many of its members were themselves lawyers. Its creation gave an unprecedented unity and identity to liberalism. Other factors helped. Both the sacrilege and the indemnification legislation helped to alarm and unite those to whom the Revolution's land settlement and affirmation of a lay state were precious. The centre-right chief minister, Villèle, in office since 1822, noting the stridency of the liberals and their successes in a number of by-elections, decided to hold a general election in November 1827. France acquired its first hung parliament, with some 160–80 royalists, an equal number of liberals, and some 60–80 ultras. Villèle resigned in early 1828.

Charles accepted the results of the election, and in conformity with established practice tried to choose ministers who could work with the new assembly. He selected a moderate royalist, Martignac, as chief minister and made the liberal leader Royer-Collard president of the Chamber of Deputies. Martignac seemed inclined to conciliate the liberals. He banned the Jesuits, held parliamentary enquiries into the problems of France's depressed industries and introduced legislation to extend the principle of election to local councils. Liberal victories in a number of by-elections forced by *Aide-toi* seemed to confirm their triumph.

Liberals seemed to be making headway elsewhere. The Greek revolt against their Turkish overlords made progress, no longer hindered by the united opposition of the Great Powers, and with the moral and poetic support of the artistic intelligentsia of Britain led by Byron. Buonarroti, who had been forced out of Switzerland in 1823 with his hopes for a European brotherhood of secret societies in fragments, had established himself in Belgium. He began to reconstruct his insurrectionary brotherhood. To rally his supporters, he brought out in 1828 through a Brussels publisher his recollections of Babeuf's 'Conspiracy of the Equals' (1796). In it he also reprinted the Jacobin democratic constitution of 1793, which had never been implemented, and urged the case for an insurrection in the name of the people.

In France, meanwhile, although the strength of the liberals in the Chamber increased with almost every by-election and reached well over 220 by 1830, the optimism of the Martignac government was not sustained. Martignac's plan for elected local councils, which liberals and ultras both wanted, was offered with an electorate limited to the quarter most rich, which suited only the ultras. Liberal criticism was so pronounced that the king withdrew the bill forthwith. Martignac then turned to the economic crisis, instituting wide-ranging government enquiries into the problems of the wine and iron industries. The effect was to increase tension and popular protest. Petitions were circulated for the abolition of the indirect taxes on wine and in some quarters demands were made for changes in tariff policies. Emphasis was laid on government culpability in the crisis. Tariffs were blamed for the high price of bread and for the depressed state of some industries, especially wine and silk.

The lengthy and inconclusive debates in parliament did not help either the government's reputation or the economic situation. The crisis caused liberal unity to evaporate. Liberals in wine and silk areas wanted to reduce tariffs, in the hope of encouraging other countries to follow suit, thus reviving the export trade in their products. Liberal ironmasters and other textile producers were generally anxious to maintain high protective tariffs, to keep out cheaper British textiles and metallurgical goods. Liberals were as worried as were royalists at the acceleration of popular unrest. Government came to a standstill and in the summer of 1829 Martignac resigned. The king, unaware that the liberals were in disagreement, was persuaded that their lively and popular newspapers and their electoral committees represented the threat of instability, even of revolution. He could not countenance a liberal government and thus broke with tradition and appointed ultraroyalists, including his close associate the prince de Polignac. In November 1829, Polignac was made chief minister. Liberal unity blossomed once more.[18]

Fearful that the Chamber of Deputies would not approve his

choice, the king delayed the opening of the parliamentary session, which should have resumed in December. In their committees and newspapers liberals spoke with one voice in opposition to the choice of Polignac and in defence of parliament. They organized petitions to refuse to pay taxes until parliament resumed. In March 1830 the delayed session opened, to be prorogued instantly by an angry king when the Chamber voted an unprecedented motion of no confidence in his government. In May 1830 parliament was dissolved and elections were held in June and July 1830. Liberal representation rose to 274.

Why had the king called an election which Polignac could not win? He refused to consider a liberal government, but hesitated how to proceed. Finally he was persuaded, or convinced himself, that the liberals posed a sufficient threat to the security of the country and the king that the constitution itself offered a way out. He was allowed to issue decree laws in an emergency. On 26 July four decree laws or ordinances appeared. The first banned the liberal newspapers; the second dissolved parliament before it could meet; the third reduced the electorate to the quarter most rich; and the fourth called new elections.

When the ordinances were published in *Le Moniteur* on Monday 27 July the liberal response was divided. The eighty or so liberal deputies, who had houses in central Paris, met together in each other's homes to discuss how to live with the decrees. The liberal journalists met and, with their livelihood threatened, published a protest claiming that the constitution did not allow the king to make law in this way, because there was no emergency. However some of the most influential papers decided to obey the first ordinance and did not publish.[19]

Open defiance came not from the beleaguered liberal elite, but on the streets. The economic crisis had made Parisian streets the focus for the protests of artisans for nearly three years. Unfortunately for the king his ordinances added newspaper workers to the crowds on a day when traditionally workers took an extra day off to recover from the week-end. Worse still for the security of the king, busy with his whist-game at his distant palace of St Cloud, the artisan quarters of central Paris were the immediate neighbours both of the newspaper industry and the centre of government. Most disastrous of all, his military commander Marmont could call on no more than 6,000 troops at a time to defend the capital. The civilian militia, the National Guard, which might have been deployed in crowd control, had been dissolved by the king in 1827, suspected of liberal disloyalty.

Protest marches quickly grew into barricades and fighting in the Three Glorious Days of the July Revolution which followed. Disillusioned and outnumbered soldiers deserted behind the safety of the barricades. National Guardsmen donned their uniforms and took the side of the protesters. The liberals, fearful at first of popular protest so close to their own front doors, gained confidence. A group of them marched to the Hôtel-de-Ville, traditional hub of insurrection, and declared a provisional government, initially just for Paris. Even the liberal deputies finally committed themselves and on 30 July accepted the journalists' suggestion that the king's cousin, the duke of Orleans, be asked to head the state. In the first week of August Charles was officially deposed and a crown of 'the French people' successfully offered to his cousin by the self-assembled parliament, suitably flanked by National Guardsmen. The constitution was reissued in a modestly revised form and the 1830 Revolution seemed over. In truth it was not, and both popular ferment and quarrels over the nature and direction of government persisted, certainly until the Lyon revolt of 1834, but since this volume must conclude in 1830, the case for revolution will have to rest with the creation of the July Monarchy.

The French example was a model for those with constitutional and liberal aspirations. The Belgians, encouraged by French left-wing liberals, and ultimately by the British and French governments, rose against the Dutch masters imposed on them in 1814. The Poles too revolted against their Russian overlords. The Belgians were able to put together an independent nation-state, the Poles relapsed under Russian control. Italian-exiled *carbonari*, promised support by republicans like Buonarroti in France, plotted the unification of the peninsula. In February 1831 a rising in Modena was followed by others in the Papal States. Harsh repression in Naples and Piedmont prevented unrest spreading. The internecine and unrealistic squabbles of the exiles and the modest and very localized expectations of the actual rebels, plus the intervention of Austrian troops in Bologna and elsewhere, ruined any chance of victory.[20]

Spanish liberals in exile tried to push their case against an elderly king whose young wife had conveniently just had a child, in a strategy to disinherit Don Carlos. In September 1832 it was thought that Ferdinand was terminally ill. Don Carlos threatened civil war unless the queen renounced her infant daughter's claim to the throne. To side-step her brother-in-law's bullying, the queen (backed by Ferdinand, who recovered briefly) adopted a liberal government, amnestied up to 10,000 liberal exiles, purged the army and exiled Don Carlos himself.[21] While it would be wrong to claim that liberalism had triumphed in Spain by 1830, it would not be unreasonable to suggest that, for the moment, the chance of thoroughgoing counter-revolution had been eliminated.

However, 1830 is by no means a terminal date in the history of either elite or popular protest, as the events of 1848 in Europe (not to mention 1851 and 1871 in France) were to show. Man is the inventor of time divisions – and students of history are perhaps more captive than most. At one level, 1830 is merely a convenient point to end this volume. The revolts of 1848 closely resembled those of 1830 in many respects. Yet there were differences, which make the selection of 1830 as a guillotine credible because 1830 signalled changes among those who sought radical reform, political or socio-economic. These included both modifications to their approach and the development of new ideas and objectives.

Movements critical of existing regimes were more substantial after 1830 than before; the drive for parliamentary reform in Britain gave a lead. The republican clubs of the 1830s and the Banquet Campaign of 1847 in France, the support for the United Diet in Prussia in 1847, were mainly limited to a wealthy elite, but there was also some mass backing. Methods were also changing. Secret conspiratorial formations persisted. But after 1830 there was a greater emphasis on specific reform of existing institutions. The Banquet Campaign is a good example. (Such comparisons cannot be pushed far; *Aide-toi* also kept within the law.) The beginnings of cheaper newspapers, often produced as well as read by artisans, gave a specific direction, purpose and publicity to artisan associations and campaigns against taxation. Moderately priced weeklies, such as *Le Charivari*, illustrated with radical caricatures, added a stroke of humour which was widely appreciated. There was even the beginning of a feminist press in France.

Objectives and aspirations were also changing. Significantly, before 1830 there was no concerted campaign by the liberals to empower themselves by pressing for change; they merely tried to preserve existing institutions. In France republicanism, an amorphous sentiment since 1814, crystallized after 1830 into aspirations for political democracy and social reform. In Italy Mazzini formed Young Italy, to try to give specificity and direction to patriotic sentiment. Neither of these projects achieved much in material results, but both were indicative of greater definition of objectives. Equally significantly, and usually closely connected, socialist ideas began to develop as solutions to the perceived problems of urban and industrial change. A terminal date of 1830 is not just the choice of editors and crabby examiners!

NOTES

1   G. Procacci, *History of the Italian People* (London, 1970), pp.280–2.
2   J. Lynch, *Bourbon Spain* (Oxford, 1989).
3   R. Carr, *Spain 1808–1939* (Oxford, 1975).
4   R.J. Rath, 'The *carbonari*: their origins, initiation rites and aims', *American Historical Review*, 69 (1963), pp.353–70.
5   P.M. Pilbeam, *Republicanism in France 1814–1871* (London, 1994), ch.4.
6   'Buonarroti's notebook 1828', in D. Beales, *The Risorgimento and the Unification of Italy* (London, 1971), pp.124–8.
7   S. Woolf, *A History of Italy 1700–1860. The Social Constraints of Political Change* (London, 1979), p.252.
8   F.J. Coppa, *The Italian Wars of Independence* (London,1992), p.10.
9   H. Hearder, *Italy in the Age of the Risorgimento 1790–1870* (Harlow, 1986), p.178.
10   D.W. Johnson, *Guizot. Aspects of French History 1787–1874* (London, 1963), pp.119–22.
11   A.H. Oliveira Marques, *A History of Portugal* (New York, 1972).
12   R.J. Bezucha, *The Lyon Uprising of 1834* (Cambridge, Mass., 1974).
13   C.H. Johnson, 'Economic change and artisan discontent: the tailors' history, 1800–48', in R.D. Price, *Revolution and Reaction. 1848 and the Second French Republic* (London, 1975), pp.87–113.
14   A.B. Spitzer, *Old Hatreds and Young Hopes. The French Carbonari against the Bourbon Restoration* (Cambridge, 1971).
15   W.J. Callahan, *Church, Politics and Society in Spain, 1750–1874* (Cambridge, Mass., 1984).
16   A. Shubert, *A Social History of Modern Spain* (London, 1990) examines the background to these conflicts.
17   S. Kent, *The Election of 1827 in France* (Cambridge, Mass., 1975).
18   P.M. Pilbeam, *The 1830 Revolution in France* (London, 1991).
19   An excellent account of the revolution in Paris in D.H. Pinkney, *The French Revolution of 1830* (Princeton, 1972).
20   C.H. Church, *Europe in 1830* (London, 1983).
21   R. Carr, *Spain 1808–1939* (Oxford, 1975), pp.129–54.

FURTHER READING

Studies which look at aspects of more than one country include J.M. Roberts, *The Mythology of the Secret Societies* (London, 1972) and C.H. Church, *Europe in 1830* (London, 1983). R.S. Alexander explores *Bonapartism and the Revolutionary Tradition in France. The Fédérés of 1815* to good effect (Cambridge, 1991). A.B. Spitzer, *Old Hatreds and Young Hopes. The French Carbonari against the Bourbon Restoration* (Cambridge, 1971) is a fascinating account of secret societies in France. D. Pinkney, *The French Revolution of 1830* (Princeton, 1972) focuses on Paris while P.M. Pilbeam, *The 1830 Revolution in France* (London, 1991) considers a regional and broader chronological span. There are useful essays in J. Merriman (ed.) *1830 in France* (London, 1975), while the early chapters of P.M. Pilbeam, *Republicanism in France, 1814–71* (London, 1994) evaluate the nature of republicanism after the failure of the First Republic.

For works on Italy, Portugal and Spain see the notes on Further Reading at the end of Chapter 6.

Chapter 8

The challenge of industrialization

Colin Heywood

Contemporaries observed the first stirrings of industrialization in Europe with some trepidation. The dilemma they faced was whether or not to grab the tail of the tiger. At one extreme stood those who were swept along by the vision of a dynamic new society. Nikolai Ivanovich Korsakov, a young Russian army officer, was one of a stream of foreign visitors who came to the industrial centres of Britain to see what the future might hold. His journal from the 1770s reveals his firm conviction that a glorious destiny awaited Russia, which his knowledge of British technology could help shape.[1] At the other extreme were those alarmed by the abrasiveness and inhumanity that seemed to go hand in hand with the spectacular creation of wealth in the industrial regions. During the 1820s, the conservative and very Catholic comte Alban de Villeneuve-Bargemont made great play of his discovery that in Lille, at the heart of one of the richest agricultural and industrial departments in France, nearly half the population was deemed to be in poverty.[2] There was, then, an awareness that industrialization involved rather more than an upheaval in the economic sphere: it also called into question the established social order, and introduced a new factor into the struggle between the Great Powers. Most people were probably ambivalent in their attitude to what was sometimes known as the 'English political and industrial system', being caught between the desire for material improvement and a yearning for stability. The challenge they faced was to adapt as best they could to the changing order around them.

Historians in their turn face a number of challenges when studying the economic history of the period. They need to be clear in their understanding of terms such as industrial revolution, industrialization and economic growth. They must choose between the traditional view that continental nations imitated the British model of an industrial revolution, and the more recent suggestion that the first shoots of industrialization appeared in various parts of Europe during the eighteenth century. They must also confront issues such as the extent to which industrialization had its origins in the countryside, the appropriateness of state-of-the-art technology for less developed economies, and the role of the state in promoting development. Finally, they can hardly avoid pondering the question of how far the new wealth being created during the early stages of industrialization trickled down to the mass of the population.

The temptation now is to caricature much of the early writing on the 'industrial revolution' period in Europe. Supposedly there was a relatively short and feverish period of activity in Britain during the late eighteenth and early nineteenth centuries, which brought a whole new world dominated by factories, canals, commercial farms, banks and international trading houses. Foreigners then attempted to apply this blueprint to their own economies. One or two did very well (the Belgians, and later the Germans); a few others made a rather modest go of it (the French, for example) and the majority were hopelessly backward for much of the nineteenth century. Elements of this picture still survive, but a number of new orthodoxies have emerged over the last few years to challenge the old ones.[3] What recent research has brought to light is the diversity of paths to development in Europe. As a result, historians have become increasingly sceptical when confronted with any attempt to outline a universal pattern to industrialization. The stages-of-growth model proposed by Rostow is the most famous casualty of this reorientation. There is also an awareness that the British industrial revolution had in effect been elevated to a 'paradigm', with the industrialization of other nations assessed according to how closely they conformed to it. No one disputes that some countries developed more rapidly than others. Bairoch finds that between 1750 and 1830 manufacturing output rose by a factor of seven in the United Kingdom, but elsewhere, 'with the exceptions of Switzerland, Belgium and to a much lesser extent, France, the growth rate of industrial output did no more than parallel population growth' (see Table 8.1). Where historians have changed their perspective is in becoming wary of suggesting that the British path to industrialization was superior to that of other nations. The so-called followers are now perceived to have adopted their own paths, in accordance with the resources available to them, and their individual legal, political and cultural traditions. For example, the very gradual (and much-maligned) French pattern has been reassessed as a 'humane' or 'unobtrusive' one; its Austrian counterpart as a case of 'leisurely' or 'persistent' economic growth.

Table 8.1 Per capita levels of industrialization, 1750–1830 (UK in 1900 = 100; triennial annual averages)

	1750	1800	1830
Austria-Hungary	7	7	8
Belgium	9	10	14
France	9	9	12
Germany	8	8	9
Italy	8	8	8
Russia	6	6	7
Spain	7	7	8
Sweden	7	8	9
Switzerland	7	10	16
United Kingdom	10	16	25
Europe	8	8	11

Source: P. Bairoch, 'International industrialization levels from 1750 to 1870', Journal of European Economic History, 11 (1982), Table 9, p.294.
Notes: 'Level of industrialization' means here the per capita volume of industrial production.
  Geographical boundaries are those at the dates given (Belgium, Italy and Germany refer to the boundaries at the time of political unification).

There are ways of avoiding the anglocentrism implicit in the term 'industrial revolution', not to mention its general fuzziness, though it must be said that they create problems of their own. One is to trace the onset of modern economic growth in the various nations of Europe, using a sustained and substantial rise in per capita product as the key indicator. Unfortunately, the scarcity of reliable data before the middle of the nineteenth century limits the scope of any survey in this area. Paul Bairoch prudently declines to calculate rates of economic growth between 1800 and 1830 from his estimates of GNP in Europe, depriving us of the most obvious way of comparing the performances of the various economies. None the less, we may note in passing some of the findings of recent 'cliometric' studies. First, they suggest that growth rates in the British economy during the classic 'industrial revolution' period were far more modest and gradual than was once thought.[4] Second, they provide evidence that the continental economies were generating a certain momentum of their own by the late eighteenth century. Bairoch calculates that by 1800 per capita incomes in continental Europe had risen to a level that was nearly a third above the average for African and Asian countries starting to industrialize in the middle of the twentieth century. As might be expected, there were considerable disparities between the various countries, the impetus to growth being more evident in western than in eastern Europe (see Table 8.2). Also, we should never lose sight of the fragile basis of these statistics: Bairoch cheerfully admits to a margin of error in the range of 20 to 30 per cent! All the same, the result has been to play down the discontinuities in European economic growth, which earlier notions of a 'great spurt' or of a 'take-off' implied, presenting instead a long-drawn-out process with its roots deep in the eighteenth century.

Table 8.2 Volume of per capita Gross National Product at market prices by regions, 1800–30 (in 1960 US dollars and prices: three-year annual averages)

	1800	*1830*
Total Europe	199	240
Western Europe	213	276
Nordic countries	193	210
Russia, Romania, Bulgaria	170	171
Mediterranean countries	203	259

Source: P. Bairoch, 'Europe's Gross National Product: 1800–1975', *Journal of European Economic History*, 5 (1976), Table 2, p.279.

At this point, we might feel entitled to ask why, if the industrial revolution was so much less dramatic than we had been led to believe, was there so much 'wonder and astonishment'[5] during the early nineteenth century? The answer, of course, is that the most spectacular changes were confined to a handful of localities: around Manchester, Birmingham, Liège, Mulhouse, Elberfeld, Brno and so on. Even when discussing Britain, in the middle of the nineteenth century, historians talk in terms of small islands of modern industrialization surrounded by a sea of pre-industrial sectors; east of the Elbe, a few corks bobbing in the ocean might be a more appropriate image. Over the short term, these isolated centres of innovation could make little impact on the huge aggregates of national income statistics – as Berg and Hudson put it, there could be 'radical change with limited growth'.[6] There are advantages, therefore, to narrowing the focus from the national to the local level, and from the broad canvas of modern economic growth to the more restricted process of industrialization. The latter is an ambiguous term. On the one hand it can mean the general shift from an agrarian economy to one based more on manufacturing and the services. On the other, it can be understood as a change in the character of industry itself, summed up by John Hicks as an 'increase in the range and variety of the fixed capital goods in which investment was embodied'.[7] That is to say, the simple tools of the craftsman were replaced by the large-scale plant and numerous types of machinery of modern industry. As for the local perspective, Sidney Pollard argues that for many purposes we should abandon our usual notions of a series of separate 'industrial revolutions' occurring within national borders. He notes that any map of industrialization during the nineteenth century would have to take the form of dots spattered across the continent. One group ran through northern France and Belgium, Rhineland-Westphalia, Alsace and parts of Switzerland. Another, to the east, covered parts of Saxony, Bohemia and Silesia. Hence he proposes 'treating the whole of Europe as one single macro-development area', with the interrelationships between the developing regions a central preoccupation. The limitations of this approach have been well rehearsed. Data on inputs and outputs are usually hard to assemble at this level; and many legal, political and even cultural influences on industrialization operate within national boundaries. These have not prevented it influencing recent historiography in Britain and abroad.

In sum, any assessment of economic change in the classic 'industrial revolution' period needs to strike a balance between conflicting influences. It is bound to imply a degree of unity by applying terms such as economic growth or industrialization to a number of countries. At the same time, it must highlight differences, given that we cannot draw up a timetable of development for an economy, in the way that we can, say, for a child. It will want to convey the momentous nature of the changes under way. Yet it can hardly avoid emphasizing the gradual nature of the transition from 'traditional' to 'modern' forms during the eighteenth and nineteenth centuries. Such considerations lead us to begin by considering the industrialization of Europe within a regional framework, along the lines suggested by Pollard, noting first the changes already under way by the 1780s, and second those more in evidence after that date. Subsequently we must revert to the national level, in order to take into account the political influences which loomed so large during the extended period of revolution and warfare between 1789 and 1815.

By the second half of the eighteenth century there were various signs of change in the economy – though where the main sources of dynamism should be sought remains a matter of controversy. One possibility is that the initial impetus towards industrialization came from an apparent backwater: the domestic workshops of the countryside. Historians have long been aware of rural industry, but recently the phenomenon has occupied centre stage after being hi-jacked, so to speak, by 'proto-industrialization' theorists.[8] They can point to its pervasive influence in early modern Europe, particularly in the north and the west of the continent and in the textile industries. The spectacular growth of cottage industries in various regions can also be documented around our period. In Flanders, in the *Châtellenie du Vieuxbourg*, for example, the number of hand looms producing linen cloth nearly doubled (from 4,976 to 8,868) between 1730 and 1792. Similarly, in Normandy, in the Pays de Caux, the total of 20,000 cottage weavers in 1780 had rocketed to 103,000 by 1810. The original schema from historians had, on the one side, merchants in the towns eager to escape from the constraints of a relatively inelastic local labour market and guild regulation; and, on the other, it had peasants in the least fertile agricultural areas desperate to escape from poverty and seasonal unemployment. The outcome was a form of industry that could be distinguished both from traditional village handicrafts and from the modern factory system. Its products were no longer bartered or sold locally: cotton cloth from Normandy was sold in the West Indies; linen from Silesia was sent to Holland, England and Spain, and from there on to their colonies. It encouraged a degree of regional specialization along lines of comparative advantage: to take the classic example, the interior of Flanders took up industrial work, while the more fertile maritime strip developed a commercial form of agriculture. And yet it remained firmly embedded in the routines of agrarian life, particularly as the villagers almost invariably continued to work part time on the land. From the late eighteenth century onwards, the system slowly buckled under the weight of rapidly mounting costs. None the less, this phase of 'proto-industrialization' allegedly facilitated industrialization proper, bequeathing a legacy of capital in the hands of merchant-entrepreneurs, commercial and mechanical skills, and a market for agricultural goods.

The theory has given important insights into the continuities of industrial development over the course of the eighteenth and nineteenth centuries – within a regional framework of analysis.[9] The flurry of research it launched into rural industry tended if anything to reinforce the impression of widespread restlessness and dynamism in eighteenth-century Europe. For example, local studies revealed cottage industry spreading into fertile regions dominated by large-scale cereal farming, such as East Anglia and the Pays de Caux, as well as to areas of subsistence agriculture. The theory could also be adapted to a variety of social and institutional contexts: to the semi-feudal environment of certain regions east of the Elbe (such as Silesia) as well as to the more emancipated west. (How far it can be extended to accommodate urban crafts and various forms of centralized production remains a moot point.) Yet while some historians were working to enlarge the scope of proto-industrial theory, others came to doubt its explanatory value. It proved most vulnerable as a further example of a stage theory whose claims to universality appeared in the end to be based on a – highly ingenious – generalization from a narrow range of examples. We might accept that in a number of regions there were links between what Mendels calls 'phase 1 and phase 2' of industrialization. Unfortunately, the model is of little help in predicting which ones will manage the transition successfully and which will fail. The recent inclination is to assert that, more often than not, rural industry proved a dead end. The logic here is that regions which had laboriously built up expertise in the low-level technologies and peculiar forms of organization associated with cottage industry might, for that very reason, be ill equipped to cope with the factory system. Bavaria, for example, has been portrayed as a region that was slow to industrialize during the nineteenth century because its population settled complacently into a self-sufficient way of life that combined peasant farming with rural handicrafts.[10] Areas of 'deindustrialization' during our period include Devonshire, Brittany, Hesse, East Westphalia and Württemberg. The implication, of course, is that the continuities between rural industry and the factory system have been much exaggerated by proto-industrial theory.

Seeking a more balanced view, historians have begun to consider other forms of industrial organization that came through from the early modern period. The communities of artisans in the towns may well have been less of an obstacle to innovation than the proto-industrialization model suggests. Michael Sonenscher has recently demonstrated the complex division of labour that had emerged in the urban trades of eighteenth-century France, and the relatively open character of their guilds.[11] As we shall see, industrialization would rely on skilled workers brought up in this tradition, as well as on semi-skilled machine operatives from outside it. The 'manufactory' or 'proto-factory' also had a claim to be considered as a 'carrier of progress'.[12] Proto-industrialization theory by no means ignores this form of production, but the stress on cottage industry risks underestimating its importance. There is no need to espouse a much older strand in the historiography which saw the manufactories of the eighteenth century paving the way for the factories of the nineteenth. Nevertheless, 'proto-factories' provide examples of development based on a concentration of labour, extensive investments in plant and raw materials, and relatively sophisticated technology. Some, such as silk mills in Bologna, the Lyonnais and Zurich, or the calico-printing works of numerous cities (London, Amsterdam, Mulhouse, Rouen, Ghent, Barcelona, Prague) operated in tandem with domestic workshops, leading to the *Gemengelage* (conglomeration) characteristic of many regions. Others, such as the ironworks of the Urals or the deep coal mines of the Borinage area in Flanders, stood apart from 'proto-industrial' forms.

In sum, there is plenty of evidence of economic change occurring on a broad front in parts of Europe by the late eighteenth century. The most clearly visible symptom was the expansion in the countryside of domestic industries orientated to distant markets. Complementing that was the more qualitative contribution from the towns, based on their skilled trades, their manufactories and their national and international commercial networks. There was also the shift towards a commercial form of agriculture in a number of regions to take into account, since it underpinned these early stages of industrialization. The fragmentary nature of the data available makes it all but impossible to measure the scale of change in these various spheres. Yet historians do not doubt the steady momentum being gained by the European economy at the beginning of our period. Few can resist a passing reference to the possibility that large areas of the continent might have continued to evolve along these lines for some time. What intervened to complicate matters was, needless to say, the pioneering of new technology in the industrial regions of Britain, and the shift to a more capital-intensive form of production. Heightened competition from this quarter forced the pace of change everywhere.

'Borrowing' technology from foreign countries was a well-established practice by the late eighteenth century. British manufacturers had in the past attempted to wrest trade secrets from more successful rivals. However, for several decades they became the principal targets of industrial espionage. Once it was clear that the Boultons, Arkwrights, Wedgwoods and others had taken a lead in their various fields, competitors from abroad rushed in to learn about the new techniques – by fair means or foul. Efforts by the innovators to distinguish between *bona fide* customers and industrial spies often met with failure. Similarly, the official policy of banning the emigration of skilled artisans and the export of unlicensed machinery from Britain proved difficult to enforce (the laws were finally repealed in 1825 and 1842 respectively). The villains of the piece, as far as the British were concerned, ranged from the aristocratic Freiherr vom Stein, acutely embarrassed when caught 'pirating' plans and parts of a Boulton and Watt steam engine for his masters in Prussia, to the Irish prisoner of war who helped construct an improved loom for muslin weaving in the French town of Tarare during the 1790s.[13] In short, access to new technical knowledge was not necessarily easy, especially during the Revolutionary and Napoleonic Wars, but somehow the flow of plans, machinery and technicians to the continent was always maintained. Crompton's mule was being manufactured in Paris ten years after its invention in 1779; Cockerill's firm at Seraing claimed a lag of only a few days before new inventions in engineering came their way during the 1830s. The British influence on industrial development was plain for all to see. Besides the ubiquitous machines, technicians and workers, there were several distinguished entrepreneurs with a British background, including the Holkers in Normandy, Heywood and Dixon in Alsace, the Cockerills in Flanders (and also in Berlin and Aachen) and Edward Thomas in Bohemia. Rouen became known as 'the Manchester of France'; Brno, in Moravia, 'the Manchester of central Europe'; by the 1840s, there was even a 'Russian Manchester', the small town of Ivanovo, in Vladimir province.

Does this mean that 'the industrialization of Europe took place on the British model'?[14] The dangers of such an assumption should be evident by now. Only those in government on the continent would be inclined to think in the national terms this implies. They might well contemplate encouraging industrial development along British lines to strengthen their military capability and their role in power politics. Inevitably, though, they would have to adapt any notion of a British model to local circumstances. The Habsburg Monarchy during the early nineteenth century, for example, was acutely aware that a policy of rapid modernization would alienate its main sources of support in the aristocracy, the Catholic Church, the army and the bureaucracy. If we return to the regional perspective, we can accept that continental entrepreneurs were eager to copy technology and institutions that they studied in, say, Lancashire or the West Midlands. However, they frequently discovered that technology introduced to solve British problems was not necessarily appropriate for their own enterprises: any transfers would require a complex process of 'creative adaptation', taking into account local factor prices, resource endowments, consumer tastes and labour relations.[15] Coke-smelting of iron provides the outstanding case here: although known to continental ironmasters from the 1780s onwards, they needed a long period of trial and error before they could put it on a profitable footing. Hence, the existence on the continent of water frames, blast furnaces and steam engines identical in appearance to those operating in Britain should not mislead us into thinking that the followers were set on a similar pattern of industrialization. Each region would have to develop at its own pace, and with its own mix of specialized industries, technologies and forms of business organization.

In some regions, it was the similarities to the British experience that stood out, notably in that cluster of regions in the Nord and Pas-de-Calais departments of France, and in the Sambre-Meuse and the Scheldt river valleys of modern-day Belgium. They harboured most of the industries that were in the forefront of development across the Channel, including coal, iron, engineering and textiles. Moreover, they were among the first to invest heavily in the type of machinery and plant pioneered by the British. There was, for example, the mushrooming of mechanized cotton spinning in Ghent and wool spinning in Verviers during the early nineteenth century; the diffusion of coke-smelting around Liège and Charleroi from the 1820s; and the steady encroachment of large-scale capitalist enterprise in the various coal fields. Other regions went in a very different direction: in Alsace, we find an example of 'upstream' development, as opposed to the 'downstream' development perceived (by Lévy-Leboyer at least) in Lancashire.[16] That is to say, entrepreneurs started by investing in a finishing process, calico-printing, and then integrated into semi-manufactures: the weaving and spinning of cotton. A similar reverse process has been noted in the central industrial region of Russia, around Moscow, where the printing and finishing of cottons preceded the diffusion of mechanized spinning during the 1830s. A further option, very different from the classic view of British industrialization, though in fact characteristic of development in Sheffield and Birmingham, involved the mechanization of handicraft production. This meant providing sophisticated versions of artisan tools for use by skilled labour on a wide range of tasks. The Jacquard loom, finally perfected in Lyon during the 1800s, provides the classic example of this 'flexible specialization'.[17] Its system of perforated cards made possible a reduction in the cost of weaving fancy silks, which enhanced the capacity of the Lyonnais industry to create new markets for its high quality range of goods. It was also compatible with a dispersed industrial structure, the small workshops of the famous *canuts* being well able to respond quickly to changes in fashion. Swiss weavers from St Gallen quickly adapted the Jacquard loom to cottons, and went on to invent their own improvements to the hand loom during the 1830s.

Everywhere in Europe, though in varying degrees, there was a coexistence of 'traditional' and 'modern' industrial forms. Sometimes the two competed with each other. During the 1800s, for example, the domestic workshops of thousands of women hand spinners in Normandy, Picardy and Flanders rivalled the water frames and mules of the cotton and woollen mills. In similar fashion, the 'archaic' method of charcoal-smelting managed to retain a firm foothold in the market well after 1830 in the Rhineland, Silesia, Lorraine and even in the Sambre-Meuse region, despite the pressure from coke-fired blast furnaces. More commonly, the old and the new engaged in a symbiotic relationship. The typical industrial region of the early nineteenth century contained a network of large- and small-scale workshops which produced goods by means of an extensive division of labour. Change can then be seen as limited to a steady grafting of the factory system on to the 'conglomerations' inherited from the past. The textile industries provide a host of examples, with their long list of preparatory, spinning, weaving and finishing processes, all of which developed at different periods across the regions. Thus in the woollen industry of Bohemia, centred on the Liberec district, carding and spinning was almost entirely mechanized by 1830; weaving remained firmly in the hands of guild craftsmen; the odd shearing machine had made its appearance, without undermining the artisanal character of this trade; and fulling was still monopolized by traditional manufactories. One result of this very gradual transition to the factory system was that increases in labour productivity were steady rather than spectacular – or so the fragmentary evidence available suggests. In Verviers (near Liège), fixed capital per worker in the woollen industry increased from 286 francs in 1780–5 to 3,286 francs in 1845–50, largely because of the mechanization of spinning; but output per worker only grew from 3.1 to 9.3 pieces over the same period, reflecting the dominance of hand loom weaving.[18]

The question that remains to be asked is why some regions in Europe were more successful than others in exploiting new technologies. The general context of a 'Gefälle', or developmental gradient, running from the north and west of the continent to the south and east, should be borne in mind (see Map 4). In the core regions of western Europe we assume that conditions were generally ripe for industrialization, but as one moves to the periphery, they became less and less promising. Following the 'regional–local' approach, the causes for any such disparities must be sought on the supply rather than on the demand side. To begin with, a couple of hoary old chestnuts need to be put into proper perspective. The first is that mineral resources were a decisive influence: Coal was King. Some of the early starters on the path to industrialization, such as Lancashire, the Sambre-Meuse region and Silesia, were indeed located on the coal fields. This factor has

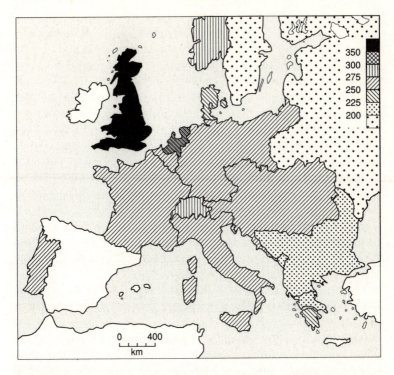

Map 4 European Gross National Product per head, *c.*1830. (The units are 1960 US dollars.)

Source: N.J.G. Pounds, *An Historical Geography of Europe, 1800–1914* (Cambridge, 1985), p.30.

returned to prominence in some of the recent literature. O'Brien noted that cheap energy from the abundant supplies of coal was 'beginning to reappear as Britain's most significant comparative advantage'.[19] It can be overplayed, none the less. Not all industries were equally affected: basic metallurgy and glass were more dependent than textiles, for example. Local supplies of both coal and iron ore certainly allowed iron industries in Charleroi and in the area around St Etienne (in the Loire department of France) to surge forward with new techniques during the 1820s, while traditional centres such as Alpine Austria, Bohemia and the Urals, denied easy access to coal by high transport costs, suffered a declining share of world markets. Yet even in these latter cases, the relative abundance of timber caused charcoal-smelting to remain more efficient economically than it would have been for their British counterparts. Thus Alpine Austria and Bohemia managed to increase their iron production by 4 to 5 per cent a year between 1815 and 1848 without a major change in technology. It was in fact entirely possible to launch the whole process of industrialization with minimal inputs of coal. The textile industries of Alsace, Lyon and the Swiss industrial region provide outstanding examples. Fuel accounted for a very modest share of total costs (the estimate in the Ghent cotton industry was 4.7 per cent during the 1830s), so that water power was a viable alternative, not to mention improved handicraft techniques.

The second 'chestnut' to consider is that certain regions were propelled along by dynamic business leadership. The archetype here would be the Protestant industrialists of Alsace and the Rhineland, with their dedication to success in business. In stark contrast was the Russian merchant of the early nineteenth century: 'bearded, patriarchal, semi-Asiatic in dress and manner, and fully versed in the arts of haggling and swindling', he resolutely clung to his 'obscurantist cultural tradition'.[20] To support this line there is a school of thought which raises entrepreneurship to the status of an independent variable in economic development, and Weber's famous thesis on the role of the 'Protestant ethic' in business. Yet it can be countered that a basic human desire to maximize one's gains will ensure that entrepreneurs will always appear when circumstances are favourable to development. Thus, in western Europe, long experience of a market economy prepared the ground for the emergence of industrial entrepreneurs during the eighteenth century. The alleged superiority of Protestant over Catholic business leaders can also be called into question, given the successful industrialization of, *inter alia*, Flanders, the Lyonnais and Alpine Austria. What we can safely point to is the prominent role of various religious and national minorities in business, including Protestant bankers in Paris, German textile manufacturers in Bohemia, and the Old Believers in the industrial communities of Moscow.

This leaves us with capital and labour, the two pillars of the emerging industrial society. The availability of venture capital might appear a key influence on regional development, given the increasing importance of fixed capital in modern industry. Cotton spinners in Zurich and calico-printers in Alsace undoubtedly benefited from ready access to the Swiss banking network when investing in new technology, while enclaves of industry in Bohemia or central Russia always struggled with an acute shortage of capital. However, the tendency in recent research has again been to play down the advantages to be gained by some regions over others in this respect. The shift from labour to capital-intensive forms of production in industry was more gradual than was once thought: the common-sense notion that vast outlays were invariably required to set up coal mines, textile mills and blast furnaces proves misleading. In cotton spinning, the early machines were similar to those found in domestic workshops, buildings could be rented, and it was not difficult to add new equipment as and when resources permitted. Somewhere between 10,000 and 50,000 francs (£400–£2,000) was generally sufficient to start a mill in Alsace during the early nineteenth century – not a daunting sum for an affluent bourgeoisie. In the iron industry, investment was 'lumpier', yet the costs of fuel and iron ore still outweighed those on plant: as in the textile industries, entrepreneurs could hope to rely on commercial credit to cover their short-term expenses, and then finance their longer-term expansion from retained profits. The Fourchambault ironworks (in the Nivernais) provides an outstanding example, as it increased its fixed capital from 800,000 to 4 million francs (£32,000–£160,000) by the system of *autofinance* between 1824 and 1835.[21] Savings in those substantial areas of western Europe with a long commercial and industrial tradition were presumably adequate to cope with this level of investment. Arguably the financial sector might have done more to channel savings to industry in some areas: Cameron implies that regions such as Normandy and French Flanders were 'imperfectly' served by the myriads of local private bankers in operation. A more common assumption would be that if banks were thin on the ground in the new industrial areas, this merely reflected the limited demands made on their services by entrepreneurs. On the whole, the informal networks of families, friends and business associates were all that were needed to mobilize capital for industry during the early stages of industrialization.

As for labour, we should think in terms of its varying skills and aptitudes, which influenced the character of industrialization in different localities. Variables included literacy, craft skills, a willingness to submit to factory discipline and freedom from feudal obligations. Literacy was less important as an influence on industrialization in the nineteenth than in the twentieth century. Below a modest threshold of literacy, development was severely constrained, the obvious example being the industrial regions of the Russian Empire, which suffered from a completely illiterate labour force. However, at the opposite end of the spectrum, widespread literacy in much of Scandinavia was not yet associated with industrialization. Leading industrial regions such as Lancashire and French Flanders could proceed with very average literacy levels by the standards of northern and western Europe.[22] More important than the formal education of the schools was the informal education young people received in their homes, in their local communities and in the workshops. J.R. Harris has demonstrated the difficulties experienced by labour (and management) when technology imported from abroad required craft skills that were alien to their traditions. Typically, managers at the famous Saint Gobain works attempting to copy British techniques for melting glass with coal during the late eighteenth century discovered that the craft skills of a furnaceman, which were taken for granted across the Channel, had to be laboriously explained to French workers – and the experiment had to be abandoned.[23] The industrial populations of continental industrial areas were often impressive in their ability to master over a short period 'coal-fuel technology' and engineering skills that had been built up over decades in Britain. Machine-building industries appearing before 1830 included those of Paris, Liège, Zurich, Wetter (in Westphalia) and Brno, for example. In this they were of course helped by their own craft traditions. Even so, for most of the nineteenth century they could never match British levels of labour productivity in basic industries such as cotton spinning and pig iron manufacture. Hence, they were often conspicuously successful in branches of industry where the British technological lead was less in evidence, or non-existent. At the lowest level of industrialization, they could import British yarns or pig iron and work them up with cheap labour in the countryside, as occurred in the cotton weaving industries centred on the Swiss textile towns and Moscow. A more sophisticated approach was to rely on the skill and inventiveness of craft labour, a strategy applied in the silk industries of Lyon and Krefeld, the metalworking trades of St Etienne and Solingen, and in the calico-printing works of Alsace.

In sum, the drift of the argument here has been to cast doubts on any suggestion that Britain had an overwhelming advantage in her factor endowment. It emerges that several regions in western Europe at least had access to cheap energy and raw materials, plus populations long accustomed to industrial and commercial activity. Hence they were well able to adapt new technologies to their own needs, given time for the laborious process of 'learning by doing'. We should recall at this stage that the model of industrialization within a regional framework necessarily plays down one further influence: that of the state. Pollard asserts that in any case during the early stages of industrialization governments were 'at best irrelevant', and overall more likely to be a hindrance than a help. Why might this be?

With half an eye on the experience of the 'first industrial nation', we might suppose that the ideal during our period would be for governments to restrict themselves to acting as policemen. That is to say, they would hold the ring for private enterprise, by defending the realm, maintaining law and order, and guaranteeing the currency, but in general they would not intervene in economic and social affairs. The assumption is that the impetus for change would have to come from the working of market forces. In this perspective, the British can be depicted as a veritable 'nation of shopkeepers', their businesses flourishing in the absence of oppressive interference from bureaucrats – and the grandiose follies of a Napoleon. However, contemporary observers were quick to point out that commercial interests in Britain only campaigned for *laissez-faire* policies after their governments had helped them build up an unassailable position in world markets. Historians in their turn have begun to nuance the contrast between market-based development in Britain and *dirigisme* on the continent. They have recognized the paradox that governments often made their most useful contribution to industrialization when they were attempting to achieve something else. On the one hand, British governments were particularly successful at creating a favourable environment for enterprise, being remarkably aggressive as 'policemen' in building a nation and carving out a world empire. Although the underlying motivation here was the pursuit of power, there were important spin-offs for commercial and industrial expansion. Their main rivals, the French, were less successful in this sphere, and the further east we move, the more there was a need for reforming governments to compromise with powerful vested interests in agrarian society. On the other hand, the British were less inclined than other nations to use the resources of the state to invest in social overhead capital (such as roads, canals and technical education), or to subsidize activities likely to bring long-term benefits for the economy. This type of state intervention could encourage rather than stifle private enterprise, particularly in less developed economies in a hurry to catch up with the leading industrial nations. There remained the problem of distinguishing projects with a long-term future on the market from those tainted by corruption, over-optimism and incompetence.

Let us begin with what Immanuel Wallerstein calls the 'Franco–British struggle for hegemony of the world economy': a struggle fought on the economic, political and military fronts, and decided in favour of the British by 1815. He considers the Seven Years' War a turning point, with victories in the colonies of India (1757) and Canada (1762) giving the British an edge over the French in overseas markets, and exposing the parlous state of French government finances. There is no disputing that, by 1780, Britain was a nation with settled frontiers, a legal and institutional framework favourable to business, a massive commercial centre in London and a formidable navy to protect its trading interests. France was not far behind, but a determined bid to catch up with the British during the Revolutionary and Napoleonic periods was ultimately unsuccessful.[24] The idea that the French Revolution of 1789 brought a wholesale shift from a feudal to a capitalist system is now out of fashion. What it did have to its credit was a series of measures (some of which were begun under the ancien regime) that were essential for further industrialization, including the liberalization of internal trade, the abolition of guilds, reform of the tax system and standardization of weights and measures around the metric and decimal systems. On the debit side, the agrarian reforms of the Revolution may have reinforced the position of a determinedly anti-capitalist group, in the shape of small peasant farmers. However, it is by no means clear that these reforms were an obstacle to industrialization: according to a recent estimate, only 10 per cent of the land was sold as *biens nationaux* (and less than half of that went to the peasants), and the inefficiency of small farms in, say, wine production or stock rearing cannot be taken for granted. Overall, the Revolution was neither the 'national catastrophe' that its critics portray, nor a wholesale liberation of productive forces. François Hincker judiciously settles for a 'half-revolution' of society, with property rather than profit, savings rather than investment, still in the ascendant.

Going to war with the British and other reactionary powers

provided further opportunities for France to promote her own industrialization. The exclusion of British competition gave her entrepreneurs breathing space to experiment with new technologies, above all in mechanized cotton spinning: the number of mills rose from 6 in 1789 to 272 in 1815. Not all of these 'hot-house' creations survived the final crises of the Empire and the return to peacetime trading conditions, but they did allow a surge of industrial development in the north and east of the country. However the costs of war were high, in terms of lost markets, shortages of labour and raw materials, and the disruption of investment: even in Britain progress was arguably slow because there were insufficient resources both to 'industrialize *and* fight'.[25] Most damaging of all for France was the dramatic decline of her maritime trade following the slave revolt of 1791 in Saint-Domingue (present-day Haiti) and the blockade of her Atlantic seaboard by the Royal Navy. At the peace in 1815 it was clear that she had been almost completely shouldered out of lucrative markets in the West Indies and Latin America by her British and American rivals. Failure on the naval front meant that her path to industrialization in the nineteenth century would be inward-looking to the continent rather than outward-looking to the Americas. Statistics for 1830 reveal that France remained a major trading power: if exports are

Table 8.3 Indicators of foreign trade around 1830 (in dollars)

	Total exports (millions of dollars)	Exports per capita	
		Dollars	Dollars per similar geographical unit
Austria-Hungary	31	1.1	1.3
Belgium	19	5.2	4.4
France	104	3.2	3.8
Germany	105	3.6	4.1
Italy	(50)	(2.4)	(1.9)
Russia	52	0.8	1.3
Spain	15	1.1	1.1
Switzerland	(30)	(14.0)	(8.8)
United Kingdom	181	7.6	6.0
Europe (without Russia)	592	3.3	3.2

Source: Paul Bairoch, 'L'Economie française dans le contexte européen à la fin du XVIIIe siècle', *Revue économique*, 40 (1989), pp.939–64 (Table 6).
Note: Figures in brackets have a particularly high margin of error.

expressed in per capita terms, and some attempt is made to take into account size of population and access to the sea, her position was close to Belgium and Germany. However, she was no longer a close rival to Britain as an Atlantic power (see Table 8.3).

French influences spilled into neighbouring territories as the Revolutionary and Napoleonic regimes embroiled the rest of Europe in their struggles. Rondo Cameron goes as far as to suggest that the greater the sway of the French during the Revolutionary era, the more likely an area was to industrialize over the following decades.[26] There is no doubt that where a population was receptive to the ideas and institutions of the Revolution, as in Belgium and the Rhineland, French occupation could be a 'blessing' (initially at least), as remnants of the feudal regime were swept away.[27] By contrast, in Spain, the kingdom of Naples and the Grand Duchy of Warsaw, the old order was sufficiently resilient to withstand the introduction of revolutionary legislation under French 'protection'. The most that can be said is that the fierce reaction to foreign domination gave some impetus to nationalist feeling, which would eventually help produce a more appropriate social and political context for economic development. The redrawing of political boundaries and the disruptions of war also had some positive results for industrial development – even if the overall balance sheet was negative. Free access to French markets was a stimulus to coal-mining interests in the Borinage and to producers of fine woollens in Aachen; a respite from British competition permitted the launching of mechanized cotton spinning in Ghent, Saxony and Bohemia.[28] As in France, the bankruptcy of many of these enterprises around 1815 raises suspicions of a misallocation of resources, but the hardier breeds were able to sustain their initial impetus in the more bracing atmosphere of the 1820s. Revolutionary France was more of a negative influence on the regimes in central and eastern Europe: absolute monarchs tended to lose their taste for 'enlightened' reforms when feeling threatened by popular radicalism. In Russia, Catherine the Great (1762–96) first backtracked on her liberalization programme in the wake of the Pugachev rebellion, and subsequently she and her son Paul sealed off the country from all subversive influences; in the Habsburg Empire, attempts by Francis I to oppose large-scale enterprises and to fix the population on the land during the 1800s contrasted with the efforts of Joseph II and Leopold II to abolish serfdom and liberalize internal trade at the end of the eighteenth century. Prussian governments stand apart for their attempt at a constructive response to the challenge from across the Rhine. Defeat at Jena and Auerstedt in 1806 convinced ruling circles that fundamental change was necessary for military and political as well as for economic considerations. The first steps towards liberating the Prussian serfs in 1807 appeared promising for the formation of an industrial labour force but, in the event, the conditions imposed left the majority dependent on the landlords. The upshot was a compromise known as the 'Prussian way' to agrarian reform: large commercial farms became numerous east of the Elbe during the 1820s, but they were owned by the Junkers, and worked by semi-servile labour.

While historians generally accept that governments have a useful role to play in clearing away institutional obstacles to industrialization, they become uneasy when assessing more direct intervention in the economy to coax out a nervous investing class. There is no shortage of examples of costly fiascos in this area: pampered companies that went bankrupt, court favourites who supplanted more competent rivals, monopolies that went on for too long, heavy-handed protectionism, and so on. Many subsidized ventures turned out to be premature, such as ill-fated attempts by governments to promote mechanized cotton spinning in Saxony during the 1780s, coke-smelting in France during the same decade, and sugar beet production in Prussia during the 1800s. Others backed unworthy individuals, such as the nobles who received state-owned iron- and copper-works in the Urals at below market prices during the mid-eighteenth century (and quickly resold them at a profit), or the equally cynical merchant Boyer-Fonfrède, whose short-lived 'free industrial school' employed hundreds of pauper apprentices as cotton spinners in a former monastery at Toulouse during the 1800s. In all cases there was the risk that government support would go to sharp operators at court or in the bureaucracy, rather than to those with business acumen. Gwynne Lewis has recently documented the harsh fate that befell the energetic, though abrasive, entrepreneur Pierre-François Tubeuf in 1788, evicted from his coal mines at Alès after being outmanoeuvred at Versailles by the powerful marquis de Castries. However, the fact remains that the state could usefully intervene on the market in circumstances where private enterprise was reluctant to act. In general, as Alexander Gerschenkron has persuasively argued, it was the more backward nations who attempted in the nineteenth century to use the resources of the state to accelerate their industrialization.[29] Before 1830, for example, the Prussian state was impressive in its investment in engineering works, the subsidies it gave to artisans wishing to study abroad, its provision of elementary and technical education, and its campaign to form a German Customs Union (the *Zollverein*). It should be added that we risk distorting motives if we attribute all government policies in follower nations to the desire to catch up with the leaders: military considerations weighed heavily on subsidies to the metallurgical industries on the continent, and the desire to raise revenue independently of parliamentary influence will partly explain the formation of the *Zollverein*. The overall result was that in the German case, as opposed to the British or even the French, the state can be described as a 'critical factor' in facilitating and promoting industrialization.[30]

By 1830, then, there was a 'core' in western Europe that was beginning to industrialize, and a 'periphery' in Scandinavia, Iberia, the Italian states, the Balkans, the eastern part of the Habsburg Empire, and Russia, which had barely started. It is conceivable that the development in the west partly depended on keeping the rest of Europe backward, exploiting it as a source of cheap agricultural produce and raw materials. There was, for example, much bitterness between the two halves of the Habsburg Empire, the Hungarians resenting the policy of giving priority to industrialization in Austria. However, the disparities can partly be interpreted as a matter of specialization according to comparative advantage, with commercial farming interests in, say, Prussia, Pomerania and Hungary drawing some benefit from new outlets for their produce. Our inclination is to accept the intermediary position of Berend and Ránki on this issue, emphasizing the varied picture of 'successes and failures, partial-successes and half-hearted tries' in the responses on the periphery to the challenge of industrialization. If relationships between countries were potentially unequal, those between classes were possibly even more so. In the long run, the political and industrial revolutions of our period would do much to emancipate the people of Europe from servitude, ignorance and poverty. In the short term, though, we may doubt whether the early stages of industrialization did much for the mass of the population. In the east, including the Habsburg realms, serfdom continued to cast its shadow over agrarian society; and in the west, long hours and miserably low wages continued to blight the existence of most agricultural workers, 'peasant–artisans', labourers in the towns, and that new spectre for the nineteenth century, the dehumanized proletariat of the factory system. For what they are worth, studies of real wages of blue-collar workers indicate that, in Britain, there was only a modest increase before the 1820s; in France, there was some increase during the Revolutionary and Napoleonic periods, but subsequently (between around 1820 and 1850) stagnation or even decline; and in Belgium 'wages failed to rise significantly between 1819 and the mid-century'.[31] Thus, appropriately enough for a study in the economic sphere, we come to an end on a dismal note!

ACKNOWLEDGEMENTS

Thanks are due to Professor Stanley Chapman (University of Nottingham), Professor Roger Price (University of Aberystwyth) and Stuart Thompstone (University of Nottingham).

NOTES

1 A.G. Cross, *'By the Banks of the Thames'. Russians in Eighteenth Century Britain* (Newtonville, Mass., 1980), pp.175–85.

2 Alban de Villeneuve-Bargemont, *Économie politique chrétienne*, 3 vols (Paris, 1834), I, pp.16, 22.

3 This section is indebted to S. Pollard, 'Industrialization and the European economy', *Economic History Review*, 26 (1973), pp.636–48; R. Cameron, 'A new view of European industrialization', *Economic History Review*, 37 (1985), pp.1–23; and P.K. O'Brien, 'Do we have a typology for the study of European industrialization in the XIXth century?', *Journal of European Economic History*, 15 (1986), pp.291–333.

4 N.F.R. Crafts, *British Economic Growth during the Industrial Revolution* (Oxford, 1985), pp.44–7.

5 P. Colquhoun, *A Treatise on Wealth, Power and Resources of the British Empire* (London, 1815), p.68, cited by P. Hudson, *The Industrial Revolution* (London, 1992), pp.9–10.

6 M. Berg and P. Hudson, 'Rehabilitating the Industrial Revolution', *Economic History Review*, 45 (1992), pp.24–50 (p.35).

7 John Hicks, *A Theory of Economic History* (Oxford, 1969), p.143.

8 See F.F. Mendels, 'Proto-industrialization: the first phase of the industrialization process', *Journal of Economic History*, 32 (1972), pp.241–61; P. Kriedte, H. Medick, and J. Schlumbohm, *Industrialization before Industrialization* (Cambridge, 1981).

9 Surveys of the literature on proto-industrialization include L.A. Clarkson, *Proto-Industrialization: The First Phase of Industrialization?*

(London, 1985); and 'Proto-industrialization in Europe', a special issue of *Continuity and Change*, 8 (1993), edited by S. Ogilvy. More critical views in a European perspective can be found in R. Houston and K.D.M. Snell, 'Proto-industrialization? Cottage industry, social change, and industrial revolution', *Historical Journal*, 27 (1984), pp.473–92; and M. Berg (ed.) *Markets and Manufacture in Early Industrial Europe* (London, 1991).

10 See Eckart Schremmer, 'Proto-industrialization: A step towards industrialization?', *Journal of European Economic History*, 10 (1981), pp.653–70.

11 Michael Sonenscher, *Work and Wages: Natural Law, Politics and the Eighteenth-Century French Trades* (Cambridge, 1989).

12 S. Pollard, 'Regional markets and national development', in Berg, *op. cit.*, *Markets and Manufacture*, p.33.

13 Fritz Redlich, 'The leaders of the German steam-engine industry during the first hundred years', *Journal of Economic History*, 4 (1944), pp.125–6; W.O. Henderson, *Britain and Industrial Europe, 1750–1870* (Liverpool, 1954), p.26.

14 S. Pollard, *Peaceful Conquest: The Industrialization of Europe, 1760–1970* (Oxford, 1981), p.v. Note that this bald statement from Pollard appears to contradict his earlier call for a European perspective; see Cameron, *op. cit.*, 'European industrialization', pp.9–10.

15 A. Maddison, *Phases of Capitalist Development* (Oxford, 1982), p.108; O'Brien, *op. cit.*, 'Do we have a typology', p.294.

16 M. Lévy-Leboyer, 'Les processus d'industrialisation. Le cas de l'Angleterre et de la France', *Revue historique*, 239 (1968), pp.281–98.

17 See C.F. Sabel and J. Zeitlin, 'Historical alternatives to mass production: politics, markets and technology in nineteenth-century industrialization', *Past and Present*, 108 (1985), pp.133–76.

18 P. Lebrun, 'Croissance et industrialisation: l'expérience de l'industrie drapière verviétoise, 1750–1850', in *First International Conference of Economic History, Stockholm, 1960, Contributions* (Paris–The Hague, 1960), pp.531–68, cited by J. Mokyr, *Industrialization in the Low Countries, 1795–1850* (New Haven, Conn., 1976), p.43.

19 O'Brien, *op.cit.*, 'Do we have a typology', p.295, n.14. See also E.A. Wrigley, *Continuity, Chance and Change* (Cambridge, 1988), p.28.

20 T.C. Owen, *Capitalism and Politics in Russia* (New York, 1981), p.1, cited by W. Blackwell, 'The Russian entrepreneur in the Tsarist period: an overview', in G. Guroff and F.V. Carsten (eds) *Entrepreneurship in Imperial Russia and the Soviet Union* (Princeton, N.J., 1983), p.13, n.1.

21 Examples taken from M. Hau, *L'Industrialisation de l'Alsace* (Strasbourg, 1987), pp.327–35; and G. Thuillier, *Georges Dufaud et les débuts du grand capitalisme dans la metallurgie, en Nivernais, au XIXe siècle* (Paris, 1959), p.40.

22 See L.G. Sanberg, 'Ignorance, poverty and economic backwardness in the early stages of European industrialization', *Journal of European Economic History*, 11 (1982), pp.675–97.

23 J.R. Harris, 'St Gobain and Ravenhead', in B.M. Ratcliffe, *Great Britain and her World, 1750–1914* (Manchester, 1975), pp.27–70 (pp.54–6).

24 This section is indebted to F. Hincker, *La Révolution française et l'économie* (Paris, 1989) and 'Révolution de 1789, guerres et croissance économique', special issue of *Revue économique*, 40 (1989).

25 J.G. Williamson, 'Why was British industrial growth so slow during the Industrial Revolution?', *Journal of Economic History*, 44 (1984), pp.687–712 (p.689).

26 R. Cameron, *France and the Economic Development of Europe, 1800–1914* (Princeton, N.J., 1961), p.26.

27 H. Kisch, 'The impact of the French Revolution on the Lower Rhine textile districts – some comments on economic development and social change', *Economic History Review*, 25 (1962–3), pp.304–27.

28 See F. Crouzet, 'Wars, blockade, and economic change in Europe, 1792–1815', *Journal of Economic History*, 24 (1964), pp.567–88.

29 A. Gerschenkron, *Economic Backwardness in Historical Perspective* (Cambridge, Mass., 1962).

30 W.R. Lee (ed.), *German Industry and German Industrialization* (London, 1991), p.3.

31 See Crafts, *op.cit.*, *Economic Growth*, ch.5; F. Braudel and E. Labrousse (eds) *Histoire économique et sociale de la France*, vol.3, part 2 (Paris, 1976), pp.785–90; Mokyr, *op.cit.*, *Low Countries*, p.189.

FURTHER READING

Works in English on European economic history are now relatively abundant, though uneven in their coverage of the various nations and topics. Fortunately, there are plenty of excellent textbooks to give an overall view, including C.M. Cipolla (ed.) *The Fontana Economic History of Europe*, vols 3, 4/1 and 4/2 (London, 1973), A.S. Milward and S.B. Saul, *The Economic Development of Continental Europe, 1780–1870* (London, 1973), and S. Pollard, *Peaceful Conquest: The Industrialization of Europe, 1760–1970* (Oxford, 1981).

Other books with an impressive sweep to them are I. Wallerstein, *The Modern World-System III: The Second Era of Great Expansion of the Capitalist World-Economy, 1730s–1840s* (San Diego, 1989), J. Goodman and K. Honeyman, *Gainful Pursuits: The Making of Industrial Europe, 1600–1914* (London, 1988), and I.T. Berend and G. Ránki, *The European Periphery and Industrialization, 1780–1914* (Cambridge, 1982). For an interesting set of national studies, focused on the Gerschenkron thesis, there is R. Sylla and G. Toniolo (eds) *Patterns of European Industrialization: The Nineteenth Century* (London, 1991).

Studies with a national focus are not always easy to find. Useful examples covering the European core include P. Mathias, *The First Industrial Nation* (London, 1969), P. Hudson, *The Industrial Revolution* (London, 1992), J. Mokyr, *Industrialization in the Low Countries, 1795–1850* (New Haven, Conn., 1976), P. O'Brien and C. Keyder, *Economic Growth in Britain and France, 1780–1914* (London, 1978), R. Price, *An Economic History of Modern France, 1730–1914* (London, 1981), C. Heywood, *The Development of the French Economy, 1750–1914* (London, 1992), and M. Kitchen, *The*

Political Economy of Germany, 1815–1914 (London, 1978). Moving towards the periphery, Austria-Hungary is well covered by D.F. Good, *The Economic Rise of the Habsburg Empire, 1750–1914* (Berkeley, Cal., 1984), J. Komlos (ed.) *Economic Development in the Habsburg Monarchy in the Nineteenth Century: Essays* (Boulder, Col., 1983), J. Komlos (ed.) *Economic Development in the Habsburg Monarchy and in the Successor States: Essays* (Boulder, Col., 1990), J. Komlos, *The Habsburg Monarchy as a Customs Union: Economic Development in Austria-Hungary in the Nineteenth Century* (Princeton, N.J., 1983). Russia also has attracted plenty of attention from economic historians: W.L. Blackwell, *The Beginnings of Russian Industrialization, 1800–1860* (Princeton, N.J., 1968), M.E. Falkus, *The Industrialization of Russia, 1700–1914* (London, 1972), and A. Kahan, *The Plow, the Hammer and the Knout: An Economic History of Eighteenth-Century Russia* (Chicago, 1985).

There are a number of monographs which adopt a European framework, notably S. Ville, *Transport and the Development of the European Economy, 1750–1918* (London, 1990), R. Cameron *et al.*, *Banking in the Early Stages of Industrialization* (New York, 1967), W.H. McNeill, *The Pursuit of Power* (Chicago, 1982), and J. Mokyr, *The Lever of Riches* (Oxford, 1990). Concise surveys of the economic impact of the Revolutionary and Napoleonic regimes can be found in G. Lewis, *The French Revolution: Rethinking the Debate* (London, 1993), and L. Bergeron, *France under Napoleon* (Princeton, N.J., 1981). Finally, local studies provide an interesting point of entry, such as R. Tilly, *Financial Institutions and Industrialization in the Rhineland* (Madison, Wisc., 1966), G.L. Gullickson, *Spinners and Weavers of Auffay* (Cambridge, 1986), G. Lewis, *The Advent of Modern Capitalism in France, 1770–1840: The Contribution of Pierre-François Tubeuf* (Oxford, 1993), and J.K.J. Thomson, *A Distinctive Industrialization: Cotton in Barcelona, 1728–1832* (Cambridge, 1992).

Chapter 9

The growth of population

Colin Heywood

'This study is not for the faint-hearted,' wrote Thomas McKeown in 1976, admitting that there were no data to provide conclusive support for his interpretation of the modern rise of population – and events were to prove him right. Recent commentators on his 'classic' work have described it as facile, inconsistent, inaccurate and 'a *tour de force* of reasoning by exclusion'.[1] Investigating population history in the late eighteenth and early nineteenth centuries is indeed a hazardous business, given the rarity of census material and the slow emergence of national systems for the registration of births, marriages and deaths. Yet this period straddled Europe's 'initial population explosion', a critical turning point in demographic history when the spasmodic growth of earlier centuries gradually gave way to a sustained increase in numbers. To varying degrees across the continent, it witnessed improved life expectancy, couples marrying earlier than in the past, and even an early resort to contraception within marriage. Needless to say, the very gradual nature of change in this field makes the isolation of any span of fifty years a somewhat arbitrary procedure. We must therefore keep in mind the long-term perspective, notably the famous 'demographic transition' from high to low birth and death rates. This chapter begins on relatively safe ground, outlining the growth of population in Europe, some contemporary reactions to it, and recent developments in historical demography. The remainder will seek explanations for the rise in numbers, partly in terms of what may be called proximate causes (changes in fertility and mortality), and partly from influences in society at large.

By present-day standards in the Third World, the population

'explosion' of the late eighteenth and nineteenth centuries looks rather tame – mercifully so, it might be added. However, compared to earlier periods of growth, the doubling of the population in Europe between 1750 and 1850, from an estimated 146 millions to 288 millions, was impressive. These figures imply an average growth rate of 0.7 per cent a year, which may be contrasted with the 0.2 per cent a year recorded in the early modern period (1600–1750).[2] This surge of growth was by no means evenly distributed across the continent. We should bear in mind some difficulty in giving precise details on the orders of magnitude here, given the slow emergence of reliable census material. Sweden led the way, with the first national census in 1749, but other countries did not follow suit until the nineteenth century: Britain and France in 1801, Belgium in 1829, and so on. Historians therefore have to rely on reconstructions for earlier periods, and these can prove to rest on shaky foundations. The 'best estimate' for the population of France on the eve of the French Revolution of 1789 has recently been raised from 25 or 26 millions to 28.1 millions![3] In the case of much of southern and eastern Europe, there is some quantitative evidence to work on, such as the *revizii* of 'male souls' in eighteenth-century Russia, but historians have been reluctant to estimate total population from such data. We can at least note from Table 9.1 the considerable disparities between countries: during the first half of the nineteenth century, for example, the English population almost doubled in size, while the French only increased by one-third (see also Map 5). Differences between the countries of Europe are assumed to have been particularly in evidence towards the end of our period. Between 1750 and 1790, growth rates were generally modest, in the order of 0.5 per cent a year. The Revolutionary and Napoleonic Wars checked growth on the continent, with French losses, for example, being put as high as 1.4 million at this period.[4] In the British Isles, meanwhile, the increases continued, paving the way for a peak in the English growth rate of 1.5 per cent a year between 1811 and 1821. The end of the wars allowed a resurgence of population growth everywhere, with Scandinavia, the Netherlands and Germany probably matching English rates. Some slowing of growth became evident during the 1830s. The exceptional position of France was fully exposed at this point, as her rate dipped below 0.5 per cent a year.

Table 9.1 Total population of Europe by country, 1750–1850 (in millions)

	1750	*1800*	*1850*
England	5.8	8.7	16.7
Austria-Hungary	5.7	7.9	12.9
Russia	35.0	49.0	79.0
Belgium	2.2	2.9	4.4
Germany	17.0	24.5	34.4
Sweden	1.8	2.3	3.5
Switzerland	1.3	1.7	2.4
Spain	8.9	10.5	15.0
France	21.7	27.0	35.8
Italy	15.3	17.8	24.0

Sources: Jan de Vries, *European Urbanization, 1500–1800* (London, 1984), p.36; J.-N. Biraben, 'Essai sur l'evolution du nombre des hommes', *Population*, 34 (1979), p.16.
Note: Estimates for Russia are based on the boundaries of the former USSR.

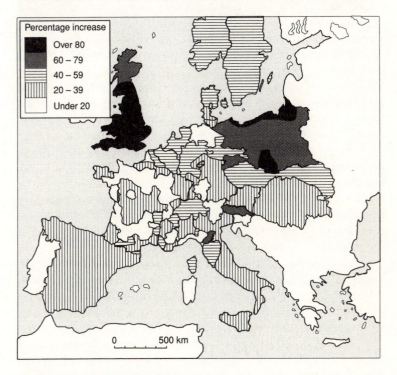

Map 5 Percentage population growth in Europe during the first half of the nineteenth century
Source: N.J.G. Pounds, *An Historical Geography of Europe, 1500–1840* (Cambridge, 1979), p.317.

Besides an increase in numbers, the late eighteenth and early nineteenth centuries also witnessed considerable migrations of population. In particular we should bear in mind the impact of migrationary movements from rural to urban areas. According to Jan de Vries, with the exception of Britain, the massive urbanization characteristic of modern society only began in earnest around the middle of the nineteenth century. He suggests that the years between 1750 and 1850 brought the final phase of 'premodern urbanization'. The salient features of this period were a steady acceleration in the pace of urban expansion and the exceptional dynamism of the smaller towns (in the range of 10,000–19,900 inhabitants). Underlying this pattern of growth was the emergence of factory towns, and the stimulus to small marketing centres from the rise of commercial agriculture.[5] Such developments had important implications for natural movements of population. Towns at this stage still had an unenviable reputation as 'consumers of people', given that their death rates tended to be higher than those of the surrounding villages, and their fertility lower.

Contemporary opinion often revealed itself to be remarkably ill informed on the population changes occurring around it, assuming stability or fearing depopulation in the midst of a rise. Among the more perspicacious, there was a considerable divergence of opinion on the implications of a rise in population. The French revolutionaries of the 1790s were typical of one well-established school of thought in being triumphantly 'populationist'. They considered large numbers a sign of strength, not least for the defence of 'la patrie'. Their assumption was that scientific and technical progress would generate sufficient resources to support the extra numbers. The Revolutionary leader Condorcet, for example, asserted optimistically that 'nature puts no limits on our hopes'. Should living standards be threatened at some far-off date, it was his belief that an obvious solution lay at hand, in the form of birth control.[6] Such arguments provoked a notoriously pessimistic riposte from Robert Malthus. His *Essay on the Principle of Population* was first published in 1798, and much expanded (after a fact-finding trip to the continent) in 1803. It continued another tradition in European thought which was concerned to counter the dangers of overpopulation. The *Essay* opened with the assertion, fundamental to his whole thesis, that 'The tendency for all animated life is to increase beyond the nourishment provided for it.' To provide a dramatic illustration of the point, Malthus used his mathematical training to set up a simple model, revolving around two contrasting progressions. On the one hand, he argued from the north American experience that 'Population when un-checked goes on doubling itself every twenty-five years, or increases in a geometrical ratio.' On the other hand, because of what is now known as the law of diminishing returns, the means of subsistence 'could not possibly be made to increase faster than in an arithmetical ratio': that is to say, instead of doubling, it would increase by the same amount every twenty-five years. Hence he calculated that:

> Taking the whole earth ... and supposing the present popu-lation equal to a thousand millions, the human species would increase as the numbers 1, 2, 4, 8, 16, 32, 64, 128, 256, and subsistence as 1, 2, 3, 4, 5, 6, 7, 8, 9. In two centuries the population would be to the means of subsistence as 256 to 9; in three centuries as 4096 to 13 and in two thousand years the difference would be incalculable.

Note that these well-known 'mathematical jingles' were used purely as heuristic devices, and so should not be taken as some iron law of nature: Malthus was careful to write of a *tendency* for population to outstrip resources, of population doubling every twenty-five years *when unchecked*, and so on. He assumed that humans, as rational beings, would perceive the advantages of curbing their reproductive instincts. His advice was to practise 'moral restraint': the preventive checks on population that applied when people delayed marriage until they could afford to feed a family, and abstained from extra-marital sexual relations. The grim alternative, of course, was to face the positive checks of war, famine and disease.[7] The shock waves of the *Essay* reverberated across the continent, with French and German translations appear-ing promptly during the 1800s, and renewed efforts to restrict the marriage of paupers in Austria and the German states.

With hindsight, it is easy to see that Malthus underestimated the potential of a modern economy to generate resources, and overestimated the fertility of the European population. Instead of the type of equilibrium familiar to Malthus from past experience, the nineteenth century brought above all a *sustained* (if un-spectacular) increase in population. For a long time his work was neglected, though interestingly it is now very much back in fashion. During the 1940s and 1950s, the prevailing model was that of the 'demographic transition'. In pre-modern societies, it was suggested, high death rates created pressure for people to reproduce themselves: various social and cultural norms in effect worked to ensure the survival of each community. The first stage of the transition involved a long-term decline in the death rate, beginning with the onset of economic development some time during the eighteenth century. A persistent decline in the birth rate, the second stage, was delayed until the late nineteenth century by the continuing influence of the age-old social and economic influences, so that in the interim there was a considerable surge in population. Finally, there was a stabilization of both the birth rate and the death rate at a relatively low level.[8] This very simple model has appeared less and less helpful as researchers probed at its various assumptions. A glance at the graphs of natural movements of population in some of the countries where national estimates are available reveals its limitations (see Figures 9.1, 9.2 and 9.3). In Sweden, there is some conformity to it during the first half of the nineteenth century, though this was a region still on the periphery of industrial Europe. In England, there is no disputing the impetus to industrialization, but the latest reconstruction concludes that it was a rise in fertility that accounts for the 'lion's share' of the acceleration in population growth. The French case was different again, with a precocious decline in the birth rate starting shortly after the long-term decline in the death rate. A further variant comes from Germany, where the assumption is that both the birth and the death rate remained high until the late nineteenth century.

To proceed beyond the demographic transition theory, historians had to abandon the thesis that population increases were invariably associated with economic development. At the same time, they had to find ways of measuring demographic variables in the various European states during their 'pre-registration' period. Everywhere, governments were slow to set up national systems of civil registration. Again the Swedes stand apart, with legislation to improve registration procedures dating from 1749; the French equivalent appeared in 1792 and 1803, while the British had to wait until 1837. What might be called without undue exaggeration the great leap forward for historians came during the 1950s, with the development of family reconstitution techniques. By searching through the birth, marriage and death

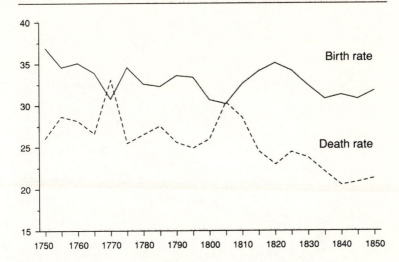

Figure 9.1 Birth and death rates (per thousand of population) in Sweden, 1750–1850
Source: B.R. Mitchell, *European Historical Statistics, 1750–1970* (London, 1978), Table A.

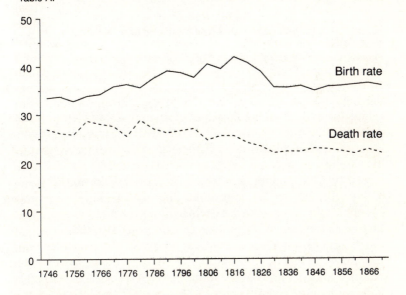

Figure 9.2 Birth and death rates (per thousand of population) in England, 1750–1850
Source: E.A. Wrigley and R.S. Schofield, *The Population History of England, 1541–1871* (London, 1981), p.529.

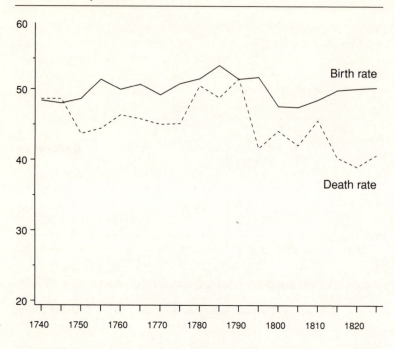

Figure 9.3 Birth and death rates (per thousand of population) in France, 1750–1850

Source: L. Henry and Y. Blayo, 'La Population de la France de 1740 à 1860', *Population*, 30 (1975), pp.108–9.

registers of a parish, they were able to assemble histories of vital events for individual families, and ultimately to calculate various demographic rates. A wealth of information became available on such population processes as changes in the age of marriage, the distribution of ages at which women bore children and infant mortality. The limitations to the technique should not be overlooked. It requires an enormous amount of skilled work to assemble and process the data, which limits the number of studies that can be produced. Family reconstitutions also fail to throw much light on important demographic phenomena such as proportions who marry, adult mortality, and migrations. Developing out of work on family reconstitutions were projects to establish national series of vital events. Still using parish registers, large teams of researchers in England and France (the Cambridge Group and the INED) set about drawing samples of these events from all regions of their countries. We now have *The Population*

History of England for the period 1541–1871 in England, and several articles covering the years 1740–1829 in France.[9] Serious gaps in our knowledge remain, the outstanding one for the period before 1830 being the silence of parish registers and civil registration on the causes of death. However, we are now in a position to make a fair stab at investigating the changes in fertility and mortality that lay behind the rise in population (the assumption being that the net balance of migrations was outwards rather than inwards for Europe as a whole).

Our first task is to discover whether there is any evidence of a rise in fertility before 1830. At first sight, this would seem unlikely. It might be assumed that, in the absence of birth control, fertility in early modern Europe would have been close to a biological maximum, leaving little or no scope for an increase.[10] However, an examination of crude birth rates during the second half of the eighteenth century rules out any such notion. What stands out is the large differences between countries: in Hungary, the rate stood at 55 per thousand; in Spain, at 43; in Lombardy and France, around 40; and in England and Sweden, around 35. It is now clear that neither in the past nor in the present have fertility levels in 'pre-modern' societies approached what is 'biologically possible'. The differences in fertility can partly be explained by variations in the proportions married at the child-bearing ages. A much-cited paper by J. Hajnal noted that west of a line running from St Petersburg to Trieste a 'European marriage pattern' prevailed, with a characteristically high age at marriage (generally over 24 for women) and a high proportion of people who never marry at all (at least 10 or even 15 per cent of women).[11] Eastern Europe stood in an intermediate position between the 'European' pattern and the African or Asian pattern (in which hardly any women over 25 remain single). During the eighteenth century, mean age at first marriage was around 26 or 27 in France and Germany, according to family reconstitutions, whereas in Hungary it was 18.6 (and in Russia women tended to marry between the ages of 17 and 22). By 1780, we may speculate, the western part of Europe had already experienced some sort of 'Malthusian' demographic transition, from early and universal marriage to a system which encouraged women to delay marriage for at least ten years after they had reached puberty. With illegitimacy still rare, the effect was to prevent women conceiving for approximately one-third of their child-bearing years. A further potential source of differences between countries was the marital fertility rate. Even within the fifteen or so years during which married women in western Europe were able to bear children, there were a number of constraints on fertility, which were likely to vary in their impact across the continent. They included religious taboos on intercourse during Lent and Advent, extended lactation and bouts of infertility due to undernourishment. Michael Flinn discerns a sufficient degree of uniformity in the age-specific marital fertility patterns in the west to justify talking in terms of a 'European demographic system'. However, this leaves eastern Europe out of the account (for lack of data), and one should add the rider that regional and inter-regional variations were important during the eighteenth century. Very broadly, village studies suggest that in France the women of Brittany, the north, the east, the Ile de France and the Lyonnais were conspicuously fertile, whilst in the German states, it was the women of Bavaria who stood out from the rest. Overall, beside national and regional differences, what needs emphasizing is the relatively low level of 'natural' fertility levels (those unaffected by deliberate family limitation) in the west of Europe around 1780.

In these circumstances, the finding by the Cambridge Group that during the 'long' eighteenth-century period (1680–1820) in England 'the fertility rise contributed about two-and-a-half-times as much to the rise in growth rates as the mortality fall' is entirely credible – though, as we shall see, it has not gone uncontested. Its data suggest that the key variable was nuptuality. Marital fertility remained stable: that is to say, married women continued to space their births much as before. Change came in the form of a drop in the average age at first marriage for women from 26 to 23, and a decline in the proportion never marrying from about 16 per cent to less than 10 per cent. Wrigley and Schofield are led to hypothesize that the English were good 'Malthusians', delaying marriage in times of declining living standards, and starting earlier during more prosperous periods. They are careful to point out that their real-wage index is not particularly robust, and they have to explain lags of at least thirty years between changes in living standards and turning points in nuptuality. Not everyone is convinced that they have overcome these obstacles. None the less, they make a strong case to show that a persistent rise in real wages over the seventeenth and the first half of the eighteenth centuries opened the way for an increase in nuptuality, and thereafter fertility. Although real wages declined after 1750, the lagged pattern of response meant that fertility continued to rise for several more decades. After 1800, Wrigley and Schofield see a 'clean break' with the age-old relationships between population and prices, as the growing momentum of economic growth in the early nineteenth century sustained the demographic increase. The extended period of adverse economic circumstances and falling nuptuality that had always appeared in the past never materialized.[12]

Nowhere else in Europe has the rise in population been attributed to increased fertility to anything like the same degree. The second half of the eighteenth century and the early nineteenth century did bring a striking increase in the proportion of illegitimate births on the continent (as in England). Reconstitutions by John Knodel in six German villages found the illegitimacy ratio rising from around 3 per cent of all births during the 1750s to a peak of over 13 per cent during the 1820s and 1830s. Similarly, the INED project in France indicated that the proportion of births out of wedlock increased from 1.3 per cent during the 1750s to 4.7 per cent during the period 1810–19.[13] However, the consensus among historians is that this shift would only have had a minor impact on the population increase, given that the vast majority of births remained within marriage. Marital fertility was also generally as stable in continental Europe as it was in England. Among the rural population of Eastern Flanders, it rose during the late eighteenth century but declined for a while after 1800;[14] in Knodel's sample of fourteen German villages there was considerable diversity of experience, but no sign of a consistent trend overall; in France (and possibly also in Spain and Switzerland) there was even a *decline*, clearly under way by the 1820s, and evident in parts of the country before the Revolution.[15] The divergence between English and continental experience was most in evidence with the mean age at first marriage among women. The decline in England contrasted with the stability, or slight tendency to rise, found elsewhere in the late eighteenth century. The upshot was that between 1740–9 and 1810–20 the gross reproduction rate (measuring the extent to which women of childbearing age are replaced by the next generation) rose in England, from an estimated 2.27 to 3.06, but declined in France, from 2.53 to 1.94.[16] It should be added that national aggregates mask considerable differences between regions. It may be, for example, that in areas where rural industry was extensively developed, couples could marry earlier, since 'niches' for a new household were easier to find than in farming or artisan communities, or support more children. Of late, however, historians have been less confident in asserting the links between 'proto-industrialization' and population increase. In some areas, such as Flanders, the mountainous zones of Zurich and Bohemia (not to mention parts of England), the evidence for them appears strong; in others, such as the Thimerais, the eastern part of Belgium and Knodel's German villages, it does not.[17]

Should we conclude with the paradoxical notion that England, conspicuous in Europe for its falling age at marriage, was the country where fertility was most sensitive to living standards? This is what Wrigley and Schofield assert in making the distinction between low- and high-pressure systems of population.[18] In the former, preventive checks act to keep population in balance with its food base. Broadly speaking, this was the position in the west of Europe, because of its peculiar pattern of delayed marriage. In the latter, the 'Asiatic' case, preventive checks are not applied, and the balance is only maintained by rising mortality: the equilibrium population is then higher than in a low-pressure system, and real incomes are pushed down. Within western Europe, Wrigley and Schofield naturally concentrate on England, stressing the 'good fortune' of its population in finding a low-pressure solution to the perennial problem in a pre-industrial society of numbers outstripping resources. By way of contrast, one can find the occasional example in western Europe of an area with a rampant 'natural' fertility that appears oblivious to the resources available. In three Bavarian villages studied by Knodel, marital fertility during the second half of the eighteenth century equalled that of the Hutterites, usually taken as the maximum on record (and hence an upper limit by which the fertility of other groups of women can be assessed). Knodel suspects that the relative absence of breast-feeding was a major influence here, since it had the effect of shortening birth intervals. He concludes from his work on German village populations that infant-feeding practices as well as nuptuality can be a critical influence on reproductive regimes:

> Where prolonged breast-feeding was the norm, both marital fertility and infant mortality tended to be moderate and thus reproduction relatively efficient; where handfeeding at early

stages commonly replaced breast-feeding, marital fertility and infant mortality were both typically high, resulting in considerably less efficient reproductive regimes.[19]

Far more voluminous is the literature on French fertility, scholarly interest being aroused by its unique decline during the early nineteenth-century period. By the 1840s, France had the lowest birth rate in Europe, which of course explains the exceptionally slow growth of her population. Wrigley and Schofield see fertility in France occupying an intermediate position in the European context, as a high-pressure equilibrium at the beginning of the eighteenth century was successfully converted to a low-pressure one by 1870. In this perspective, the originality of the French compared to the English was that they finally resolved the problem of maintaining a balance between population and resources by resorting to family limitation rather than by delaying the age of marriage. Specialists in French history have been noticeably cool on this line of interpretation. They have cast doubts on the contrast between low- and high-pressure systems on the two sides of the Channel, noting that the French population no less than the English delayed marriages in times of crisis. An interesting case study of this process, in the Thimerais (a small *pays* near Chartres), suggests that it was the poor rather than the well-off who bore the brunt of these adjustments during the eighteenth century. Dividing his village populations into *laboureurs* (substantial farmers) and *journaliers* (agricultural labourers), Bernard Derouet notes that the average age of marriage for women in particular was relatively stable among the former, but among the latter it fell during prosperous times and rose sharply during lean years. David Weir goes as far as to argue that marriages in France were more responsive to pressures from the economy than those in England. His calculations imply that between 1740 and 1789 a doubling of prices in one year would lead to a 61 per cent shortfall in marriages over the following five years in France, compared to only 11 per cent in England. Weir is also unconvinced by the thesis that French controls on fertility can be seen as a variant on traditional systems for maintaining an equilibrium between population and resources. He points out that, contrary to the expectations of a 'Malthusian' model, during the early nineteenth century marital fertility in France was falling while living standards are assumed to have been rising.[20] (We

might note in passing that most interpretations of the early resort
to family limitation in France see it as a sign of new attitudes, say,
to religious authority or to children – though a convincing
interpretation has yet to emerge.)[21] At this stage in the debate,
therefore, it is an open question whether the 'Malthusian' framework proposed by Wrigley and Schofield can be applied to the
whole of Europe. The favoured alternative is the 'Boserupian' one.
Instead of seeing increases in the food supply as the determining
influence on population growth, Ester Boserup reverses the line
of causation, and argues that an increase in population is likely to
stimulate development in agriculture.[22] To understand this line of
reasoning, we need to consider the reasons for the general decline
in mortality in Europe during our period.

Death was still taking a terrible toll on the people of Europe in the
middle of the eighteenth century. The early stages of life were
particularly precarious. Efforts to measure infant mortality rates
(the number of deaths of infants under the age of one, expressed
per thousand live births) are hampered by under-registration of
the deaths of unbaptized children. The results vary disconcert-
ingly between the parishes studied, ranging from around 100 to
over 400. English reconstitutions suggest a relatively benign
rate of around 160 (between 1740 and 1790); but in France during
this period it stood at 280, and in parts of southern Germany,
somewhere between 350 and 425. The age-group 1–5 was also
highly vulnerable to a premature death. As a result, it is possible
that in much of western Europe half of all children were dying
before they reached the age of ten. Communities also had to
contend with massive surges in mortality from time to time, as
infectious diseases cut huge swathes through their ranks. Whereas
normal levels of mortality carried off around 3 per cent of the
population each year, the onset of a crisis could double or treble
the proportion.[23] Life could indeed be 'nasty, brutish and short'.
We would do well to bear in mind that mortality levels remained
high throughout the period 1780 to 1830. Arguably, the most
important turning point in the transition to lower rates would not
come in Europe until the late nineteenth century: the long-run
series available for England suggest that expectation of life in the
middle years of the nineteenth century was much the same as it
had been during the period 1566–1621.[24] Although some of the big
'killer' diseases receded into the background during the eight-

eenth century, others were on hand to replace them. Bubonic plague was one traditional scourge that had been largely eradicated by the eighteenth century. It continued to run rampant in the Ottoman Empire until the 1840s, for want of administrative measures to isolate infected areas, but the last major outbreak in the west was recorded at Cadiz in 1800. Smallpox was also on the retreat from the middle of the eighteenth century onwards, partly, it seems, in the face of efforts to encourage inoculation and vaccination. On the debit side, though, typhus, tuberculosis and, from around 1830, cholera came to the fore as causes of death.

The eighteenth and early nineteenth centuries did bring some decline in mortality. Taking the continent as a whole, the consensus among historians is that this decrease was the main reason for the growth in population during our period. We may note in passing that Peter Razzell has consistently championed the view that England was no different from continental Europe in this respect. In so doing, he now stands as something of a lone voice, challenging the virtual orthodoxy of a stress on rising fertility which the Cambridge Group established during the 1980s.[25] Two sets of changes were under way in parts of Europe during our period. First, there was some 'stabilization' of death rates, as the jagged peaks characteristic of pre-industrial societies gave way to a smoother and more consistent pattern (see Figure 9.4). Second, the 'normal' rate began a secular decline that would continue into the twentieth century. Needless to say, these broad generalizations cover a multitude of local variations: in the original level of mortality, in the timing of the first major downturn, and in the rate of decline. Sweden endured a high and fluctuating death rate during the second half of the eighteenth century, but in the nineteenth century the decline was continuous. England experienced an early start to the fall in her death rate, around the middle of the eighteenth century. She apparently began with a relatively low level of mortality (though the figures from the Cambridge Group may be an underestimate) and, after an initial decrease, underwent a long phase of negligible progress between the 1820s and the 1870s. France set out during the 1740s (when national series first become available) with a considerably higher crude death rate than England, in the range of 32 to 35 as opposed to 25 to 28. Her rate was also slower to stabilize, partly because of the disastrous impact of political and military events, and partly because of continuing problems with the food supply in certain regions. However, she too was an early starter, and by the middle of the nineteenth century her mortality level was close to that of England (see Table 9.2). Other countries are less easy to study, in the absence of national estimates of mortality. What evidence we have points to an end to the extreme variability of death rates from the 1740s, but little in the way of a secular decline before the middle of the nineteenth century. In the German states, for example, the death rate stayed well below the birth rate, even with the occasional peak from a crisis, but only a few areas registered a sustained decrease between 1750 and 1850.

Table 9.2 Life expectancy at birth in England and France

	England	France
1750–9	36.9	27.9
1760–9	34.6	27.7
1770–9	36.9	28.9
1780–9	35.3	27.8
1790–9	37.0	31.1
1800–9	37.3	33.9
1810–19	37.7	36.5
1820–9	39.6	38.8
1830–9	40.5	38.1
1840–9	39.9	39.9

Source: M. Livi-Bacci, *Population and Nutrition: An Essay in European Demographic History* (Cambridge, 1991), p.70.

So far, so good: the real difficulties arise when we try to explain the changes in mortality. Historians have tended to divide into at least two warring camps, which operate by first dismissing the opposition case, and then asserting their own. The key question is whether the incidence of infectious diseases declined because of improved nutritional standards or because of advances in medicine and public health – or perhaps even because of biological changes, acting independently of social and economic forces, which affected the relationship between infectious agents and their human hosts. McKeown is invariably cited as the leading light in the camp stressing the importance of nutrition during the eighteenth and early nineteenth centuries: a thesis he first documented with English material, and later extended to cover the Swedish, French, Irish and Hungarian cases.[26] Although historians often suggest that his approach is the most widely accepted,

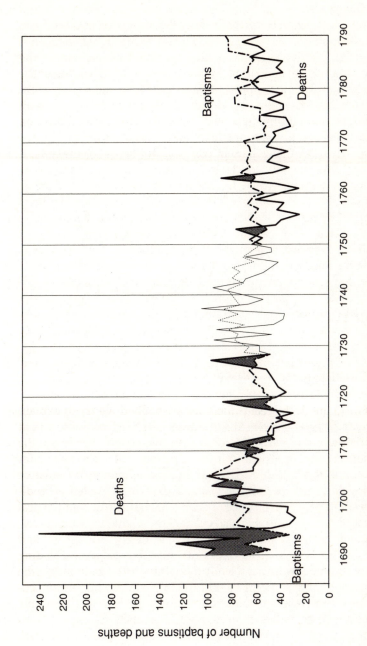

Figure 9.4. A new demographic regime in the eighteenth century: the case of Breteuil, in the Beauvaisis
Source: P. Goubert, *Beauvais et le Beauvaisis de 1600 à 1730*, 2 vols (Paris, 1982), vol.II, pp.60–1. Copyright of the Ecole des Hautes Etudes en Sciences Sociales.

it has been the target of a growing volume of criticism during the last few years.

McKeown began by virtually demolishing an earlier orthodoxy: that the modern rise of population could be attributed to medical advances (in the prevention and treatment of disease in the individual). Armed with his knowledge as a physician, he noted that before 1850 medical practitioners were ignorant of the nature of infectious diseases, and deprived of any effective forms of immunization and therapy. Such medical advances as did occur, in the fields of midwifery, medicine and inoculation, he considered insignificant for the welfare of patients, and hence for the decline in mortality. His only concession concerned medical measures to combat smallpox, which he deemed to be of some influence, particularly in France and Ireland. Much of this argument has been accepted by historians. McKeown also doubted whether a change in the character of certain diseases, occurring independently of medical intervention or environmental influences, would go far to explain a long-run fall in mortality. In his view, such movements must have occurred throughout human evolution, and so are inadequate to explain the unprecedented expansion of population. Partly by a process of exclusion, he readily admitted, McKeown finally settled on a third possible explanation for the decline in deaths from infectious diseases: improvements in the environment. Of these, public health measures would be a major influence, but not until late in the nineteenth century. Hence his conclusion that 'The reduction of mortality and rise of population in the eighteenth and early nineteenth centuries were probably due to a significant increase in food supplies.' To buttress this case for rising living standards, and in particular for an improvement in diet, he gave a cursory account of agricultural developments and industrialization in his selected countries. Discounting the influence of the latter during the early period, he claimed that there existed a broad correlation between the pace of change in agriculture and the rate of population growth. He also examined the links between nutrition and mortality, and in particular speculated, 'not too wildly', on those between food shortages and infectious diseases. The drift of his argument was that the nutritional state of an individual was 'important and sometimes critical' in determining his or her response to an epidemic infection, such as typhus or smallpox, and especially to an endemic infection, such as tuberculosis.

Such a wide-ranging yet simple exposition gave rather too

many hostages to fortune. Critics were quick to point out his lack of evidence for the eighteenth century (the Swedish case excepted), and his inability to explain mortality declines among infants or wealthy groups in society. In an extended debate, three areas have recently been examined in some detail. First, there is the impact of agricultural advances on nutrition in the eighteenth century. There is no disputing the movement to bring marginal land under cultivation, to introduce new crops and to increase productivity. However it is conceivable that additional food supplies simply allowed the population to grow without any improvements in nutrition. Taking the French case, one can cite the work of Michel Morineau, which dismissed many eighteenth-century developments on the land as ambiguous in their effects: 'the progress of misery', as opposed to the abundance of an agricultural revolution. Thus innovations such as the introduction of the potato to Lorraine or buckwheat to Brittany arguably boosted the population but depressed living standards. It is also likely that everywhere in Europe increases in food production were unevenly distributed across the population. In other words, 'food entitlements' varied according to what people owned, what they were able to trade and what they could obtain from communal sources. An extreme case comes from Prussia, where substantial increases in agricultural output (135 per cent between 1816 and 1865) coincided with rising infant mortality and 'inflated' child mortality rates. The reason, according to Robert Lee, was that the agrarian system rested on the expansion of large, export-orientated estates owned by the Junkers, at the expense of peasant property. The growth in output was achieved by increasing inputs of labour rather than by technical progress, which meant less time for child care among the hard-pressed labourers, and possibly also a deterioration in their diet.[27]

Second, historians have sought more direct evidence on living standards. The most conclusive indicator for this debate would of course be data on food intakes, but it must be admitted that the available sources are not particularly helpful. The best-documented case is France, where there is no sign of improvement until the 1830s and 1840s. J.-C. Toutain estimates that between the end of the eighteenth century and 1830, the average intake of calories per person hovered around 1,700 to 2,000 per day: a barely adequate ration, particularly for those of low nutritional status (in other words, people who had to cope with the burdens of heavy manual labour and intensive exposure to infectious diseases). The French peasantry during the second half of the eighteenth century faced a monotonous diet based almost exclusively on cereals, eaten either as bread or some form of gruel, eked out with a few vegetables, a little milk and cheese, and tiny amounts of pork and fish. In the Gévaudan, for example, adults worked their way through at least 500 grammes of a heavy rye bread each day, adding some fat or cheese. As elsewhere, their diet was excessively reliant on carbohydrates and fats, and deficient in protein, vitamins and minerals. Town dwellers were generally better fed than villagers, but it is interesting to note that a study of Paris suggests declining standards during the early nineteenth century. Thus in the 1780s the Parisians were 'almost comfortable' on around 2,000 calories a day, with 'bread, always bread, and more bread' for the poor, and plenty of fish and meat for the rich. By the 1850s, the upheavals of revolution and mass immigration had undermined the old infrastructure, leaving the population vulnerable to tuberculosis and cholera.[28] The Russian diet had much in common with that of the French peasantry, if an English governess is to be believed in her observation that the people 'can make an hearty Meal on a Piece of black sour Bread, some Salt, an Onion, or Garlick' – though there was also an addiction to strong liquor to cloud the picture.[29] A more recent development in the literature, which has brought to light some interesting results in a number of countries, involves the use of data on height to investigate nutritional status. The general picture is one of declining age-by-height profiles among the lower classes of Europe during the early stages of economic development in the late eighteenth century. Military records from the Habsburg Monarchy show a trend towards smaller stature among the male population born between the 1750s and the 1790s. Similarly, the records of the Marine Society in London show that mean heights of adolescent boys from the labouring classes changed little between 1775 and 1790, but then declined for two decades – to a level so low that it is rarely encountered anywhere in the world today.[30] These findings tie in with our previous conclusion that the early stages of economic development brought few benefits for the lower orders in society.

Finally, historical research and recent medical investigations suggest that the relationship between nutrition and disease is more complex than McKeown would allow. This is not to deny that malnutrition could lower resistance to infectious diseases.

There are plenty of studies which will demonstrate that sharp increases in grain prices were followed by a notable increase in mortality, or that the chances of a premature death were greater in a poor than a well-off section of a town.[31] For example, French scholars have a long tradition of treating grain prices as a demographic 'barometer' under the ancien regime, and even as late as 1816–17 there was 'the last great subsistence crisis in the western world' which particularly affected mortality in Switzerland, the Italian peninsula and parts of the Habsburg Monarchy. The Swiss case in 1817 reveals a population weakened by lack of food, or by eating 'scarcely any thing but boiled nettles', succumbing in droves to typhus and tuberculosis.[32] However, as McKeown himself realized, the poor, besides being less well fed than the rich, were also more likely to be exposed to infection. Even today it is not easy to disentangle malnutrition from other influences on mortality such as a lack of sanitation, overcrowded housing, harsh working conditions and ignorance of the rules of hygiene. The main impact of a famine could conceivably have been to increase the risk of infection, as hordes of desperate people took to the road. Furthermore, all commentators are aware that there were epidemics that occurred independently of food shortages (such as the outbreaks of dysentery in western France around 1779 and in Krefeld during the early 1780s, and the devastating 'fevers' of rural Catalonia in 1800–3) and periods of dearth that made little impact on mortality (for example, in the *généralité* of Paris in 1699–1700).[33] The latest statistical studies in fact tend to play down the links between prices and mortality: Galloway concludes from a survey of several European countries between the 1750s and the 1870s that fluctuations in grain prices would only explain between 20 and 40 per cent of the variance in non-infant mortality.[34] To make sense of these findings, we should bear in mind that while some diseases are strongly influenced by nutritional status (notably tuberculosis, bacterial diarrhoea, cholera and respiratory infections), others are much less so (typhoid, plague and smallpox, for example). There is also the suggestion that humans are capable of adapting to food shortages, so that above a certain level of severe malnutrition their immune system will always function.[35] Hence there is the conclusion from Livi-Bacci that 'Mortality seems largely independent of the availability of food resources.'

When it comes to putting forward explanations of their own,

critics of McKeown often give the impression of being on shaky ground themselves. (Alfred Perrenoud even manages to sound slightly dotty in noting 'an amazing coincidence between the annual mean sunspot numbers and the course of mortality'.)[36] They generally give more weight than McKeown to medical advances and public health measures, though not always with great conviction. J.C. Riley gave a full account of 'environmental engineering' in eighteenth-century Europe, including projects to drain swamps (and the moat of the Bastille), to ventilate public buildings and to move burial sites away from centres of population. However, he did not attempt to measure their impact on mortality, and freely admitted that his evidence was 'circumstantial'. Above all, they tend to emphasize the ebb and flow of the major diseases. In their view, the transmission of, say, typhus or smallpox is partly determined by the resistance of the population, but for the most part by the virulence of the infectious agents and the frequency of contacts with carriers.[37] Of late, there are signs of claws being retracted among the main protagonists, with the recognition that the debate was becoming unduly polarized. There is a growing consensus that the decline in mortality must have been caused by a multiplicity of factors. These will certainly include nutrition and public health, but also living and working conditions, medical advances, infant-feeding practices, personal hygiene, education, the rise and fall of various diseases, and changes in climate. How these influences combined remains to be explored in different settings: we still have to admit to our limited knowledge in this area.

An understanding of the relationship between population and the economy is arguably one of the 'grand themes' of history.[38] The fact that the population increase of the late eighteenth and early nineteenth centuries can be observed right across Europe, in countries at widely differing levels of social and economic development, gives a hint that the relationship was by no means straightforward. On the one hand, as we have seen, agricultural and industrial development could encourage a growth in population, by improving the production and distribution of food, diversifying employment opportunities and paving the way for advances in medicine and public health. However, demographic increases could also be found in less developed countries such as Spain, Italy and Russia, where there were few signs of an agricultural revolution during the eighteenth century, let alone an industrial one. Even in the more developed parts of the continent, signs of a better standard of living for the 'big battalions' of peasants and workers were painfully slow to materialize. On the other hand, a rising population could stimulate economic development in various ways, giving a boost to demand for foodstuffs and manufactured goods, for example, or promoting investment in housing and the infrastructure. From the perspective of continental Europe, these latter influences loom large during our period. The 'population and industrialization' debate which has so enlivened the British literature is generally irrelevant to other countries before 1830. Given that the population increase started well before industrialization, and that the decline in mortality which caused it can be attributed at least partly to forces exogenous to the economy, the theoretical framework provided by Ester Boserup comes to mind once again. The pressure was on the agricultural and industrial sectors to respond to the stimulus of rising numbers.

ACKNOWLEDGEMENT

Thanks are due to Professor Robert Lee (University of Liverpool).

NOTES

1 T. McKeown, *The Modern Rise of Population* (London, 1976), p.4; R. Schofield and D. Reher, 'The decline of mortality in Europe', in R. Schofield, D. Reher and A. Bideau (eds) *The Decline of Mortality in Europe* (Oxford, 1991), pp.1–17.
2 J.-N. Biraben, 'Essai sur l'évolution du nombre des hommes', *Population*, 34 (1979), p.16.
3 See C. Langlois, '1790: La Révolution de vingt-huit millions de Français?', *Annales de démographie historique* (1976), pp.215–58, and J. Dupâquier et al., *Histoire de la population française*, vol.2, 'De la Renaissance à 1789' (Paris, 1988), pp.61–8. Note that matters are complicated by the use of contemporary frontiers by some authors, those of 1861 (or present-day France) by others.
4 L. Henry and Y. Blayo, 'La Population de la France de 1740 à 1860', *Population*, 30 (1975), pp.71–122 (p.107).
5 J. de Vries, 'Patterns of urbanization in pre-industrial Europe, 1500–1800', in H. Schmal (ed.) *Patterns of European Urbanization since 1500* (London, 1981), pp.77–109.
6 A.-N. de Condorcet, *Sketch for a Historical Picture of the Progress of the Human Mind* (1795), (London, 1955, trs. J. Barraclough); M. Reinhard

and A. Armengaud, *Histoire générale de la population mondiale* (Paris, 1961), pp.213–22; Dupâquier, *op.cit.*, *Population française*, vol.2, ch.XI.

7   T.R. Malthus, *An Essay on the Principle of Population* (Cambridge, 1992, ed. D. Winch), pp.13–19; W. Petersen, *Malthus* (London, 1979), pp.61–5.

8   A.J. Coale, 'The demographic transition', in *International Population Conference*, vol.1 (Liège, 1973), pp.53–72 (pp.53–4).

9   E.A. Wrigley and R.S. Schofield, *The Population History of England, 1541–1871* (London, 1981); for progress in France, see Dupâquier, *op.cit.*, *Population française*, vol.2, pp.3–4.

10 This section is indebted to Coale, *op.cit.*, 'Demographic transition'.

11 J. Hajnal, 'European marriage patterns in perspective', in D.V. Glass and D.E.C. Eversley (eds) *Population in History* (London, 1965), pp.101–43.

12 Wrigley and Schofield, *op.cit.*, *Population History*, chs 7, 10, 11; E.A. Wrigley, 'The growth of population in eighteenth-century England: a conundrum resolved', *Past and Present*, 98 (1983), pp.121–50. See also R. Schofield, 'English marriage patterns revisited', *Journal of Family History*, 10 (1985), pp.2–20, and J.A. Goldstone, 'The demographic revolution in England: a re-examination', *Population Studies*, 40 (1986), pp.5–33.

13 Dupâquier, *op.cit.*, *Population française*, vol.2, pp.111–12.

14 C. Vandenbroeke, 'Caractéristiques de la nuptialité et de la fécondité en Flandre et en Brabant aux XVIIe–XIXe siècles', *Annales de démographie historique* (1977), pp.7–20 (pp.12–14).

15 A.J. Coale and R. Treadway, 'A summary of the changing distribution of overall fertility, marital fertility, and the proportion married in the provinces of Europe', in A.J. Coale and S.C. Watkins (eds) *The Decline of Fertility in Europe* (Princeton, 1986), pp.31–181 (pp.37–9).

16 Wrigley and Schofield, *op.cit.*, *Population History*, p.230; J. Bourgeois-Pichat, 'The general development of the population of France since the eighteenth century', in Glass and Eversley, *op.cit.*, *Population in History*, pp.474–506 (p.506).

17 Cf. W. Fischer, 'Rural industrialization and population change', *Comparative Studies in Society and History*, 15 (1973), pp.158–70; and R. Houston and K.D.M. Snell, 'Proto-industrialization? Cottage industry, social change, and Industrial Revolution', *Historical Journal*, 27 (1984), pp.473–92. Case studies include P. Deprez, 'The demographic development of Flanders in the eighteenth century', in Glass and Eversley, *op.cit.*, *Population in History*, pp.608–30; R. Braun, 'The impact of cottage industry on an agricultural population', in D.S. Landes (ed.) *The Rise of Capitalism* (New York, 1966), pp.53–64; M.P. Gutmann and R. Leboutte, 'Rethinking protoindustrialization and the family', *Journal of Interdisciplinary History*, 14 (1984), pp.587–607.

18 This section relies on Wrigley and Schofield, *op.cit.*, *Population History*, ch.11; and E.A. Wrigley, 'The fall of marital fertility in nineteenth-century France: exemplar or exception?', in *People, Cities and Wealth* (Oxford, 1987), pp.270–321.

19 John E. Knodel, *Demographic Behaviour in the Past* (Cambridge, 1988), p.456.

20 Bernard Derouet, 'Une Démographie sociale différentielle: clés pour un système auto-régulateur des populations rurales d'ancien régime', *Annales E.S.C.*, 35 (1980), pp.3–41; David R. Weir, 'Life under pressure: France and England, 1670–1870', *Journal of Economic History,* 44 (1984), pp.27–47.

21 See, for example, P. Ariès, 'An interpretation to be used for the history of mentalities', in O. and P. Ranum (eds) *Popular Attitudes toward Birth Control* (New York, 1972), pp.100–25, J.-L. Flandrin, *Families in Former Times* (Cambridge, 1979), ch.4, and Dupâquier, *op.cit.*, *Histoire de la population*, vol.3, 'De 1789 à 1914', ch.VII.

22 E. Boserup, *The Conditions of Agricultural Growth* (London, 1965), p.11.

23 See M.W. Flinn, *The European Demographic System 1500–1820* (Brighton, 1981), pp.14–15.

24 R. Schofield, 'Population growth in the century after 1750: the role of mortality decline', in T. Bengtsson *et al.*, *Pre-Industrial Population Change* (Stockholm, 1984), pp.17–39 (p.35).

25 See P.E. Razzell, *Essays in English Population History* (London, 1994).

26 T. McKeown, R.G. Brown and R.G. Record, 'An interpretation of the modern rise of population in Europe', *Population Studies*, 26 (1972), pp.345–82; T. McKeown, *The Modern Rise of Population* (London, 1976).

27 See M. Morineau, *Les Faux-semblants d'un démarrage économique: agriculture et démographie en France au XVIIIe siècle* (Paris, 1971); A. Sen, *Poverty and Famines: An Essay on Entitlement and Deprivation* (Oxford, 1981); W.R. Lee, 'Mortality levels and agrarian reform in early nineteenth-century Prussia: some regional evidence', in Bengtsson, *op.cit.*, *Pre-Industrial Population*, pp.161–90, and 'The mechanism of mortality change in Germany, 1750–1850', *Medizinhistorisches Journal* (1980), pp.244–68.

28 J.-C. Toutain, *La Consommation alimentaire en France de 1789 à 1964* (Geneva, 1971), p.1979; O.H. Hufton, *The Poor of Eighteenth-Century France, 1750–89* (Oxford, 1974), pp.44–8; R.-J. Bernard, 'L'Alimentation paysanne en Gévaudan au XVIIIe siècle', *Annales E.S.C.*, 24 (1969), pp.1449–67; R. Philippe, 'Une Opération pilote: l'étude du ravitaillement de Paris au temps de Lavoisier', *Annales E.S.C.*, 16 (1961), pp.564–8.

29 E. Justice, *A Voyage to Russia* (2nd edn, London, 1746), p.18, cited by R.E.F. Smith, *Bread and Salt: A Social and Economic History of Food and Drink in Russia* (Cambridge, 1984), p.178. For a more optimistic view, see I. Blanchard, *Russia's Age of Silver* (London, 1989), ch.5.

30 J. Komlos, *Nutrition and Economic Development in the Eighteenth-Century Habsburg Monarchy* (Princeton, 1989), ch.2; R. Floud, K. Wachter and A. Gregory, *Height, Health and Nutritional Status in the United Kingdom* (Cambridge, 1990), pp.163–75.

31 See, for example, E. Vedrenne-Villeneuve, 'L'Inégalité sociale devant la mort dans la première moitié du XIXe siècle', *Population*, 16 (1961), pp.665–98. The findings of this Parisian study are not corroborated in the case of Rouen, where 'mortality responses among the rich and

poor to higher grain prices are virtually the same in terms of both magnitude and timing'; P.R. Galloway, 'Differentials in demographic responses to annual price variations in pre-Revolutionary France', *European Journal of Population*, 2 (1986), pp.269–305.

32 Dupâquier, *op.cit.*, *Population française*, vol.2, ch.v; John D. Post, 'Famine, mortality, and epidemic disease in the process of modernization', *Economic History Review*, 29 (1976), pp.14–37.

33 P. Kriedte, 'Demographic and economic rhythms: the rise of the silk industry in Krefeld in the eighteenth century', *Journal of European Economic History*, 15 (1986), pp.259–89 (pp.274–5); P. Vilar, 'Essai d'un bilan démographique de la période 1787–1814 en Catalogne', *Annales de démographie historique* (1965), pp.53–65 (p.60); J. Dupâquier, 'Demographic crises and subsistence crises in France, 1650–1725', in J. Walter and R. Schofield (eds) *Famine, Disease and the Social Order in Early Modern Society* (Cambridge, 1989), pp.189–99 (p.198).

34 P.R. Galloway, 'Basic patterns in annual variations in fertility, nuptuality, mortality, and prices in pre-industrial Europe', *Population Studies*, 42 (1988), pp.275–303 (p.291).

35 P.G. Lunn, 'Nutrition, immunity and infection', in Schofield, *op.cit.*, *Decline of Mortality*, p.137; M. Livi-Bacci, *Population and Nutrition* (Cambridge, 1991), ch.2.

36 A. Perrenoud, 'Mortality decline in its secular setting', in Bengtsson, *op.cit.*, *Pre-Industrial Population*, pp.41–69 (p.65).

37 Livi-Bacci, *op.cit.*, *Population*, pp.119–20.

38 R.S. Schofield and E.A. Wrigley, 'Population and economy', in R.I. Rotberg and T.K. Rabb (eds) *Population and Economy* (Cambridge, 1986), pp.1–9 (p.1).

FURTHER READING

Fine introductory surveys to European demographic history are provided by M.W. Flinn, *The European Demographic System, 1500–1820* (Brighton, 1981), M. Anderson, *Population Change in North-Western Europe, 1750–1850* (London, 1988) and W.R. Lee (ed.) *European Demography and Economic Growth* (London, 1979). More general works that are useful as introductions include E.A. Wrigley, *Population and History* (London, 1969), and N.J.G Pounds, *An Historical Geography of Europe, 1500–1840* (Cambridge, 1979). For an update on theory, there is D. Coleman and R. Schofield, *The State of Population Theory: Forward from Malthus* (Oxford, 1986).

Much important work appears in specialized journals, but some of it is conveniently assembled in D.V. Glass and D.E.C. Eversley, *Population in History* (London, 1965), R.I. Rotberg and T.K. Rabb, *Hunger and History* (Cambridge, 1983), and *Population and Economy* (Cambridge, 1986).

Some key aspects of population history are covered in European perspective in T. Bengtsson, G. Fridlizius and R. Ohlsson (eds) *Pre-Industrial Population Change* (Stockholm, 1984), J. Walter and R. Schofield (eds) *Famine, Disease and the Social Order in Early Modern Society* (Cambridge, 1984), A.J. Coale and S.C. Watkins, *The Decline in Fertility in Europe*

(Princeton, 1986), R. Schofield, D. Reher and A. Bideau (eds) *The Decline of Mortality in Europe* (Oxford, 1991) and M. Livi-Bacci, *Population and Nutrition* (Cambridge, 1991).
Other works which cover Europe on a particular theme include D. Grigg, *Population Growth and Agrarian Change* (Cambridge, 1980), J.D. Post, *The Last Great Subsistence Crisis in the Western World* (Baltimore and London, 1977), and J.C. Riley, *The Eighteenth-Century Campaign to Avoid Disease* (London, 1987). On urbanization, see J. de Vries, *European Urbanization* (London, 1984) and P.M. Hohenberg and L.H. Lees, *The Making of Urban Europe, 1000–1950* (Cambridge, Mass., 1985). National studies in English are few and far between. E.A. Wrigley and R. Schofield, *The Population History of England, 1541–1871* (London, 1981) is outstanding for its broad perspectives on demographic history. Like T. McKeown, *The Modern Rise of Population* (London, 1976), it makes some comparisons between England and other European countries. J.E. Knodel, *Demographic Behaviour in the Past: A Study of Fourteen German Village Populations in the Eighteenth and Nineteenth Centuries* (Cambridge, 1988) contains a wealth of data, though it declines to make any links to social and economic forces.

Chapter 10

European society in revolution

Pamela M. Pilbeam

Human society tends to be grouped in a series of elements from the family upwards, interconnected like the rings caused by pebbles dropped into water. How still was the water of the late eighteenth century? What were the main features of society and social change in these years? What were the links between economic and social developments? In what ways did radical alterations in the role and power of the state have a bearing on society? Normally fifty years would be too short a span of time to note any real differences, but the unprecedented upheaval in ideas, institutions and frontiers produced by the French Revolution and the Napoleonic Empire, which have been described elsewhere in this book, need to be taken into account as catalytic accelerators of development throughout much of western Europe.[1]

The most talked-about changes were the social repercussions of economic development and increasing urban growth. The major perceived impact was in social relations, increasingly defined in confrontational and antagonistic class terminology. Contemporaries were inclined to contrast a 'lost' social harmony, or society of 'orders', with a new dynamic but divisive concept of class. Was this a meaningful comparison, or mere political rhetoric? This was an age of conflict between and within states, some of which has already been discussed. This chapter will investigate the structure of society and the relationship between social groups.

What is social history? Definitions have changed dramatically in the last generation. The expectation of database analysts that full statistical social assessments would be possible have been rendered more modest and realistic by the very limited and incomplete information available. Gender, family, ethnic and broadly political issues are now explored, adding balance and depth to the study of past societies. Some European societies are better documented than others.[2] That this essay focuses largely on France is not solely the consequence of the author's own research interests!

In 1780 writers often still used the language of orders or estates to describe European society west of Russia, although the original medieval belief that society was an organic whole had long been forgotten. In Catholic states three orders were included. The clergy were the first, because in a fundamentally religious/superstitious world their spiritual responsibilities were presumed to be paramount. Second came the nobility, once the organizers of military defence, still vital in that role on the borders of the Russian Empire. Finally came everyone else, lumped together as the third estate, whose role was to feed, clothe and generally labour for the rest. By 1780 the justification for these groupings, based on assumptions of moral responsibility, had dissolved into myth, although they were to have some appeal to right-wing Romantic writers a generation later. They were unhelpful as indicators of relative wealth and were imperfect as guides to where power lay. The social reality behind the idea of orders was a series of sometimes interlinked hierarchies, distinguished by degrees of privilege, occupation and income.

At the apex of pre-Revolutionary European society were competing powerful corporations. In Catholic countries the most dominant of these was the Catholic Church, rightly labelled the first order.[3] Over the centuries the church had negotiated enormously valuable privileges, the most detested of which by these years was the right to collect a tenth of everyone's income, the tithe, together with manifold tax exemptions. The first order was not homogeneous, but reflected the divisions of society as a whole. At the peak of its hierarchically structured pyramid were rich senior clerics, regular and secular who were powerful influences on central government and were themselves members of wealthy, noble, landowning families. The mass of the clergy were habitually of peasant stock and had no chance of promotion to senior posts. They tended to have a secure, if sometimes modest, income from the tithe. In Catholic countries the church was normally the largest single landowner, a major landlord and employer and thus a powerful economic as well as social and political force. Church lands, such as those in the Ile de France, were likely to include large sections which were commercially farmed by prosperous tenants. Through endowed hospitals and schools religious orders provided for the corresponding social needs of the community. In an embryonic sense the church undertook many of the social functions of the modern state. In its spiritual capacity the church baptized, married and buried everyone, providing the ceremonial framework and support for society and exercising a powerful control over private norms and morals. Most ordinary folk had far more contact with the church than with the state.

During the eighteenth century the Catholic Church had come under increasing attack from Enlightened writers for its failure to perform its social role adequately, and from the state for its unwillingness to contribute equitably towards national expenditure. Criticism of the inadequacies and neglect of hospitals and schools was legion. The corporate privileges of the church, with the exception of the tithe, were of little benefit to the vast majority of clergy, some of whom were as critical of them as were the lay community. Religious orders, especially the Jesuits, were criticized for placing their papal connections above loyalty to the state. There were attempts to expel the Jesuits from most states in the second half of the eighteenth century. The role of the Inquisition, where it remained influential in state circles, particularly in Spain and Portugal, was curtailed.

If the senior echelons of the Catholic hierarchy thought of themselves as the first order in 1780, Protestant and Russian Orthodox clergy could make no such claims. In Lutheran Prussia toleration of recently acquired Catholic enclaves and Jewish populations was assured, but so was the dominance of the state over churches of all kinds. In Russia the Tsar was head of church and state. Peter I ensured a subservient clergy when he set up the Holy Synod, while Catherine II deprived the church of its lands, substituting state salaries for the clergy. Exemption from income tax remained a prerogative, but the ordinary priest continued to receive such a pittance that he was barely distinguishable from the rest of the peasant community. Orthodoxy was held in esteem and the clergy had an important role in supporting the autocracy. In return the Orthodox clergy were encouraged to enforce the view that 'Holy' Russia had to be Orthodox. By 1830 religious tolerance was growing elsewhere, but in Russia Old Believers might still be deported to Siberia and Jews were denied the right to run their own schools.

The nobility or aristocracy, the second order or estate in Catholic countries, constituted a highly privileged corporation everywhere. They had the right to collect feudal dues from tenants, who were in various stages of legal servitude, ranging from the technical, but costly obligation to pay money-dues in France, to bodily servitude in Russia where a different form of serfdom had been imposed only in the seventeenth century. In Russia nobles counted their wealth not in land, but in the souls, or bodies, who worked the soil for them. Tsars were accustomed to rewarding nobles with gifts of people, to whom parcels of land were attached. Nobles had also acquired huge privileges, the most valuable of which tended to be tax exemptions. Nobles and clergy both paid tax, but, unlike the rest of the population, in some states they had the right to nominate assemblies, which negotiated terms with the ruler.

The nobility were deeply stratified by antiquity and origin of title, as well as by function and financial standing. The term gentry is sometimes used to describe those who were less rich and whose influence was usually local. The poorest nobles farmed their own land; in Brittany this group were very numerous and were called *hobereaux*. Nobles were typically landowners and often legislation had been enacted to protect their right to land; in Russia only nobles could buy serfs and thus own land. Regulations reciprocally prevented nobles engaging in business. By the 1780s, however, nobles had diversified into finance, commerce and industrial investment, using their land as a vital asset in textile and metal-lurgical activities, although usually their industrial concerns would be run by managers or tenants. The massive growth in Europe's world trade over the previous century was often noble-financed.

Curiously, in Russia, this was a period of retrenchment. Traditionally nobles had acquired the right to run foreign trade ventures and to set up iron and linen production. Towards the end of the eighteenth century the initiative passed to their managers, foreign, including Jewish entrepreneurs and in some cases serfs, such as the Old Believer group in the Moscow region, some of whom went on to become cotton millionaires. Meanwhile many nobles were taking out mortgages to the state to survive. In France in the 1780s, while noble families fought against attempts by the ruler to tax more rationally and effectively, the privileges of the nobility, particularly the right to collect feudal dues, were increasingly resented. In France these had often been sold and up to 20 per cent were owned by members of the middle class. They were collected purely as a dividend, having become quite divorced from traditional concepts in which the lord had owed protection and charity to those who paid the dues.

If poorer nobles sold feudal titles, richer bourgeois also bought nobility. The French crown sold titles along with venal, sometimes only honorific, office. The longer established nobles, the *noblesse d'epée*, despised this *noblesse de robe*, though they intermarried with its upstart members (often lawyers). The purchase of nobility through venal office bought privileges such as tax exemptions. On the eve of the 1789 Revolution sixty out of just over a hundred local noble families in Lille, a region acquired by France only in 1667, had gained their titles by purchase of office,[4] but the promised fiscal immunities evaporated as the crown invented new taxes to finance its war programme. In the half-century before the Revolution the burden of royal taxation tripled in Lille, robbing the elites of fiscal immunity, leaving them with only the lacquer of privilege. Their powerlessness to resist the fiscal exactions of the crown provoked a variety of groups to adopt the language of the *philosophes* and to identify their situation with such novel and amorphous concepts as the 'nation' and the 'citizen'.

Thus in the late eighteenth century the wealthy elite in western Europe was part noble, part bourgeois. In recent years revisionist historians of France, anxious to unpick a Marxist analysis of the French Revolution as a bourgeois takeover, have emphasized that by the 1780s there were no fundamental economic or fiscal distinctions between second and third estate.[5] Families were distinguished by self-perception and how they were seen by others. Life-style, education and marriage alliances were the keys. By the 1780s the concept of a single 'third' estate was entirely meaningless.

Although the first two orders might pay lip service to the remnants of internal cohesion, the third estate had none, but was clearly divided into a large number of elements. A wealthy minority of the third estate were substantial landowners; many were office-holders and as privileged as any members of the first two orders. In France an elite section of the judiciary also had direct political power, which many older established nobles considered they lacked. The twelve *parlements*, or appeal courts, run by *noblesse de robe*, had the right to register all decree law. In the years before 1789 they exercised increasing control over the king – filling a vacuum left by the Estates General that had last met in 1614. Prosperous lawyers, professionals, businessmen and merchants were keen to acquire land for the security and status which it conferred; the right to collect feudal dues was treasured. Even more attractive was one of the many expensive venal privileged state offices, which conveyed nobility and coveted tax exemptions. Thus in France the richest segment of the third estate shared many of the economic and political concerns of the nobles, with whom they intermarried when the impoverishment of a noble family matched their own status ambitions.[6] In the later decades of the twentieth century 'révisionist' historians were inclined to lump both groups together and call them 'notables'. Napoleon's officials had a habit of doing the same, but only when drawing up lists of the most wealthy inhabitants of a region for bureaucratic or other fiscal purposes. In their social relations eighteenth-century nobles and rich non-nobles were very conscious of the differences in status between them. They would have found the idea that they were all united by being 'notables' meaningless except in a financial and fiscal sense.

The third estate included merchants, businessmen, industrialists, professionals, officials and artisans as well as all sorts of landowners, tenants and labourers. In Russia, non-noble and non-serf social groups were carefully, systematically and minutely graded according to both prosperity and economic function.[7] Elsewhere, too, this was usually the case in practice. In France every group, however tiny, sought corporate status. There the urban guilds had acquired tax exemptions and other privileges in return for the right to organize their trade and were often powerful bodies in spheres far beyond their own craft. In many Italian cities the wealthy elites who ran municipal administration were powerful and closed corporations.

Towns would contain skilled artisans, journeymen, apprentices, large numbers in domestic service, unskilled labourers and the invisible and uncounted, who survived by their wits and by begging. Their numbers varied according to the general level of prosperity. By the end of the eighteenth century an increasing proportion of industry was located outside towns. Villages might contain specialized full-time craftsmen like shoemakers, but also many families who would take on both agrarian and industrial work depending on season and opportunity. In some of the poorest rural areas the migration of a large part of the adult male population to neighbouring and far distant towns in search of work was the norm. In Italy there were growing numbers of day-labourers, pushed off the land by capitalist agriculture, who would migrate for a few months each year to Naples, Rome, Palermo, Genoa and Milan in the agricultural dead season. Contemporaries could identify their origins by their craft and vice versa. Milanese chimney-sweeps hailed from the valleys of Onsernone, Canobbio and Valvigezzo, fruit and wine sellers from Ossola and Lake Maggiore, while porters, pot-makers, builders, painters and woodcutters were drawn from other poor rural areas. Over half the servants in Naples were migrants.[8] Seasonal migration was a feature of poor land, as well as rising numbers and agricultural change.

Within the third estate many were entirely dependent on farming. They ranged from landless labourers to those who survived as part-owners, part-tenants or, as was the norm on poor land, share-croppers. There were also prosperous tenants and large landowners. Many, but not all, owed feudal dues, payable in labour or cash. In western Europe such dues were largely commuted to cash, and resented because they had become merely an additional rent. In France violent peasant resistance to feudal dues ensured that their abolition came high on the agenda of revolutionary politicians in 1789. In Spain widespread peasant rioting against these dues was temporarily diverted by the struggle to drive out Napoleon, but after 1814 was directed against conservative and liberal regimes alike with increased virulence.[9]

The Revolutionary period witnessed the transformation of labour service into rents in most of the German states. This, linked to population increase, led to a by now familiar increase in the numbers of landless peasants, particularly in Pomerania, Silesia and the Mecklenburgs, but also in southern areas like Thuringia and Hesse-Darmstadt.[10] In Russia the vast majority of the population were serfs, although a small number of the more enterprising paid an *obrok*, or cash in lieu of work in preference to bodily service, both for themselves and for their own employees. Most communes would include land for common pasture, and often also woodland, whose use was shared by the community and was vital for the survival of the poorest members.

Throughout Europe most agricultural and industrial production was largely subsistence or directed to a very local market, but proto-capitalism was well advanced in limited areas and sectors of the economy such as wheat and silk production in the Ile de France and Lyon. Craftsmen were increasingly, and often unhappily, dependent on merchants and the vagaries of the market. There was also widespread resentment that the sale of feudal titles with no reciprocal obligations had degraded a relationship of mutual dependency into a totally commercial one. In this half-century in Italy and elsewhere in western Europe the better-off members of rural communities, or even outsiders, pressed to enclose common land for their own exclusive use. By 1780 those who were the losers from such processes yearned for a past 'moral' economy which was often wistfully, if misleadingly recalled as a society of settled 'orders'.

By the 1780s in France both were mere dreams. In 1788 when Louis XVI decided to revive the moribund Estates General in an attempt to solve the crown's financial problems, men were grouped in orders for the election and the initial assembly. The abbé Sieyès, in his widely influential contribution to the debate on how elections should be conducted,[11] used the language of orders to describe the society of classes which actually existed. The third estate, he claimed, included the vast majority of people and should properly be considered as constituting the nation. However, when he discussed the actual election and later when he helped to draw up a constitution, it was apparent that Sieyès was determined only to include the wealthy, educated and privileged middle-class element.

Contemporaries like Adam Smith and other economists who first began to write about 'classes' offered a fairly specific, predictably economic, explanation for their evolution. Class divisions, they argued, were a product of the growing gap between wealth and poverty which contemporaries believed to be the consequence of the development of a market economy. These observers disapproved of the growing disparities of income and resultant poverty, but thought them temporary and viewed capitalism itself as desirable. Class came to be defined more precisely and more politically during the French Revolution, when many of the social tensions implicit in the contemporary definitions of the term were visible.

The details of the French Revolution and the Napoleonic Empire have been dealt with elsewhere. The bloody confrontation of the 1790s helped to focus concepts of class, giving them political as well as socio-economic perspectives. The first order, the clergy, disappeared as a separate element. The concept of a 'second estate' disappeared: the nobility was formally abolished. For a time 'aristo' was used merely as vituperative abuse for anyone, titled or not, who was suspected of being hostile to the Revolution. No one talked about a third order any more, but of 'citizens'.

The Catholic Church was eliminated as an economic force in France and its power was reduced elsewhere in proportion to the success of French armies, vastly accelerating a trend begun in Catholic states before 1789. All of its French lands were sold in the 1790s and although individuals were again permitted to donate property to the church after 1814, it was never to recover independent economic power. The German Catholic Church lands were also sold. In Italy the Revolutionary armies encouraged seizures of church lands and the imitation of Jacobin-style anti-clerical policies. In 1804 Napoleon signed a Concordat with Pius VII on the French model. The bishops' authority over priests was restored, Catholicism was recognized as a state religion, while the Pope accepted loss of territory, the right to nominate bishops and acceded to the sale of church lands. Napoleon ignored his side of the Concordat, however, and in 1809 the Pope was imprisoned. In contrast the Spanish church, which led a crusade against Napoleon, remained enormously wealthy, monopolizing 20 per cent of the nation's income.

While the Catholic Church disappeared as a separate estate, the nobility Europe-wide was transformed from an order into the apex of the upper class. In France noble persecution of the 1790s was short-lived and by the turn of the century it was clear that their social and economic pre-eminence was unchallenged and their political power recoverable if the right compromises were reached.[12] The existence of different strata within the nobility was even more perceptible than before the Revolution, particularly as Napoleon created his own brand of titles. The financial consequences of the abolition of feudal rights in 1789 were smoothed away by estate managers who simply raised rents when new leases were due. In France and in other conquered territories, the land of émigrés was liable to be sequestrated, if the head of the house left the country, but compared with the church, the nobility got off very lightly. In France it is calculated that noble landownership probably fell from 25 to 20 per cent of the total and some of the more pushy losers were paid compensation after 1825.

The French nobility retained its social status undinted, perhaps even enhanced by the persecution of the 1790s. In 1831 when the Orleanists decided that only life-peers should sit in the Upper

House, the Chamber of Peers lost its kudos, but the idea of nobility did not. Snobbish bourgeois simply invented titles. In 1841 spurious ones were sported by about ninety of the elected Chamber of Deputies. Landownership became even more the litmus test of noble status. Detailed research is lacking, but it appears that, aside from the richest European noble families where diversification into business had been the norm, snobbery encouraged a partial rejection of the entrepreneurial world, at a considerable economic cost. In the second half of the nineteenth century, an increasing number of impoverished noble families in Prussia and Russia were obliged to sell their estates. To compensate and survive nobles became, if anything, more entrenched in these countries as the senior figures in the fast-growing bureaucracies.[13]

In some states wealthy non-nobles also occupied the top rank as members of the upper class, intermarried with the nobility, bought landed estates and jostled for social elevation, but only in France was bourgeois status and wealth sufficient to qualify for membership of the ruling elite after 1830. Elsewhere, whether in the Italian and Iberian peninsulas or in Germany and Russia, members of the nobility, sometimes admittedly with recent titles, continued to occupy the top jobs.

The middle classes were a rambling element, with no real distinguishing features beyond the desire of the most wealthy for nobility and the fears of the most poor of being regarded by others as artisans or peasants. The middle classes grew rapidly during these years. Historians habitually divide them into upper, middling and lower strata, sometimes even making the interchangeable terms 'bourgeois' and 'middle class' steps in a hierarchy of classification.[14] Contemporaries were more inclined to define themselves by function as landowners, state servants or members of the professions. Because one man might be all of these, and perhaps a forge-owner as well, class analysis, especially by computer, is quite tricky. The middle classes liked to imitate the nobles' life-style, trimmed according to income. The better-off acquired land. This was particularly important after 1814 when the growing trend towards elected legislative assemblies, launched by the French, meant that the right to vote and sit in the assemblies was dependent on the size of a man's tax bill, in which land taxes were almost invariably the major component.

The French Revolution had offered immense scope to the

landowning ambitions of the middle classes in France and in conquered territories. Sequestrated church (and to a lesser extent noble) lands were mainly acquired by the propertied middle classes, particularly by those further enriched by compensation paid for their loss of venal office. But the largest single occupational group within the middle classes were public officials. In the 1820s 40 per cent of the French Chamber of Deputies indicated a variety of official appointments as their main 'profession'. The enlargement of the modern state, much accelerated by the panoply of new centralized institutions created everywhere by the French during the Revolutionary decades, led to an astronomical growth in official jobs. There was a new air of professionalism about these bureaucracies. Everywhere it became customary for senior officials to have undertaken legal training at a university. But this trend did nothing to democratize them. It was an age of 'careers open to talent', but only for those whose families could afford to cultivate that talent. Junior official posts, whose numbers grew even more rapidly, were reserved for the lower middle class, with career grades so rigid that no clerk could aspire to serious promotion.

The professions were another area of growth and definition within the middle classes, but one where there were some problems in the years after 1814. In both of the senior professions, law and medicine, numbers expanded, as they did also in engineering. Standardization of entry requirements (in the German states the *abitur*, in France the *baccalauréat)* and of the ensuing training in faculties and universities added to the sense of prestige and of measurable professionalism. However, throughout the professions the expansion of the role of the state seemed a threat to independence and corporate autonomy. The state itself oversaw the new tests. In Prussia no one could enter state service without the *abitur*, nor could a qualified lawyer begin to earn money until he obtained a state appointment, which might add ten further years to a decade of legal training. Traditionally senior lawyers, and those who staffed courts of appeal in particular, visualized themselves as independent arbiters, almost Platonic Guardians.[15] In the early nineteenth century in France, Prussia and other German states, lawyers were incensed by restrictions on the number of appointments and promotions available to an increasing pool of trained practitioners.

In these years centralization of government resulted in the

rationalization and the standardization of law and legal systems. Written codes became the norm, with the French setting an example which they imposed on conquered territories. Such rationalization gave status to the law, but made the state, not the courts, the law-makers. In addition the officials in the new courts of the Napoleonic era in France and dependent territories were state appointed. Venality of office was abolished and with it went lifetime, hereditary appointments. Asserting the Enlightened principle of the separation of powers in the state, the French legal profession ensured that government-appointed members of courts could not be dismissed, but a refusal to promote, or a sideways move to an unattractive area, could have the same effect.

Medical men, who enjoyed a similar autonomy if less status in the ancien regime, also found these years ones of uncomfortable adjustment. German doctors were angered by state intervention to limit the number of doctors being trained. In France the creation of the less qualified *officier de santé*, to cope with the wartime crisis, led to an over-large pool of medical men once the battles were over and, ironically, to complaints that the state refused to limit numbers in training. Governments also intervened in the development of specialized higher education institutes in France, Germany and Russia to train top level engineers for state civil and military functions. Like the other professions, the cost of education and training ensured that recruits were predominantly from the rich middle class, often following the same calling as their fathers.

Up to 1830 these were contentious issues. Over the next half-century the professions were able to develop such respect for their calling and status that they managed to preserve corporate privileges and professional autonomy. They became vital elements in the centralized bureaucratic state, where they were not only unchecked by elected assemblies, but also often (particularly the lawyers) played an important role within those bodies in Germany, Italy, France and elsewhere. The survival and revamping of corporate autonomy placed such severe limitations on the openness and democracy of new structures later in the century that the result has been referred to as a 'stalled society'.[16]

No united middle class emerged, either in this half-century or later. However the educated elites convinced themselves that they were threatened by the 'popular' or 'dangerous' classes. In the years after 1820 educated contemporaries were becoming concerned that industrial change and urbanization were leading to such visible extremes of wealth and poverty that social stability was threatened. On the right and left of politics class consciousness and differentiation appeared a danger to the state. Contemporary social critics, from Babeuf, the 'communist' insurgent of the 1790s, to Saint-Simon, aristocratic social reformer, were inclined to echo the economists and define class purely with material criteria. They used simple polemical divisions which implied not only distinctions but also confrontation, such as the 'idle' rich of all kinds, and the 'active' of all varieties, from lawyer and journalist to rural labourer. From the start observers saw class as contentious. Babeuf and all the later socialists who revered his name thought radical measures were needed to eliminate or reduce class divisions. Saint-Simon argued that the answer lay in including all property-owners, including industrialists, in government. Liberals thought that the problem of poverty was a temporary phenomenon to be alleviated by private charity and that the popular unrest it created should be controlled by detachments of troops.

There is evidence of some rudimentary class consciousness among the elites in Restoration France, obviously learned from the French Revolution. Ultra-royalist officials habitually referred to their liberal opponents as 'the commercial and industrial middle class', totally ignoring the fact that the liberals were nearly all substantial landowners and that most were professional men, usually lawyers. The liberals liked to picture themselves as bourgeois sons of 1789, although most wanted strict limits on future revolution, and a number were of noble rather than middle-class origins. The height of propaganda nonsense in the use of class phraseology by the educated was the description of Louis-Philippe, duke of Orleans, and cousin to the Bourbon king Charles X, as a 'bourgeois' monarch in 1830. Thus the elites were sensitive to the language of class, although often word-blind.

There was far less class awareness among the victims of economic change and depression in France, the 'popular classes' of the elites' nightmares. Artisans in small-scale wine production, silk, tailoring and so on, would band together locally to protest to government representatives about the perceived injustice of official commercial policies, but spasmodically, briefly and in a fragmented way. In the 1780s it was well-established practice for artisans within a single craft in an area to combine for mutual protection. In the following half-century the issues of new techniques – such as the introduction of 'off-the-peg' tailoring, new machines, cheap female and foreign labour – were to become contentious matters in different crafts, although a quarter-century of war distorted the issues. Traditional small-scale mutual insurance schemes grew as rapidly as suspicious officials would allow. Poorer country-dwellers tried to oppose the erosion of communal rights which accompanied the abolition of feudal institutions. Thus there were numerous factors which made popular unrest endemic, but they did not lead to any sense of class consciousness among the 'popular' classes.

The educated feared that economic change would lead not only to revolution but also to declining moral standards and the demise of the family. In reality, down to 1830, dramatic economic transformation was concentrated in Britain, and even here almost exclusively in the cotton industry. However the commentaries of doctors like Kay, who described the horrors of cotton-mad Lancashire, stimulated the moral conscience of his continental colleagues, who led the way to middle-class awareness and, shortly, to institutional reform. In the 1820s bourgeois ladies still read Sir Walter Scott, but within a few years Hugo, See and the factual reports of Villeneuve-Bargemont and Villermé would be thrilling them with the horrors endured by women and children workers in industry. As we have seen, industrial growth was largely in rural areas, and rapid urbanization belonged far more to the later years of the century. But capital cities were expanding and poverty was more visible, as the post-war depression of 1816–18 was quickly followed by a similar collapse in 1827.

Contemporaries were beginning to note the scale of women's and children's employment; up to 30 per cent of the French workforce was female, 12 per cent children. Far more worked in agriculture, in domestic service and in rural artisan industry than in cotton factories. Their employment was the long-established norm and no innovation. But their educated brethren were more aware of their presence in newer industries and moralized about the decline of the family, increased sexual immorality, drunkenness and, what was indisputably correct, the unhealthy conditions of an industrial environment.

Whereas women had always worked in domestic industry, their position was qualitatively altered by the development of cotton spinning mills (although these existed only in very limited areas, such as Mulhouse, Rouen, Moscow, parts of Saxony, etc.). Often a minority of workers were men, and the displacement of the latter seemed to turn the world upside down for educated observers. Additionally female and child labour was beginning to be seen as inhumane. It involved very long hours, and was very poorly paid, sometimes less than a quarter of the man's rate.[17] Such low payments forced parents to be hard task masters when their fellow-workers were their own offspring.[18] Observers were also shocked to realize that the protests of enlightened writers about wet-nursing had been to no avail. French women workers continued to hand their infants to a wet-nurse, although in Britain female cotton operatives rarely worked when they became mothers.

Statistics on infant mortality, illegitimacy and prostitution were beginning to fuel middle-class outrage. Observers assumed that recent industrial innovations were wholly responsible. Probably the main change was that figures were now being assembled and that, in these years, the collators were men like Villeneuve-Bargemont[19] who were entirely opposed to industrialization and yearned for a paternalistic golden age. In the 1820s female and child labour in new factories had little more of an impact on family structure than had the domestic system, for families continued to work in teams, even in factories. Women were no more immoral; appallingly low wages forced them, as always, to make ends meet in whatever way was possible and domestic service, still the biggest employer, provided far more occasions for sexual harassment than did the factory. Mulhouse cotton kings were disposed to heed the warnings of reformers who urged them to improve the morality of their workers by setting up schools. It was the Mulhouse Industrial Society which began the impetus for government legislation to restrict child labour, first introduced in 1841.

Arguably industrial change was beginning to have an impact on middle-class families. As industrial, commercial and retail concerns grew beyond the limits of family organization, wives were needed less as book-keepers and shopminders, at least until widowhood obliged them to take over. The age of a leisured female middle class was arriving, divided between domestic management, piety and charitable works – a golden age indeed! There has been a tendency among late twentieth-century historians, notably feminists, to stress the emergence of separate spheres for the sexes. In the eighteenth century, when neither sex had direct access to legislative power outside Great Britain, wealthy aristocratic ladies presided over *salons* and apparently exercised

considerable informal political influence thereby. In the nineteenth century parliaments were male preserves, but the churches
increasingly female in terms of their active membership. The
education of women by female religious orders intensified the
separation of spheres. Earlier some enlightened writers, of whom
Rousseau is best remembered, had argued that there was a
biological gender bias in the distribution of that prized commodity, reason, and that women should be educated for motherhood
and family exclusively.

Women were very visible in revolutionary crowds in 1789, 1830
and 1848, as surviving illustrations bear witness. However, their
presence was not necessarily a political act. It was traditionally
accepted that women had the right to protest about high food
prices as part of their family role.[20] Yet it seems clear that some
were demanding more than fair bread prices.[21] In the 1790s their
political presence was sufficient for two of the three portraits
included by Lamartine in his history of the Revolution to be
Madame Roland, wife of the Girondin minister, and Charlotte
Corday, Marat's assassin. Olympe de Gouges published a Declaration of the Rights of Women in 1791, Pauline Léon petitioned that
women be allowed to join the National Guard, women's clubs
were formed, and Condorcet offered some support.

After some slight hesitation, the revolutionaries rejected such
demands. Most women apparently shared the common Jacobin
view that their role was to breast-feed the next generation of
soldiers of the Republic. The attack on the Catholic Church turned
many women against the Revolution, which of course strengthened
the voice of Jacobins who had already been convinced that the
power to reason was gender-specific.[22] On the other hand, the
legalization of divorce in 1792 might be interpreted as a feminist
measure. Three-quarters of those who petitioned for divorce in
Rouen were women, and before the withdrawal of the legislation
in 1803 there was one divorce for every eight marriages.[23] However, the measure was chiefly designed to curb clerical power. The
codes of law completed in the early 1800s confirmed the reduction
in the status of women in society. The creation of representative
systems and elections even excluded the wealthy females who
would have had the right to delegate a male to vote on their behalf
in ancien regime estates. It is a curious irony that the symbol of
1789 was female.

In the early 1830s the Saint-Simonians reintroduced the idea of women's rights in France,[24] although the personal behaviour of Enfantin and some of his female acolytes provided fuel for traditionalist comments that feminism licensed whores and harpies. In the 1840s politically aware women, such as Flora Tristan and Jeanne Deroin were more preoccupied with trying to form unions, of men and women, to fight against exploitation, although in 1848 Jeanne Deroin did speak up for votes for women and tried to stand as a candidate. That she only received one vote and was condemned by George Sand for her efforts, indicates the divisions, even among feminist women. The social question of the years which followed 1830 was not the emancipation of the female, but of the poor from the impact of economic change.

NOTES

1 A useful survey is W. Doyle, *The Old European Order. 1660–1800* (Oxford, 1978).
2 See Further reading, pp.221–2.
3 W.J. Callahan and D. Higgs (eds) *Church and Society in Catholic Europe of the Eighteenth Century* (Cambridge, 1979).
4 G. Bossenga, *The Politics of Privilege. Old Regime and Revolution in Lille* (Cambridge, 1991), p.70.
5 See D. Johnson (ed.) *French Society and the Revolution* (Cambridge, 1976).
6 D.C. Higgs, *Nobles in Nineteenth Century France. The Practice of Inegalitarianism* (Baltimore and London, 1987), p.194.
7 C.E. Timberlake,'The middle classes in late Tsarist Russia', in M.L. Bush (ed.) *Social Orders and Social Classes in Europe since 1500* (London, 1992), pp.86–113.
8 S. Woolf, *A History of Italy 1700–1860. The Social Constraints of Political Change* (London, 1979), p.289.
9 A. Shubert, *A Social History of Modern Spain* (London, 1990), pp.93–5.
10 T.S. Hamerow, *Restoration, Revolution and Reaction. Economics and Politics in Germany 1815–1871* (Princeton, New Jersey, 1970), pp.51–2.
11 *Qu'est-ce-que le tiers état?* (Paris, 1788).
12 D.C. Higgs, *Nobles in Nineteenth-Century France. The Practice of Inegalitarianism* (Baltimore and London, 1987).
13 A balanced survey of recent thinking on noble survival in D. Lieven, *The Aristocracy in Europe 1815–1914* (London, 1992).
14 A comparative perspective can be found in P.M. Pilbeam, *The Middle Classes in Europe 1789–1914: France, Germany, Italy and Russia* (London, 1990).
15 A lucid synthesis of German research can be found in M. John, 'Between estate and profession: lawyers and the development of the legal profession in nineteenth-century Germany', in D. Blackbourn and R.J. Evans (eds) *The German Bourgeoisie* (London, 1993), pp.162–97.
16 M. Crozier, *The Stalled Society* (New York, 1974).

17 L. Tilly and J. Scott, *Women, Work and Family* (London, 1978).
18 C. Heywood, *Childhood in Nineteenth-Century France: Work, Health and Education among the 'Classes Populaires'* (London, 1988).
19 Legitimist prefect of the Nord who sustained his war against the regime which unseated him in *Economie politique chrétienne*, 2 vols (Paris, 1834).
20 O. Hufton, 'Social conflict and the grain supply in eighteenth century France', in R.I. Rotberg and T.K. Rabb (eds) *Hunger and History* (Cambridge, 1985), pp.103–35.
21 H.B. Applewhite and D.G. Levy, *Women and Politics in the Age of the Democratic Revolution* (Ann Arbor, Michigan, 1990).
22 O. Hufton, *Women and the Limits of Citizenship during the French Revolution* (Toronto, 1992), pp.104–18.
23 R. Phillips, 'Women and family breakdown in Rouen, 1780–1800', *Social History* (1976).
24 C. Moses, 'St Simonian men/St Simonian women: the transformation of feminist thought in 1830s France', *Journal of Modern History*, 54 (1982).

FURTHER READING

Incisive and stimulating essay collections which offer insight into more than one country include M.L. Bush (ed.) *Social Order and Social Classes in Europe since 1500. Studies in Social Stratification* (London, 1992) and G. Crossick and H.-G. Haupt, *Shopkeepers and Master-Artisans in Nineteenth Century Europe* (London, 1986). Comparative studies of social groups are provided in D. Lieven, *Aristocracy in Europe 1815–1914* (London, 1992) and P.M. Pilbeam, *The Middle Classes in Europe 1789–1914* (London, 1990).

French society has been well served by French, British and North American historians, with a wealth of regional studies in addition to the small selection included here. Two recent surveys of France offer contrasting approaches: R.D. Price, *Social History of Nineteenth Century France* (London, 1987) is thematic in structure, while P. McPhee, *A Social History of France 1780–1880* (London, 1992) attempts a chronological format and is more linked to political developments. An essential starting point for French approaches to social history is M. Agulhon, *The Republic in the Village: The People of the Var from the French Revolution to the Second Republic* (Cambridge, 1970, trs. Janet Lloyd). Two invaluable mines of information have been translated: A. Moulin, *Peasantry and Society in France since 1789* (Cambridge, 1991) and G. Noiriel, *Workers in French Society in the 19th and 20th Centuries* (New York, 1990). W.H. Sewell, *Work and Revolution in France: The Language of Labor from the Old Regime to 1848* (Cambridge, 1980) is thought-provoking. K.A. Lynch, *Family, Class and Ideology in Early Industrial France. Social Policy and the Working-Class Family 1825–1848* (Wisconsin, 1988) merits attention. The Catholic Church has been well documented in R. Gibson, *A Social History of French Catholicism 1789–1914* (London, 1989) and F. Tallett and N. Atkin, *Religion, Society and Politics in France since 1789* (London, 1991).

Those interested in the German states would do well to begin with H. Bohme, *An Introduction to the Social and Economic History of Germany* (Oxford, 1978) and T.S. Hamerow, *Restoration, Revolution and Reaction. Economics and Politics in Germany 1815–1871* (Princeton, New Jersey, 1970) is still well worth hunting for. D. Blackbourn and R.J. Evans (eds) *The German Bourgeoisie. Essays on the Social History of the German Middle Class from the Late Eighteenth Century to the Early Twentieth Century* (London, 1991) is immensely lucid and informative, based solidly on recent German research. A number of excellent regional studies have appeared including T.C.W. Blanning, *Reform and Revolution in Mainz, 1743–1803* (Cambridge, 1974), T.C.W. Blanning, *The French Revolution in Germany* (Oxford, 1983), J. Whaley, *Religious Toleration and Social Change in Hamburg, 1529–1819* (Cambridge, 1985), J.M. Diefendorf, *Businessmen and Politics in the Rhineland, 1789–1834* (Princeton, 1980) and Mack Walker, *German Home Towns: Community, State and General Estate, 1648–1871* (Ithaca, 1971).

S. Woolf, *A History of Italy 1700–1860. The Social Constraints of Political Change* (London, 1979) makes up for the lamentable lack of work in English on Italian society. Also of value are K.R. Greenfield, *Economics and Liberalism in the Risorgimento: A Study of Nationalism in Lombardy 1814–48* (Baltimore, 1965) and J.A. Davis, *Merchants and Contractors: A Study of Economic Activity and Society in Bourbon Naples 1815–1860* (New York, 1981).

Students of Russian society might begin with C.E. Black (ed.) *The Transformation of Russian Society* (London, 1960) and M. Raeff, *Understanding Imperial Russia. State and Society in the Ancien Regime* (New York, 1984). A.J. Rieber, *Merchants and Entrepreneurs in Imperial Russia* (Chapel Hill, North Carolina, 1982) is an excellent example of an increasing number of English language investigations into the pre-Revolutionary middle class.

An essential work on Spain is A. Shubert, *A Social History of Modern Spain* (London, 1990), which is indispensable, not only for its quality, but also for the lack of other work in English on Spanish society in this period.

Chapter 11

Reason and romanticism: currents of social and political thought

Michael Biddiss

THE ENLIGHTENMENT AND THE ROMANTIC MOVEMENT

Europe of the eighteenth century bequeathed to the nineteenth a rich and complex legacy. It included not only political revolution in France and industrial revolution in Britain but also challenges from two broad currents in the realm of ideas. One became known as the Enlightenment, the other as the Romantic Movement. Their moods were in some ways mutually irreconcilable. Yet there were significant points of convergence too, especially where they each called into question many entrenched habits of eighteenth-century life and thought, society and government. This essay will outline something of their ambivalent interrelationship, and of their dual influence upon European social and political thinking down to the revolutions of 1830.

In examining the Enlightenment, we must not exaggerate either its doctrinal or its organizational coherence. The *philosophes* who promoted it came from the aristocracy as well as the educated middle class. They were also participating in a phenomenon of truly European scope which exhibited great variety of detail according to local circumstance. For example, the religious scepticism characterizing the movement in its French heartland needs to be contrasted with both the Catholic and the Protestant brands of Enlightenment developed across the German states. The depiction of the *philosophes* as a tightly coordinated phalanx of plotters, aiming to impose standardized dogma, was largely the product of their opponents' anxious imaginations. What did draw the enlightened together was a shared attitude of mind reflecting some broad consensus about the nature of contemporary problems and about the strategies required to solve them. At the core lay their belief in the connection that must be secured between critical thinking – firmly founded on reason treated not as a vague *a priori* force but as something linked to experience and experiment – and forms of effective action. In a famous essay of 1784 Immanuel Kant answered the question 'What is Enlightenment?' by defining it as 'the emergence of mankind from its self-imposed immaturity'.[1] He proposed that it should borrow a motto from the Latin poet Horace: *sapere aude* (dare to know!). Kant glossed this as meaning that all should have the courage to use their own rational judgement. So viewed, the Enlightenment meant a systematic questioning of all traditional authority – a plea for critical (and, at its best, *self*-critical) attitudes throughout every sphere of thought and action.

The intent was far from being merely negative. Especially in social matters, criticism served essentially as a foundation for more positive attempts at rational construction. 'Progress' was now a real possibility, but never an inevitability attainable without intelligent striving. The multi-volume *Encyclopédie* (1751–80), edited by Denis Diderot as the central collaborative enterprise of the French Enlightenment, showed concern not merely to catalogue the ancien regime's abuses but also to draw guidelines for humane reform. In such searching for a 'science' of man and society, the movement was crucially influenced by two Englishmen whose careers ended early in the eighteenth century. The achievement in physics of Isaac Newton (d.1727) had prompted greater confidence in the scope of all human understanding. Similarly, the political, psychological and educational treatises of John Locke (d.1704) had encouraged greater expectations about the improvement that might stem from conscious alterations to a social environment whose defects now seemed not intrinsic but man-made. On this basis, the *philosophes* aimed to alter attitudes not just towards the desirability of social change but also towards the practicability and pace of its attainment. Eventually, they helped to unleash in France a more sudden upheaval than most of them had bargained for. Yet, just as surely, they assisted with the evolution of a wider European transformation, involving an erosion of the persuasive power of mere tradition and an encouragement of the newer habit of experimental innovation.

Enlightened reform had as its goals both freedom and felicity. The *philosophes* tended to assume over-readily that liberty must necessarily lead towards happiness, and they often found it difficult to reconcile the individual and collective dimensions of each. None the less they were right to recognize strong similarities between the factors that were frustrating freedom and those that were prolonging misery. That awareness underpinned the Enlightenment's protests against unthinking deference to secular or spiritual authority, arbitrary applications of power and privilege, restrictions on speech or belief or trade, judicial whims and delays, and many other disorderly and irrational features of European society and governance. The criticisms ranged wide, yet they were largely the protests of reformers rather than conscious revolutionaries. Voltaire and his fellows did not intend that their militant moderation should be a mere prelude to fanatical excess. However, that upshot became more probable once the assault on current social and political defects developed so pervasively as to encourage condemnation of the whole framework. By the 1780s it was increasingly doubtful whether the goals of Enlightenment really could be attained without some more dramatic reconstruction than that originally envisaged.

The movement had been forthright in pursuit of religious toleration, penal reform and equality before the law. Yet it had not generally abandoned the idea of hierarchy as such. In economics, where *laissez-faire* principles were its beacon, the Enlightenment showed much respect for property and little enthusiasm for thoroughgoing redistribution of wealth. As for schooling, the *philosophes* certainly wanted to reduce illiteracy, yet their overall attitude towards the educational and moral capacities of the masses showed strong elements of hesitancy, ambiguity, and even fear. Voltaire was typical in wondering just how much illumination the bulk of humanity could bear. Similar caution prevailed in regard to popular political involvement. The enlightened tended to view the conduct of public affairs in the classical fashion – as the preserve of men practised in the arts of leisure and refinement. Thus the obvious instrument of change was not the people at large, but a sympathetic monarch or minister wielding an authority commensurate with the scale of the reforming tasks ahead.

The term 'Enlightened Absolutism' still has some value in suggesting this real, if always problematic, convergence of interest between rulers and *philosophes*. The former were often keen to enhance efficiency through a rationalization of institutions and procedures, as witnessed by the *Cameralwissenschaft* ('science of administration') promoted in a number of the German states. Enlightened thinkers, for their part, greeted opportunities to contribute directly towards improved government. Their inspiration was apparent in the reforms of such rulers as Joseph II in the Habsburg Empire, his brother the Archduke Leopold of Tuscany (briefly Emperor Leopold II), Charles III of Spain, and the Margrave Charles Frederick of Baden. Yet, generally, the liaison was more a matter of convenience than conviction. When tensions arose, monarchs preferred traditional kingship to innovative philosophy. Diderot rightly doubted the sincerity of Catherine the Great; Voltaire felt misused by Frederick II of Prussia; and in France the Turgot ministry was abruptly terminated by Louis XVI. On the whole, as Peter Gay argues, such collaboration led the *philosophes* 'through the devious and embarrassing detours of repression and manipulation that were a denial or a mockery of the world they hoped to bring into being'.[2]

Another brand of potential distortion was also evident. If reform did not come quickly enough from the top, there was risk of it being violently pursued from elsewhere. This was particularly so in the case of France, whose monarchy lacked the nerve to be either effectively despotic on the one hand or consistently enlightened upon the other. The country also had higher literacy and a more politically alert middle class than was generally the case elsewhere in continental Europe, and thus it supplied particularly fertile ground for that central feature of the Enlightenment epoch which Roy Porter characterizes as the growth of 'the secular intelligentsia . . . as a relatively independent social force'.[3] By 1780 the intellectual life of France, reflected in such features as its journals and provincial academies, had come to centre upon enlightened ideas. The *philosophes* had won an audience extending beyond the third estate to many aristocrats and clergy. The Enlightenment's topicality was enhanced by the fact that the government itself repeatedly publicized the need for reforms, even while failing properly to pursue them whenever privileged interest groups resisted. Relevant too was Louis XVI's support for the American colonial revolt against Britain. This not only brought France close to bankruptcy, but also confronted her with an ideological paradox full of subversive potential. How wise had it been to assist the triumph of a new republic which, claiming rationalist principles of foundation, was now (for the benefit of whites, but not black slaves) implementing many enlightened ideas and promoting the rhetoric of Liberty and Equality?

As deadlock developed within France, notions derived from the Enlightenment were expressed in an increasingly populist way. What the *philosophes* had uttered in salons or relatively expensive books could acquire a more crudely radical meaning elsewhere. The less comfortable sections of urban society provided the chief audience for the *libelles*, and other forms of cheap literature dedicated to diffusing the habit of criticism. Here authors expressed mordant contempt for polite society at large, including those circles where the *philosophes* themselves had become too cosily domesticated. The French Revolution owed much to both of these brands of writing. Yet at many points, and especially during the phase of radical Jacobinism, it would explore the implications of Enlightenment in a spirit closer to the *libellistes* than to the *philosophes*.

As for the Romantic Movement, this was even more lacking than the rationalist one in tight organizational or doctrinal structures. It is as a loose cluster of attitudes, a shared mood and manner of feeling, that we see romanticism coming to affect not only political thinking but every other genre of intellectual and creative endeavour. The intensity of impact differed from country to country, but none entirely escaped its influence. This process was not, chiefly, a matter of direct importation from one area to another. Romanticism developed, rather, as a series of largely spontaneous expressions of some common temper that had native roots within nearly every land. The word itself assumed its modern meaning only after 1800. However, the substance of the phenomenon had clearly begun to emerge during the last third of the eighteenth century – at the epoch when most of the principal *philosophes* were already reaching the end of their careers.

In some respects, romanticism – like the Enlightenment – repudiated the conventions of the ancien regime. In others, it signified equally some rejection of the *philosophes* as well. The latter attitude did less than justice to the complex, and often positive, nature of the relationship between the two intellectual currents. The Enlightenment did not totally spurn the imaginative faculties, nor did romanticism condemn outright the reasoning ones. Each movement, at its best, explored the senses in which heart and head might be consorts, not rivals. As Diderot observed, reason should serve to harmonize the passions. The ambivalence of the situation was well exemplified by the case of the Genevan writer Jean-Jacques Rousseau, whose influence grew even after his death in 1778. Especially through his novel *La nouvelle Héloïse* (1761), he contributed much to the ethos of romanticism. While never quite comfortable in *philosophe* circles, he none the less left his imprint on the Enlightenment too. He made a romantic cult of individual emotion and sensibility, yet also strove to contain its consequences within a rational framework. The ensuing ambiguities pervaded his political classic on *The Social Contract* (1762). One unequivocal conclusion that did come through, however, was Rousseau's conviction that the procedures of the ancien regime in Europe could satisfy neither enlightened nor romanticist principles. Not surprisingly, during the French Revolution his ideas would be invoked at moments both of moderation and of frenzy.

Romanticism's critique of the Enlightenment, even if sometimes overplayed, did score some palpable hits. There was accusation about narrowness of vision, particularly regarding the status of reason. The approach of the *philosophes* was deemed to be not so much false as inadequate, in so far as they mistook a portion of the truth for the whole. The romantics, for their part, were not generally hostile to reason, nor to science. Yet they did warn against crediting such things with supreme authority, and treating them in that mode of mechanistic materialism towards which the Enlightenment tended. This had produced a version of rationalism which must now be condemned as a desiccating spirit set to drain all beauty from the world. Was there not more to nature than the analytic approach could ever reveal? Romanticism stressed the need to combat the habit of accepting as real only that which accorded with a shallow view of what was factual or fitting. Thus its supporters indulged the rhetoric of heart and soul, of passionate and intuitive compulsion. They championed, far more fully than any *philosophe*, the vital revelatory quality of the emotive and imaginative faculties. Now, as Hugh Honour has proposed in ironic echo of Kant, the motto would be, 'Dare to feel, have the courage of your own intuition.'[4]

The romantics revelled in the sheer diversity of human experience, thrilling not least to things historically or geographically remote. 'Primitive' societies became one of the chief focal points of their search for harmonious conditions of uncorrupted simplicity. There was also enhanced concern with the origins and development of the sense of nationhood. This involved a form of consciousness that bound past and present together in the kind of organic continuity undervalued by the Enlightenment's rationalism. The contrast with the *philosophes* was further demonstrated through the kind of responsiveness to the Middle Ages well exemplified in *The Genius of Christianity* (1802) by François de Chateaubriand. These centuries were now rehabilitated as an era of spiritual sensitivity, rather than derided for their unenlightened superstition. Romanticism urged that much could still be learned from medieval humility in face of the mysterious and the infinite. Those who, in the spirit of Enlightenment, pursued the mere domination and dissection of nature tended to neglect the kind of emotional response to it that might reveal still greater truths. As William Wordsworth reproachfully observed:

> One impulse from a vernal wood
> May teach you more of man,
> Of moral evil and of good,
> Than all the sages can.[5]

Thus, at every turn, the Romantic Movement aspired towards a larger cognitive range, illuminating the deeper realities lying beneath the level of mere appearances.

This emphasis on varieties of experience was also evident in criticisms of the enlightened concern to render the world tidy and to establish universally valid principles in politics, morals or whatever. Such regularity appealed little to the romantics, who preferred to make a merit of diversity. They delighted in a world not of static 'being' but of dynamic 'becoming'. Here reality was something constantly remoulded by the play of mind and imagination – part of the creative disorder stemming from each individual's uniquely subjective interpretation of experience. Nothing was more characteristic of romantic literature than its confessional quality and its lyric expression of an inner voice. It probed into the realms of the unconscious, and of ecstasy and madness too. Similarly, it thrilled to the perils of night, to the season of dreams and ghosts, and even to the mysteries of the ultimate darkness – death itself as the gateway to another, and alluringly unpredictable, world of experience.

The application of these insights to debate about society and politics was no simple matter. As Porter and Teich put it, romanticism was 'neither uniformly progressive nor reactionary, neither wholly liberal nor authoritarian, neither unequivocally republican nor monarchist'.[6] The concern with diversity, for instance, could inspire empathy towards the customs of other lands; but, in an era of rising nationalism, it could just as easily promote arrogance about the unique worth and superiority of one's own people. Again, the romantics' passion for individual self-fulfilment obviously had positive implications for liberalism; yet these could be negated either through failure to cope with situations where the self-fulfilment of one person worked at the expense of this same virtue in others, or through an attempt to deal with that problem by establishing some potentially illiberal super-organism to whose higher purposes all must sacrifice themselves. Similar ambiguities pervaded the romanticist responses to major events, and to the French Revolution especially. It could certainly be viewed in terms of that blissful dawn which Wordsworth originally perceived. Alternatively, it might appear – either from its very origins, or merely from its lapse into terror – as nothing less than the deplorable outcome of attempts to rupture a proper organic continuity with the past.

REVOLUTIONARY IDEAS AND CONSERVATIVE REACTIONS

The upheaval in France made profound impact upon the whole conceptual structure of modern political debate. One example was the slogan of 'Liberty, Equality, Fraternity', widely current after 1791. Another was the imagery of 'Right' and 'Left' which, originating in the seating arrangements of the Convention, thereafter haunted the rhetoric of confrontation between advocates of continuity and those of change. Not least, 'Revolution' itself assumed a deeper significance, reflecting visions of social as well as political transformation on a greater scale than previously envisaged. The term now expressed, even beyond particular risings, some powerful force constantly in being – like the spectre with which in 1848 Karl Marx would threaten the European bourgeoisie.

Those who, during the nineteenth century, drew on the ideas of the French Revolution revealed much diversity in their political attitudes. Thus they mirrored differences of emphasis already evident through the period 1788–94. Liberals harked back to the opening phase, when attempts at constitution-making owed much to the prescriptions about balance and moderation derived from Montesquieu. Enthusiasts for more drastic change admired, rather, the epoch of Jacobin ascendancy dominated by Robespierre's interpretation of Rousseau. After that experience, many of the 'letters of complaint' which had been submitted on the eve of the Revolution looked, with hindsight, remarkably temperate. Their main political focus had fallen neither on republicanism nor radical egalitarianism. What they tended to demand were restrictions on the arbitrary operation of royal authority, attainable through a representative system spreading power among those with a propertied stake in society. That was the aim of Abbé Sieyès when he answered the question posed by his famous polemic – *What is the Third Estate?* (1789) – by saying that it wished to be something, instead of nothing.

The Declaration of the Rights of Man and of the Citizen similarly indicated some measure of moderate intent. Yet, having been approved by the National Assembly late in August 1789 and thus only six weeks after the fall of the Bastille, this charter-document of the Revolution also carried a more radical potential. It provided not only a summary critique of current abuses but also a positive statement of principles that should now be deemed universally valid. Most of the text stemmed from axioms proclaimed in the opening articles:

I   Men are born, and remain, free and equal in rights. Social distinctions can be based only on public utility.

II The aim of all political association is the preservation of the natural and imprescriptible rights of man. These rights are liberty, property, security, and resistance to oppression.

III The principle of all sovereignty resides essentially in the nation. No body or individual may exercise any authority which is not expressly derived from it.[7]

Mirabeau was one prominent member of the Assembly who feared that the Declaration might impose precipitate demands on a people still unversed in the arts of representative government. However, by the time that the Convention met in 1792, leadership of the Revolution had clearly fallen into more radical hands. France now declared itself a republic – and one that executed its deposed monarch early the following year.

During 1793–4 the revolutionary drive was sustained by the dogmatic Robespierre, who treated politics as an arena for essentially moral activity. Echoing both Rousseau and the Declaration, he insisted upon the people as the source of all sovereign authority. He and the Jacobins strove to liberate a natural good-ness whose possession by the masses had been obscured amidst the corruptive circumstances of the ancien regime. Under con-ditions of equality, it was claimed, citizens would put public benefit above private interest and, by demonstrating their *amour de la patrie*, would launch the Reign of Virtue. In reality, Jacobinism became increasingly authoritarian. Robespierre concluded that its aims must be promoted through the use of terror – defined, conveniently, as the form that virtue itself must take in a time of national peril. However, this temporary expedient soon hardened into a whole way of life – or, indeed, death. As Jacobin violence grew more indiscriminate, not even the undoubted personal integrity of 'the Incorruptible' could check the frenzy of his moral fervour. By the time of his fall, Robespierre had effectively expropriated from the people that sovereignty with which he theoretically endowed them, and the fanaticism of his new secular ideology had made him more of a threat to civil liberties than Louis XVI ever managed to be.

One victim was the Marquis de Condorcet. Known as a *philosophe*, he was a supporter of the Revolution but not of its Jacobin manifestation. Even as the agents of the Terror pursued him, he wrote a work which revealed him as a still greater optimist than Robespierre concerning the scope for a transformation of human potential. His *Sketch for a Historical Picture of the Human Mind* (posthumously published in 1795) interpreted past, present and future in essentially progressive terms. As mankind ap-proached its 'tenth epoch' of development, he summarized his expectations in terms of three goals: 'the destruction of inequality between nations; the progress of equality within a single nation; finally, the real perfecting of man'.[8] For Condorcet, even the Revolution which betrayed him had a dynamic role to play in the consummation of such hopes. A wiser author might have been more sceptical, especially about the potential discrepancies be-tween technical and moral improvement. Yet his strident confid-ence helped to set the tone for much nineteenth-century talk of 'progress'.

Beyond France, '1789' was championed most articulately by a number of British writers. Foremost among them was Tom Paine, a supporter of the American revolt who had strengthened his contacts with radical groups in Paris during the 1780s. The first part of his *Rights of Man*, dedicated to George Washington, appeared in February 1791; the second, honouring Lafayette, followed twelve months later. Paine saw in the Revolution a prospect of human regeneration, whose attainment was dependent on people's willingness to make their own judgements even in defiance of long-standing custom or prescription. As he declared near the start of his work: 'Every age and generation must be as free to act for itself, *in all cases*, as the ages and generations which preceded it. The vanity and presumption of governing beyond the grave is the most ridiculous and insolent of all tyrannies. Man has no property in man; neither has any generation a property in the generations which are to follow.'[9] On this basis Paine advocated universal suffrage, and denied legitimacy to all forms of inherited monarchical, aristocratic and ecclesiastical authority. Nor did he neglect the economic dimension. While not condemning private property as such, *Rights of Man* offered to the lower orders an alluring prospect of wealth less unevenly distributed, within a system involving graduated income tax, family and pension allowances, public provision of housing and education, and other features foreshadowing later schemes of 'welfare'. The book attained almost instantly the status of a radical classic on both sides of the Channel. Threatened with arrest at home, Paine became an elected member of the Convention. Yet, by 1794, even he was a prisoner of the Jacobins. Thus, although he survived to end his days in Thomas Jefferson's new republic, he shared something of Condorcet's experience of the process whereby revolution could devour its own makers.

The British radical literature also includes James Mackintosh's *Vindiciae Gallicae* (1791) – later recanted – and Mary Wollstonecraft's *Vindication of the Rights of Woman* (1792), a pioneering protest against the marginalization of her whole sex. Just before her death in 1797 she 'legitimized' through marriage her partnership with Thomas Godwin. Four years earlier he had published his own remarkable *Enquiry Concerning Political Justice*. Influenced by Locke, he affirmed that character was largely the product of 'external circumstances'; and, like Condorcet, he suggested that these could be so fundamentally transformed as to free humanity for the fulfilment of its self-perfection. The real distinctiveness of Godwin's argument stemmed from the anarchist flavour of his insistence that the greatest present obstacle was nothing less than the institution of government itself – as the root of all human evil. Thus he urged for the equalization of property in small communities, where one could dispense with the necessarily oppressive mechanisms of governmental authority. As Basil Willey observes, 'Godwin caught the ardent tone of 1793', and assumed representative significance as one who, just as the tide was turning against revolution, 'enunciated the extreme conclusions of eighteenth-century rationalism'.[10]

Much of the conservative response to revolutionary ideas was crudely repressive. The kind of censorship which Paine suffered in Britain was even more burdensome in those parts of Europe where autocracy held sway. In Russia, for example, it was only through a bureaucratic lapse that Alexander Radishchev managed to bring out *A Journey from St Petersburg to Moscow* (1790), an assault on the evils of serfdom by that country's leading representative of the 'Age of Reason'. This earned him a death sentence, eventually commuted into Siberian exile. It was not the case, however, that all conservatism proved so dismally negative. In some ways the Revolution had simply added new urgency to questions already being thoughtfully addressed in the 1780s. How could the defenders of traditional values counter the case for radical innovation by the use of argument rather than mere force? What ideas might they formulate to surpass in comprehensiveness and cogency those available to the champions of change?

Answers involved appeal to a more refined sense both of community and of history. Conservatives argued that '1789' had encouraged forms of abstract and self-centred individualism which culminated inevitably in anarchy. There had been too much talk of rights, too little of duties. Proper fulfilment could occur only when individual and instant desires were subordinated to the longer-term purposes of society at large. The latter was not a mere aggregation of people, but an organic whole. Some change within it was unavoidable, but this needed to run along – and not against – the grain of history. The required rhythms were those of nature, not of man-made machinery – those marked by evolution, not by the fury of revolutionary convulsion. The reasonableness of most established institutions was demonstrable from their proven capacity to survive, adapt and render useful service over long tracts of time. For the conservative, this seemed a better guide to worth than any criterion which was more rigidly rationalistic and thus unresponsive to changing historical circumstance.

Along these lines Edmund Burke pursued his *Reflections on the*

French Revolution. It was this work, published in November 1790, which had largely provoked Paine to compose his own *Rights of Man.* Like the latter author, Burke had sided with the American colonists during the 1770s. But he believed that their defence of 'manly, moral, regulated liberty' against the injustices of George III deserved far better than to be compared with '1789'. Three years before Robespierre's rule, the *Reflections* warned of the ease with which Louis XVI's opponents might convert 'democracy' into an oligarchical dictatorship harsher than the pre-revolutionary regime. Not the least of Burke's targets were the *philosophes* themselves – as embodiments of intellectual arrogance, as wreckers wildly pursuing their goals whether 'by the thunderbolt of despotism, or by the earthquake of popular commotion'. Above all, they were said to demonstrate how abstract political reasoning must always remain arid because of its insensitivity to lived historical experience. Burke's own preferred approach was superbly expressed in the most celebrated passage from the *Reflections*, where he declared society to be a partnership 'in all art . . . in every virtue, and in all perfection'. Since its goals must take many generations to fulfil, this was also a partnership 'not only between those who are living, but between those who are living, those who are dead, and those who are to be born'.[11] Burke thus accepted as readily as the *philosophes* that society had a contractual basis, yet it was also one relating to matters more organic and less mechanistic than they had ever grasped. Similarly, he was advocating a more modest assessment of human capabilities, and a less turbulent tempo of expectation about improvement, than the Enlightenment had inspired.

Among the French, suffering directly the upheavals of revolution and war, the conservative cause tended to be more stridently expressed. For example, Abbé Barruel's *Memoirs contributing to the History of Jacobinism* (1797) presented a synthesis of current conspiratorial explanations for the destruction of the old order: this work not only heaped blame upon the *philosophes* and the reformist ministers they had captivated across Europe but also presented the extraordinarily durable vision of a masonic plot against Catholicism. Such combined defence of throne and altar was similarly vital to the concerns of Louis de Bonald. His *Theory of Political and Religious Power in Civil Society* (1796), and later works, made him an intellectual prop to the Bourbon restoration of 1814–15. An even more passionate champion of reaction was

Joseph de Maistre, a Savoyard who in 1796 published *Thoughts on France* that aimed to show how the Revolution had already gone brutally astray. Subsequent writings, such as *The Soirées of St Petersburg* (1821), helped to consolidate his influence as an opponent of the Enlightenment's presumptuous challenges to the proper authority associated with papal infallibility and monarchical absolutism. He repeatedly expressed his faith in the ability of prelates and nobles to act as the guardians of wisdom. Whatever our scepticism about that claim, we might yet acknowledge that de Maistre also recorded some important insights of a socio-psychological kind – concerning particularly the circumstances under which the mass of men might even crave to be dominated, and the disorientation that they might suffer once a sense of religious awe was destroyed.

From 1802 to 1817 de Maistre was Sardinia's diplomatic envoy to Russia. Thus he had first-hand experience of a Romanov court that became a focal point of rivalry between various liberalizing and repressive factions, all competing for the support of the mercurial Tsar Alexander I. Out of this milieu there emerged Nikolai Karamzin's *Memoir on Ancient and Modern Russia*, another classic contribution to the literature of conservatism. Though not properly published until long after its composition in 1811, the text was promptly given private circulation around the court as part of a successful campaign to oust the reformist minister, Michael Speransky. A visit to France early in the revolutionary period had cured Karamzin of his initial sympathies for liberalism. He now contended that Russia should draw inspiration from the superior values of its own tradition, rather than adopt 'westernizing' innovations. Thus the *Memoir*, written when tsardom stood close to humiliation by Napoleon, possessed xenophobic features that recurred in the same author's monumental and semi-official *History of the Russian State* (12 vols, 1816). Karamzin reasserted the identity of interest that had long existed between an autocratic Tsar-patriarch, the Orthodox Church and the older aristocracy (as distinct from the 'service' nobility tainted with western ideas). In that context the continuance of serfdom was as crucial to him as its destruction had been for Radishchev. Here was a case where foreign travel had clearly narrowed the mind. Above all, it intensified that resistance to western models which surfaces so often in the political thought of Russian conservatives both before and after Karamzin's own epoch.

NATIONALISM, LIBERALISM AND SOCIALISM

Beyond France, it was the German states which not only felt most directly the impact of Revolutionary and Napoleonic upheaval but also responded in the most complex way. There particularly close links were forged between political thinking and other aspects of philosophical activity, and enlightened influences were not so much repudiated as increasingly overlaid by strongly romanticist features. A major point of common reference was the legacy of Kant. The process whereby his initial enthusiasm for the French Revolution turned into disillusionment was one that many fellow-Germans also experienced. Yet few of them shared his scrupulousness in recognizing that this shift might be accompanied, far too casually, by a shallow optimism not just about human nature at large but also about the uniquely high value of their own national contribution to the store of human wisdom. When Johann Gottfried Herder embarked on his renowned delvings into the roots of Teutonic culture, he had done so in a spirit largely compatible with liberal cosmopolitanism. However, in 1806 – three years after his death, and only two after Kant's – the Prussian defeat at Jena generated across the German regions a powerful and far less tolerant clamour of nationalistic self-assertion. This was voiced most famously by Johann Gottlieb Fichte, through a series of *Addresses to the German Nation* (1807–8) delivered in Berlin. According to H.S. Reiss, although their author still 'generally expressed his ideas in the terminology of the Enlightenment',[12] the substance of these speeches revealed his conversion to romanticism. Fichte's compatriots were urged to build upon their cultural triumphs in the era of Goethe and Beethoven, by developing a unified state structure worthy of their homeland's potential destiny in terms of political nationhood too. Only within such a framework, joining individuals to their wider national community, could the German people find its proper fulfilment. It was a linkage expressed in those essentially organic terms that would soon run as a recurrent motif through the rhetoric of romantic nationalism elsewhere in Europe too.

Fichte's hostility towards particularism within Germany was also endorsed by Georg Wilhelm Friedrich Hegel, a philosopher who would eventually exert almost as much posthumous influence as Kant on the course of European thought. In 1821, three years after succeeding to Fichte's former professorship at Berlin,

Hegel published *The Philosophy of Right* as his central contribution to political theory. Here he focused on the workings of reason, yet also treated these as essentially processes of 'becoming'. Thus he adopted an approach which we have noted already as characterizing much romanticist thinking. In the Hegelian scheme of things, history amounts to the progressive actualization of freedom through the 'spirit' (or *Geist*) of reason. This is a movement driven by the logic of 'the dialectic'. The latter involves the ceaseless conflict of opposites and their (usually transient) resolution in forms of higher synthesis. On such a reading, it was possible to find oneself confusingly welcoming, in turn, the French Revolution *and* the Napoleonic Empire *and* the Vienna Settlement of 1815, each as a manifestation of some awkward combination between divine providence and the latest 'cunning of reason'. Similarly, Hegel saw the dialectical tension between 'family' and 'civil society' as being resolved in the modern nation-state. More puzzling, however, were his hints that this particular example of a hitherto incessant logic might come to a halt right there – leaving us, indeed, with a political construct curiously similar to the constitutional forms and militaristic ethos of the contemporary Prussian monarchy!

Henceforth Hegel's legacy was available to encourage all those who, whatever their political goals, favoured a synthesizing and 'total' explanation of historical and social processes. On the Left, for example, Marxists would exploit his mechanism of dialectic, albeit after revamping this to operate in largely materialistic terms. Conversely, on the Right, his belief that individual fulfilment was attainable only through subordination to the higher purposes of the state would survive to inspire such 'philosophy' as eventually underpinned the twentieth-century fascist creed. Yet, if Hegel himself was often ambiguous about such issues as revolution and reaction, he was hardly more so than the one great contemporary whom he was prepared to include among his 'world-historical figures'. Here, in Napoleon, we do indeed find (as Robert Alexander has stressed elsewhere in this volume) both a continuer and a destroyer of the spirit of '1789' – and, moreover, someone who emerges both as a potential romantic hero and as a promoter of bureaucratic rationalization. Under the Empire, his professions of faith in universal principles seemed increasingly at odds with his imposition of a merely French hegemony over other nations. During the Napoleonic era nearly every European country had experienced at least one cycle of invasion, occupation and liberation, when the established order had been shaken and the scope for change revealed. However selectively the Emperor might seek to export the principles of the Revolution, neither he nor the rulers who often re-established themselves in the wake of his retreat could ever feel secure concerning the effectiveness of such limitation. The heightened political consciousness which clearly developed over these years was not simply the outcome of widespread European sympathy for the Rights of Man. Within the context of nationalism especially, it also stemmed from general resentment against alien military power – not just among Germans but also among others such as Italians, Spaniards or Russians. Partly by intent, though more by inadvertence, Napoleon had strengthened everywhere in Europe new energies and expectations whose force, over the longer term, would prove to be uncontainable.

More immediately, following the Vienna Congress of 1814–15, it was conservatism that held the upper hand. At the heart of Europe's post-Napoleonic system stood Metternich, chief minister of the Habsburg regime. This made him the servant not merely of autocracy but also of Austrian–German hegemony over Slav, Magyar and Latin populations. Thus, within and beyond his Emperor's domains, he was determined to resist liberalism and nationalism alike. It is vital to realize that, just as he believed these forces to be inseparable, so too did those who actually championed them as manifestations of 'progress'. Why should Lord Byron and all the others who during the 1820s supported the Greek revolt against the Ottomans think otherwise? Was not the Belgian liberation from Dutch rule in 1830 driven by a similar conviction? And is it not readily understandable that, in the following year, Giuseppe Mazzini should have felt confident about founding 'Young Italy' under a motto of 'Freedom, Equality, Humanity, Independence and Unity' whose elements seemed entirely reconcilable one with another? Yet, with hindsight, we know that all these examples betray a dangerous innocence. Only in the decades after the revolutionary pandemic of 1848–9 would it begin to become clear that the patterns of relationship – positive *and* negative – between nationalism and the promotion of freedom were far more dependent on particular contingencies of circumstance than most liberals had cause to appreciate during the age of Metternich.

Reactionaries of his kind found it easier to retard the pace of direct political change during the generation after 1815 than to control the processes and effects of socio-economic transformation. Most notable were the accelerating rises in European population, urban settlement and industrial activity (themes directly explored by Colin Heywood in earlier chapters). While such trends certainly imperilled Metternich's quest for stability, they were also a challenge to the wisdom of those who wanted to align themselves with 'progress'. How, by 1830, had the anti-conservatives begun to adapt their own analyses to these changing circumstances? To what extent, moreover, was liberalism starting to be rivalled by something called 'socialism'? It is true that the latter term came into use only towards the end of this period, and that it did not seem readily separable from the former one until 1848 or so. Yet there was already some prefiguration of that divorce between liberalism and socialism which, increasingly over the second half of the nineteenth century, would make them into mutually competitive versions of progressive political inspiration.

Liberals had readily available to them the Enlightenment's legacy of economic theory. Support for *laissez-faire* principles could be derived not only from the work of the French 'physiocrats' but also from Adam Smith, author of *The Wealth of Nations* (1776). His superior understanding of the manufacturing and commercial – not simply the agrarian – bases for prosperity made him the principal influence on that 'classical economics' which during the early nineteenth century developed most strongly in Britain, the first of Europe's industrial nations. One notable contributor was Thomas Malthus, whose two essays on *The Principle of Population* came out in 1798 and 1803. These focused attention on the disparity between two tendencies: the geometrical progression of demographic growth, and the merely arithmetical increase of food resources. As a partial response to Malthus, the work of David Ricardo on *The Principles of Political Economy and Taxation* (1817) was less obviously pessimistic. Yet, even while exploring prospects of much greater productive potential, the latter was also voicing anxieties about the ill-effects of any systematic maldistribution of the total wealth that free trade might yield. In this respect, as well as through his attachment to a labour theory of value, he soon became as important to socialists as to liberals. Much of the credit for popularizing Ricardian economics must rest with James Mill. It was he, moreover, who served as the principal link between two broad epochs of 'philosophical radicalism'. He not only helped the ageing Jeremy Bentham (who himself survived until 1832) to promote the highly rationalistic 'utilitarian' version of the quest to maximize human happiness, but also produced and educated the son – John Stuart – who would eventually be the most influential figure in adapting this whole tradition of liberalism to the changing circumstances of the mid-Victorian age.

In the political domain, most liberals of the period up to 1830 were far more cautious than Bentham about the desirability of giving the vote to every man. Their moderation was typified by the Swiss-born Benjamin Constant, who became a notable publicist within France. Having been used by Napoleon to lend respectability to the concept of a 'liberal Empire' during the Hundred Days, he strove thereafter to limit the authoritarian pretensions of the restored Bourbon monarchy. Commentators such as he were searching after 1815 for middle ground somewhere between their hatred of rule by the few and their fear of rule by the many. Liberals certainly resisted the Metternich system by standing for freedom of the press, for the removal of religious intolerance and for equality of treatment before the law; and they were similarly unequivocal as advocates of more effective constitutional restraints upon executive power. Yet their creed could also look like something sustained chiefly by the narrow self-interest of the professional and commercial classes. Liberalism favoured, for example, concepts of active political participation which would still be linked to the possession of wealth and property. From such a standpoint, was it not prudent to develop parliamentary institutions essentially on the basis that some such material stake in society should remain the precondition for direct electoral involvement? As the circle of property and ownership was enlarged through the successful operation of liberal–capitalist principles, it was indeed conceivable that all disturbing questions about wider enfranchisement would then settle themselves in a suitably gradualist way.

Towards 1830, however, this potentially reassuring interpretation of political and economic advancement was starting to be challenged from a socialist quarter. Here was a critique of liberalism that had very similar roots in the Enlightenment, and, as Eric Hobsbawm remarks, 'Reason, science, and progress were its firm foundation.'[13] At the heart of the evolving separation between the two doctrines was socialism's contention that appeals to Liberty must remain meaningless so long as they were unconnected with a commitment to Equality and Fraternity as well. It was argued that, while the rapid advances in industrial production over the previous half-century or so had undoubtedly enriched some people, they had impoverished many more. The remedy lay partly in a quest for social equality on a scale generally unacceptable to the bourgeois reformers. Yet it depended also on a desire for fraternal 'community' which, in paradoxical ways, brought the socialists closer to Burke's conservative rhetoric about organic partnership – and even to the wider romanticist nostalgia for a lost golden age – than to the discourse of unfettered competition associated with liberal individualism. According to this same socialist analysis, the most brutalized victims of the mismatch between the accumulation and the distribution of wealth were to be found in the ranks of the ever-growing urban proletariat. It was time to ask whether these workers – and indeed Europe's rural masses too – could ever enjoy the properly harmonious combination of Liberty, Equality and Fraternity without the attainment of a triple transformation. In its most radical forms, this would involve the overthrow of the whole capitalist system as a matter of economics, the implementation of a thoroughgoing version of popular sovereignty as an issue of politics, and the achievement of communal cooperation as an embodiment of man's natural potential for sociability.

It was only in 1828 that the Italian-born Filippo Buonarroti, by then an activist among the various secret societies working across much of Europe to subvert Metternich's restored conservative order, made fully public the scope and aims of the failed socialist plot that he and other ex-Jacobins had prepared in France over thirty years before. One element in this conspiracy of 1796 against the Directory had been the composition (though not the wider publication) of Sylvain Maréchal's *Manifesto of the Equals*. Another was the leadership of François 'Gracchus' Babeuf. Thus, after the appearance of Buonarroti's account, it was under the guise of 'Babouvism' that the plotters' ideas came to influence the later development of the French revolutionary socialist tradition, particularly as embodied by Auguste Blanqui. The thinking behind this 'Conspiracy of the Equals' was clearer about the need to achieve a thorough levelling in the distribution of material resources than about the means of actually enhancing the overall amount of wealth available to a society. In this sense, Babouvism was typical of the first phase of socialist ideas when, as Leszek Kolakowski observes, 'Moral indignation at poverty and inequality was not distinguished from economic analysis of capitalist production, but rather took the place of such analysis.'[14]

That criticism was, however, less applicable to two other figures whose work from the first decades of the nineteenth century also proved influential in laying the foundations for socialism. A visit to England in 1818 – amidst the commercial crisis that followed the ending of the Napoleonic Wars – led the first of these, the Swiss economist Jean Charles Sismondi, to sharpen his anxiety about forms of capitalism that were becoming increasingly linked to the industrial mode of production. In essence, were these still governed by the beneficial self-equilibrating mechanisms that had been generally postulated in 'classical' theory as developed all the way from Smith even down to the most recent work of Ricardo? The upshot was a book that went beyond the latter, even as hinted by Sismondi's choice of title: *New Principles of Political Economy* (1819). This work argued for greater awareness of the possibility – even the inevitability – of chronic underconsumption and cumulative disequilibrium. Sismondi hinted also at the frailty of *laissez-faire* principles. While these might promote aggregate production, there was also a moral need for government to concern itself directly with the issue of just distribution. He believed that the continuation of present trends would threaten an increasingly conflictual polarization between enriched capitalists and impoverished workers. The nineteenth-century Left certainly valued the diagnostic insights present in his work, but he was less trenchant about recommendations for cure. When in 1848 Marx and Engels came to associate him essentially with 'petty-bourgeois socialism',[15] they were suggesting that, in the last resort, Sismondi preferred merely to limit the drawbacks of capitalism rather than to destroy the system as such.

The socialist credentials of the second analyst, Claude-Henri de Saint-Simon, are similarly far from unproblematic. He saw civilization as alternating between 'organic' and 'critical' phases. At certain times social and political institutions were harmoniously geared to man's requirements, but at others not. For him, the principal task of the epoch after '1789' was that of building up a new condition of organic wholeness, concordant with the recent and prospective achievements of scientists and captains of commerce and industry. Saint-Simon (who was assisted from 1817 to 1824 by Auguste Comte, the eventual pioneer of positivistic 'sociology') produced little that was unequivocally socialist in tone. His writings, culminating in *The New Christianity* of 1825 (the year of his death), certainly stress the need for a planned economy and the pivotal historical significance of transition from a feudal to a predominantly bourgeois order. Yet there seems scant enthusiasm for radical social equalization or for any decisive shift of political authority into the hands of the labouring classes. Saint-Simon argues, rather, that capital and labour are potentially complementary forces which, in an organic community, will have a shared commitment to successful production. Only by harnessing the guiding talents of an educated elite could society assure the well-being of proletarians or peasants alike. He recommended the establishment of three chambers: one element composed of engineers and artists to propose plans of reform, a second comprising scientists to assess these projects, and a third drawn from the ranks of all those involved in the productive process who would implement the resulting schemes for the benefit of the whole community. Administered in this way and strengthened by the consensual ethos of his 'New Christianity', societies would no longer need coercive machinery. Thus government in the conventional sense would dwindle to the most residual functions.

Much of the linkage between Saint-Simon's name and early socialism was due to the band of disciples – many trained at the Ecole Polytechnique in Paris – who radicalized his ideas immediately after his death. By 1830 a group headed by Olindes Rodriguez, Armand Bazard and Barthélemy-Prosper Enfantin had issued the first part of its collective *Exposition of the Saint-Simonian Doctrine*. This drove further the attack upon the principle of inheritance and demanded that the state should assume responsibility for redistributing capital according to capacity and need. The authors of the *Exposition* had no direct hand in the July Revolution of 1830, and they soon succumbed to quarrels amongst themselves. Even so, they managed to make a more plainly socialist version of Saint-Simon's ideas better known not just in France but also amongst many of the British, German, Polish and Russian radicals who would be active during the following decades.

Another important facet of early socialist idealism is evident from the abortive endeavours of 'Père' Enfantin to establish an actual settlement where, on a small scale, the faithful might try to put the 'New Christianity' into practice. Even earlier, Robert Owen had similarly aspired to make his Scottish textile factory at New Lanark into the basis for a model productive community. That was an experience which encouraged him to write *A New View of Society* (1813) and, in the late 1820s, to make an unsuccessful effort at developing a socialistic settlement in the USA. Far more 'utopian' still was the vision of restored communal harmony cherished by Charles Fourier, who himself had little time either for Owenites or Saint-Simonians. He claimed that his contemporaries, once they were properly organized into his ideal 'phalansteries' of some 1,600 souls, could enjoy the full actualization of their natural cooperative potentialities by means of an unfettering of their passions. Indeed, through such works as *The New World of Industry and Sociability* (1829), Fourier seemed to be promising everyone a constant feast of good food and free love. He went so far as to advertise for a financial sponsor, but, surprisingly or otherwise, none ever appeared. Thus it was less as the father of the failed 'phalanstery' than as the producer of occasionally brilliant psychological insights into social 'alienation' and 'repression' that, over later generations, Fourier would come to be cited from time to time by Marxists as well as Freudians, and by surrealists as well as publicists of 'flower-power'. Despite his eccentricities, he serves to remind us of a vital concluding point. This involves recognizing that early nineteenth-century socialism, while drawing principally on the rationalist and materialist legacy of the Enlightenment, derived a good measure of its growing strength from that alternative source whose influence we have also been tracing. In short, the socialists and other radicals of this epoch owed more than they sometimes acknowledged to that search for organic wholeness, harmony and belonging which, even beyond 1830, the Romantic Movement itself would continue to inspire.

NOTES

1 Quoted as epigraph in P. Gay, *The Enlightenment* (London, 1970), vol.2, p.7.
2 *Ibid.*, p.497.
3 R. Porter, *The Enlightenment* (London, 1990), p.11.
4 H.Honour, *Romanticism* (Harmondsworth, 1981), p.282.
5 'The tables turned', in W. Wordsworth and S.T. Coleridge, *Lyrical Ballads* (London, 1991, eds R.L. Brett and A.R. Jones), p.106.

6 R. Porter and M. Teich (eds) *Romanticism in National Context* (Cambridge, 1988), p.3.

7 J.M. Roberts (ed.) *French Revolution Documents* (Oxford, 1966), vol.1, p.172.

8 Quoted in J. Lively (ed.) *The Enlightenment* (Harlow, 1966), p.74.

9 T. Paine, *Rights of Man* (Harmondsworth, 1969), pp.63–4.

10 B. Willey, *The Eighteenth-Century Background: Studies of the Idea of Nature in the Period* (Harmondsworth, 1962), pp.223, 207.

11 E. Burke, *Reflections on the French Revolution* (Harmondsworth, 1968), pp.194–5.

12 H.S. Reiss (ed.) *The Political Thought of the German Romantics, 1793–1815* (Oxford, 1955), p.11.

13 E.J. Hobsbawm, *The Age of Revolution: Europe, 1789–1848* (London, 1962), p.241.

14 L. Kolakowski, *Main Currents of Marxism: Its Origins, Growth, and Dissolution* (Oxford, 1981), vol.1, p.186.

15 K. Marx and F. Engels, *The Communist Manifesto*, in D. McLellan (ed.) *Karl Marx: Selected Writings* (Oxford, 1977), pp.239–40.

FURTHER READING

The best form of further reading involves examining some of the 'primary texts' from the period 1780–1830 which have been cited in this essay. The preceding reference notes indicate some anthologies of such source material as variously edited by Roberts, Lively and Reiss.

Among the 'secondary' materials, E.J. Hobsbawm, *The Age of Revolution: Europe, 1789–1848* (London, 1962) is a general history that takes a broadly Marxist approach, but also produces an outstandingly stimulating assault on the problem of relating social and political thinking to the wider fabric of the age. Two standard textbooks in the history of ideas are R.N. Stromberg, *An Intellectual History of Modern Europe* (New York, 1966), and F.L. Baumer, *Modern European Thought: Continuity and Change in Ideas, 1600–1950* (London, 1977). For brief analytical essays on particular thinkers reference can most usefully be made to D. Miller (ed.) *The Blackwell Encyclopaedia of Political Thought* (Oxford, 1987), and J. Wintle (ed.) *Makers of Nineteenth-Century Culture, 1800–1914* (London, 1982).

There is a wealth of good material on the *philosophes* and their legacy. P. Gay, *The Enlightenment*, 2 vols (London, 1967–70) provides a wide-ranging treatment. Admirable shorter studies include N. Hampson, *The Enlightenment* (Harmondsworth, 1968), and R. Porter, *The Enlightenment* (London, 1990). Two parallel volumes of essays collected by R. Porter and M. Teich under the titles *The Enlightenment in National Context* (Cambridge, 1981) and *Romanticism in National Context* (Cambridge, 1988) help to illuminate some of the comparative issues pursued in the present chapter. H.G. Schenk, *The Mind of the European Romantics: An Essay in Cultural History* (Oxford, 1979), and H. Honour, *Romanticism* (Harmondsworth, 1981) are similarly very useful.

A very wide range of relevant articles will be found in K. Baker, C.

Lucas, F. Furet and M. Ozouf (eds) *The French Revolution and the Creation of Modern Political Culture* (Oxford, 1987–9). Reading on conservative thought might well begin with the survey of 'The Counter-Enlightenment' included in I. Berlin, *Against the Current: Essays in the History of Ideas* (Oxford, 1981). The same volume also contains a valuable piece on 'Nationalism', and this current of political ideas is covered in a similarly illuminating way by E.J. Hobsbawm, *Nations and Nationalism since 1780: Programme, Myth, Reality* (Cambridge, 1990). E.K. Bramsted and K.J. Melhuish (eds) *Western Liberalism: A History in Documents from Locke to Croce* (London, 1978) includes a substantial analytical introduction as well as a wide range of extracts from contemporary sources. Other studies of 'progressive' ideas include A. Arblaster, *The Rise and Decline of Western Liberalism* (Oxford, 1984); L. Kolakowski, *Main Currents of Marxism: Its Origins, Growth, and Dissolution*, vol.1 (Oxford, 1978); and two works by G. Lichtheim, *The Origins of Socialism* (London, 1968) and *A Short History of Socialism* (London, 1970). G.D.H. Cole, *A History of Socialist Thought*, 7 vols (London, 1953–60) remains very helpful as a work of detailed reference, and there is good material in Chapters IV and V of another well-established classic, E. Roll, *A History of Economic Thought* (new edn, London, 1973).

Conclusion: Liberty – and order?

Pamela M. Pilbeam

On the well-known principle, hammered into this editor by her sixth-form and undergraduate progeny, that students only read introductions and conclusions, what above all do we learn from the half-century under review? Two issues stand out. First, the long-term and linked impact of the 1789 Revolution and the protracted European war which followed it. Second, the huge difference in the scale of its repercussions in eastern and western Europe. The reader will be curious to explain the difference. Both Julian Swann and Brendan Simms make it clear that pressure for change in the structure of government and society already existed Europe-wide before the French Revolution, the latter noting that the Austrian Emperor believed that France in 1789 was on the verge of imitating his own reforming efforts. In the ensuing fifty years the directions taken by the eastern empires and western Europe diverge. Despite extensive military commitment and temporary devastating defeat, the eastern states emerge from the wars barely touched by the ideas of the Revolution.

In the west the effects of 1789 were everywhere. Julian Swann stresses the contribution of accidental and personal factors in bringing about revolution from below, rather than the reform from above attempted variously in eastern Europe. Louis XVI is described as well meaning, but weak. The chance for reform slips by in May–June 1789 and France seems to slither into half a century of revolution and war. In 1814 Louis XVIII and his politicians try to merge revolutionary and old regime institutions, but his brother Charles X loses his throne hesitantly attempting to unmake the Revolution. In the eastern empires, despite extensive humiliation by Bonaparte's armies, the old dynasties survive, with minimal modifications to their power after 1814. Was France possessed of particularly whimpish kings, or did other factors swirl the country into repeated revolution?

Diversified and broad-based economic development bestowed on France a substantial educated and politically ambitious elite. In 1789 wealthy property-owners, most, but not all of them middle class, wanted a share of the political action. Scenting royal weakness, they pushed for an end to hereditary privilege and the creation of representative elected assemblies and a written constitution. But it soon became clear that there was far more to running a large and populous state than the influence of the spoken and written word. Escalating popular violence, combined with the lack of any means of physically controlling it, gave the aspiring politicians both more – and less – than they had dreamt of. The political ambitions of the rich were transparently selfish and ended in dictatorship in both 1799 and again in 1851 as the scrabbling statesmen successively failed to convince their rivals of the justice of their definition of who should exercise power.

If the route from reform to revolution was an accidental wrong turning in 1789, the ideals which quickly emerged had, and still have, an irresistible potency and appeal. By 1830 it was obvious that the attempt to reconstruct old regime Europe embarked on in 1814 had failed. A new generation formed secret, idealistic sects (like the *carbonari*), for whom the slogans of Liberty, Equality, and particularly Fraternity, had a new meaning. Revolution was also kept alive by frustrated ambition. In France and the Italian states restored monarchs deposed politicians and administrators who became centres of opposition and discontent.

Thus in western Europe men had been shaped both by the Holy Grail and the job prospects of revolution. Prolonged war reinforced changed attitudes and ambitions and France was at war for nearly half of this period. Former soldiers were at the centre of subversive activities after 1814 in both France and Italy. The defection of army units and the National Guard, usually led by former soldiers, was conclusive in the success of the 1830 Revolution in France. Service in the Imperial army seemed to contribute more than Rousseau to the survival of the French Revolution.

But all of this is inadequate to explain the political volatility of western Europe and the conservatism of the east. One must turn to Colin Heywood's accounts of economic and demographic developments and Pamela Pilbeam's excursions into social change to understand the effervescence. Europe was moving, patchily and tentatively, from a semi-subsistence to a market economy and her population was growing at an unprecedented rate. The livelihood and survival of the uneducated majority of the population was increasingly threatened by the erosion of communal rights and traditions, new methods of industrial production and temporary but painful shortfalls in food supply due to climatic disasters and the absence of alternative sources of supply. The slogans of 1789 added political aspiration to economic deprivation. The recipe for repeated popular upheaval, the vital underpinning of all revolutionary experience in this half-century, was complete.

Chronology of main events

1780		Joseph II sole ruler in Austria
1781		Joseph abolishes serfdom and decrees religious toleration
1782		Necker's *Compte Rendu* of French finances
1784		German decreed the official language in Hungary
1785		Charter making Russian nobility an estate
1786		Calonne's reform attempts in France
1787	Feb	Assembly of Notables meets in France
1788		Sieyès, *What is the Third Estate?*
1789	May	Estates General
	July	Fall of Bastille
	Aug	Abolition of feudal rights
		Declaration of Rights of Man
	Oct	March to Versailles
	Nov	Decrees of church in France securalizing church land
1790	Feb	Joseph II dies. Leopold II Emperor
	June	Abolition of nobility in France
	July	Civil Constitution of Clergy in France
1791	June	Flight to Varennes
	Sept	Constitutional Monarchy begins in France
	Oct	Legislative Assembly
1792	Mar	Francis II succeeds Leopold as Emperor
	Apr	Declaration of War of Liberation of the Peoples of Europe by French State. War with Austria

	June	Invasion of Tuileries (royal palace)
	July	Prussia declares war on France
	Aug	Revolution 10 August; king suspended
	Sept	September Massacres
	Sept	Battle of Valmy – Prussian advance on Paris held
		Convention meets
		Republic declared. Year I of Republic
	Nov	Austria defeated at Jemappes
1793	Jan	Execution of Louis XVI
	Jan	First partition of Poland by Russia and Prussia
	Feb	France declares war on Britain and Holland
	Mar	France declares war on Spain
	Apr	Committee of Public Safety
	June	Girondins defeated; Jacobin Constitution
	Sept	Year II of Republic
		Second partition of Poland
1794		Prussia – Basic Law *Allgemeines Landrecht*
	July	Robespierre arrested and executed
	Dec	Armistice – France and Austria
1795		Treaty of Basle – France and Prussia and Holland, later with Spain
	Aug	Constitution of Year III
	Oct	Directory begins
		Third partition of Poland
1796	Mar	Bonaparte commander of army in Italy
		Paul Emperor of Russia
1796–9		French military victories
1797	Feb	Frederick William IV king of Prussia
1799	Nov	*Coup d'état* 18 Brumaire
	Dec	Constitution of Year VIII. Consulate begins
		Napoleon First Consul
1801	Feb	Treaty of Lunéville between France and Austria
	Mar	Deposition and murder of Paul I of Russia
		Alexander I Emperor of Russia
		Internal reforms in Russia
	July	Napoleon signs Concordat with papacy

1802	Mar	Peace of Amiens between France and Britain
	May	Napoleon Consul for life
1803		Abolition of territorial sovereignty of ecclesiastical princes in Holy Roman Empire
1804	Mar	Civil Code
	May	Empire proclaimed
	Aug	Proclamation of Austrian Empire
	Dec	Napoleon crowned
1806	July	Confederation of Rhine formed by Napoleon
	Aug	Abolition of Holy Roman Empire (founded AD 800)
	Oct	Battle of Jena
1807		Treaty of Tilsit
		Baron Stein begins reform programme in Prussia
		Speransky reforms in Russia
1808	Dec	Invasion of Spain
1809		Count Metternich Austrian foreign minister
1812		Invasion of Russia
1813		Wars of 'Liberation' against Napoleon
	Oct	Battle of Leipzig, 'of the Nations'
1814	Apr	Napoleon abdicates
		First Restoration of Bourbons, Louis XVIII king
	May	First Treaty of Paris
	June	Constitutional Charter
	Sept	Congress of Vienna
1815	Mar	Napoleon back. Hundred Day rule begins
	June	Battle of Waterloo. Napoleon's second abdication
		Second Restoration of Bourbons
		White Terror in Midi
	Sept	*Chambre Introuvable* elected in France
	Nov	Second Treaty of Paris
		German Confederation founded under Austrian presidency
1816	Sept	*Chambre Introuvable* dissolved

1816–17		Economic crisis
1818	Sept	Congress of Aix-la-Chapelle
	Nov	Allied troops leave France
1819		Karlsbad Decrees
1820–2		Liberal revolts in Spain, Italian states, Greece
1820	Feb	Murder of duc de Berri; law of double vote
	Oct	Congress of Troppau
1821	Jan	Congress of Laibach
		Death of Napoleon
		Carbonari formed
	May	Metternich chancellor of Austrian Empire
		Greek revolt
1822	Oct	Congress of Verona
	Sept	Villèle head of government in France
1823	Apr	French military expedition to Spain
1824	Mar	Right-wing election victory in France
	Sept	Charles X king of France
1825	Jan	Francis I succeeds Ferdinand I as king of Two Sicilies
		Law against sacrilege – France
		Law indemnifying émigrés – France
	May	Coronation of Charles X
		Nicholas I Tsar of Russia
	Dec	Decembrist rising in Russia
1826		John VI replaced by Maria II (regency) – Portugal
1827	July	Greek autonomy accepted by Britain, Russia, France
1827–32		Economic crisis; harvest failures; commercial/industrial recession
1827	Nov	General election – France
1828	Jan	Martignac head of government in France
1829	Aug	Ultra-royalist government in France

	Nov	Polignac head of government in France
1830	Feb	Greece independent
	Mar	Vote of 221 against Polignac in France
	May	French Chamber of Deputies dissolved
	July	Four Ordinances of St Cloud
		Revolution in France; 'Three Glorious Days'
		Louis-Philippe, duke of Orleans king of the French
	Aug	Belgian revolt
	Sept	Revolts in Hesse, Brunswick and Saxony
	Nov	Polish revolts
	Dec	Belgian independence agreed – London Conference

Index